CITIES IN A
WORLD ECONOMY
THIRD EDITION

Sociology for a New Century Series

SOCIOLOGY FOR A NEW CENTURY

CITIES IN A WORLD ECONOMY

THIRD EDITION

Saskia Sassen
University of Chicago

PINE FORGE PRESS
An Imprint of Sage Publications, Inc.
Thousand Oaks • London • New Delhi

For information:

Pine Forge Press
An imprint of Sage Publications, Inc.
2455 Teller Road
Thousand Oaks, California 91320
E-mail: order@sagepub.com

Sage Publications Ltd.
1 Oliver's Yard
55 City Road
London EC1Y 1SP
United Kingdom

Sage Publications India Pvt. Ltd.
B-42, Panchsheel Enclave
Post Box 4109
New Delhi 110 017 India

Printed in the United States of America

Library of Congress Cataloging-in-Publication Data

Sassen, Saskia.
Cities in a world economy / Saskia Sassen. — 3rd ed.
    p. cm. — (Sociology for a new century series)
Includes bibliographical references and index.
ISBN 978-1-4129-3680-4 (pbk.)
    1. Urban economics. 2. Metropolitan areas—Cross-cultural studies.
3. Cities and towns—Cross-cultural studies. 4. Sociology, Urban.
I. Title. II. Series: Sociology for a new century.
HT321.S28 2006
330.9173'2—dc22   2005034084

This book is printed on acid-free paper.

09 10 11   10 9 8 7 6 5 4 3

Acquiring Editor:	Ben Penner
Editorial Assistant:	Annie Louden
Production Editor:	Sanford Robinson
Copy Editor:	Teresa Barensfeld
Typesetter:	C&M Digitals (P) Ltd.
Indexer:	Julie Sherman Grayson
Cover Designer:	Michelle Kenny

About the Author

Saskia Sassen is the Ralph Lewis Professor of Sociology at the University of Chicago and Centennial Visiting Professor at the London School of Economics. Her recent books are *Territory, Authority, Rights: From Medieval to Global Assemblages* (2006), *A Sociology of Globalization* (2006), *Digital Formations* (coeditor, 2005), *Global Networks, Linked Cities* (editor, 2002), and *Guests and Aliens* (1999). Her books have been translated into 16 languages. She is the editor of the volume on urban sustainability in the new 14-volume *Encyclopedia of Life-Systems* being produced by UNESCO and EOLSS (2006), for which she coordinated a network of researchers and activists in 30 countries.

Contents

Preface to the Third Edition

L ittle did I know that 15 years after the original version I would find
myself working on a third edition of this book. The two preceding prefaces contain much of what I would like to repeat here, but the occasion
demands brevity. Besides a thorough updating, bringing in the latest available data, this new edition addresses some of the critical questions about a
range of processes that have gained prominence over the last several years.
One of these is international migrations, examined in Chapter 7, a whole
new chapter, and through new material in several other chapters. Women
have emerged as key actors in migration processes and in some of the labor
markets growing fast in global cities. When it comes to new trends, the
second edition showed a strengthening of patterns that had been only dimly
detected in the first edition. The data for the late 1990s and into 2005 examined in this third edition show a further strengthening of some of those patterns, such as the sharp concentration of global wealth and the growth of
various forms of inequality, as well as the emergence of new patterns.
Perhaps most notable among the latter is the rapid growth in the network of
global cities and the addition of several new major centers at the top of the
system. Further, some of the leading centers, such as Tokyo, have lost
ground, while others, such as New York after the attacks of September 11,
2001, have regained power. The data covering social variables show a sharpening in several alignments, further suggesting the emergence of new types
of social formations inside these cities.

Much was said already in the prefaces to the two preceding editions,
particularly the first, about the genesis of the book and all the institutions
and people who made it possible. They made all the difference, and I remain
grateful to them. Here, I would like to acknowledge the encouragement
of teachers and students who have used the book. Their praise and their
comments mean a lot to me. I would like to single out several users of the
book for their most helpful suggestions: Professors Rhacel Parrenas (University of California, Davis), Jan Nijman (University of Miami), Daniel Monti

(Boston University), Gerry Sussman (State University of New York, Oswego), and Peter Taylor (Loughborough University, United Kingdom). They wrote detailed comments and suggestions that I have tried to follow.

Finally, the people who made this third edition happen: I am most grateful to the editors of the Series, York Bradshow (University of South Carolina, Upstate), Vincent Roscigno (Ohio State University), and Joya Misra (University of Massachusetts, Amherst), for asking me to do a third edition. It is not really easy or comfortable to go back to an old book, and to do so word by word, number by number. They persuaded me it was a good idea. Ben Penner, the Pine Forge editor of the series, was contagious in his enthusiasm and was a generous supporter of the project, especially of the vast research necessary to do the updates. Annie Louden of Pine Forge was extremely helpful. The single largest thank you goes to David Lubin, who did much of the research for the tables and their final preparation; it could not have been done, certainly not on time, without him. Zachary Hooker, Vikas Chandra, Danny Armanino, and Nilesh Patel were enormously helpful at various stages of the work. Last but not least, copyeditor Teresa Barensfeld made all the difference.

Preface to the Second Edition

Since I completed this book in the early 1990s, the world has seen a recession come to an end, a boom in global financial transactions, and a major crisis in Southeast Asia, parts of Latin America, and Russia. Yet throughout these often sharp and massive shifts, we have also seen the continuation of the major developments that I used to specify the features of the global economy that have made cities strategic. Indeed, many of the updated tables in this edition show the accentuation of some of the trends identified in the earlier edition. They also show the growth of the cross-border network of cities that constitutes a transnational space for the management and servicing of the global economy. As countries adopt the new rules of the global game, their major business centers become the gateways through which capital and other resources enter and exit their economies.

A major new trend that is becoming evident over the last few years is the strengthening of the networks connecting cities, including a novel development: the formation of strategic alliances between cities through their financial markets. The growth of global markets for finance and specialized services, the need for transnational servicing networks due to sharp increases in international investment, the reduced role of the government in the regulation of international economic activity, and the corresponding ascendance of other institutional arenas, notably global markets and corporate headquarters—all these point to the existence of a series of transnational networks of cities. We can see here the formation, at least incipient, of transnational urban systems. To a large extent, it seems to me that the major business centers in the world today draw their importance from these transnational networks. The global city is a function of a network—and in this sense, there is a sharp contrast with the erstwhile capitals of empires. This subject is sufficiently new and so little known that I have added a whole new section on it in Chapter 5.

These networks of major international business centers constitute new geographies of centrality. The most powerful of these new geographies of centrality at the global level bind the major international financial and business centers: New York, London, Tokyo, Paris, Frankfurt, Zurich, Amsterdam, Los Angeles, Sydney, and Hong Kong, among others. But this geography now also includes cities such as Bangkok, Seoul, Taipei, São Paulo, Mexico City, and Buenos Aires. The intensity of transactions among these cities, particularly through the financial markets, trade in services, and investment, has increased sharply, and so have the orders of magnitude involved. At the same time, there has been a sharpening inequality in the concentration of strategic resources and activities between each of these cities and others in the same country.

One of the more controversial sections of the first edition of this book proved to be my analysis and conceptualization of the growth of inequality within these cities. Then and now, the data are inadequate to have definitive proof. Yet I would argue that we continue to see this trend toward inequality. There is an ongoing growth of the highly paid professional classes connected to leading sectors of the global economy and of national economies. And there is also continuing growth of low-wage service workers, including industrial services. In many of these cities, we continue to see a fairly large middle class. But on closer examination, a good part of this middle class is still living at the level of prosperity it gained in the earlier economic phase. It is not certain at all that the sons and daughters of these aging middle classes in various cities around the world will have the, albeit modest, prosperity enjoyed by their parents. Furthermore, the growth of disadvantaged sectors, many excluded from a growing range of institutional worlds—of work, education, and politics—continues to be evident in many of these cities.

It has been fascinating to revisit the earlier empirical information and bring it up to date. The strengthening of many of these patterns took even me a bit by surprise.

Preface to the First Edition

Sociologists have tended to study cities by looking at the ecology of urban forms and the distribution of population and institutional centers or by focusing on people and social groups, lifestyles, and urban problems. These approaches are no longer sufficient. Economic globalization, accompanied by the emergence of a global culture, has profoundly altered the social, economic, and political reality of nation-states, cross-national regions, and—the subject of this book—cities. Through the study of the city as one particular site in which global processes take place, I seek to define new concepts useful to understand the intersection of the global and the local in today's world—and tomorrow's.

It is helpful in this context to recall Janet Abu-Lughod, a leading urban sociologist, who has commented that it is impossible to study the city only from a sociological perspective because it requires an understanding of many other realities. Manuel Castells, another major urban sociologist, has added that it is impossible to study the city only from an urban perspective. These two observations mark an empty space in urban sociology, which I seek to address in this book.

Although there has been an international economic system for many decades and a world economy for many centuries, the current situation is distinct in two respects. On the one hand, we have seen the formation of transnational spaces for economic activity where governments play a minimal role, different from the role they once had in international trade, for instance. Examples of such spaces are export processing zones, offshore banking centers, and many of the new global financial markets. On the other hand, these transnational spaces for economic activity are largely located in national territories under the rule of sovereign states. There is no such entity as a global economy completely "out there," in some space that exists outside nation-states. Even electronic markets and firms operating out of the World Wide Web have some aspect of their operation partly embedded in actual national territories. Yet the location of the global largely in the national happens through a significant new development: a change in the ways in which the national state regulates and governs at least part of its economy. Deregulation and privatization are but partial descriptions of this change. The outcome is the formation of transnational spaces inside the national. This new configuration is increasingly being called a global economy to distinguish it from earlier formations such as the old colonial empires or the international economic system of the immediate post-World War II period, in which governments played a crucial regulatory role in international trade, investment, and financial markets.

Understanding how global processes locate in national territories requires new concepts and research strategies. The global city is one such new concept; it draws on and demands research practices that negotiate the intersection of macroanalysis and ethnography. It presumes that global processes, from the formation of global financial markets to the rapid growth of transnational labor markets, can be studied through the particular forms in which they materialize in places.

This book shows how some cities—New York, Tokyo, London, São Paulo, Hong Kong, Toronto, Miami, and Sydney, among others—have evolved into transnational "spaces." As such cities have prospered, they have come to have more in common with one another than with regional centers in their own nation-states, many of which have declined in importance. Such developments require all those interested in the fate of cities to rethink traditionally held views of cities as subunits of their nation-states or to reassess the importance of national geography in our social world. Moreover, the impact of global processes radically transforms the social structure of cities themselves—altering the organization of labor, the distribution of earnings, the structure of consumption, all of which in turn create new patterns of urban social inequality. In *Cities in a World Economy,* I seek to provide the vocabulary and analytic frames with which students and the general reader can grasp this new world of urban forms.

List of Exhibits

1

Place and Production in the Global Economy

I n the late twentieth century, massive developments in telecommunications and the ascendance of information industries led analysts and politicians to proclaim the end of cities. Cities, they told us, would become obsolete as economic entities. The growth of information industries allows firms and workers to remain connected no matter where they are located. The digitizing of services and trade shifts many economic transactions to electronic networks, where they can move instantaneously around the globe or within a country. Indeed, from the 1970s onward, there have been large-scale relocations of offices and factories to less congested and lower-cost areas than central cities, as well as the growth of computerized workplaces that could be located anywhere—in a clerical "factory" in the Bahamas, China, or a home in the suburbs. Although these trends may be sharpest in the United States, they are evident in a growing number of countries around the world. Finally, the emergent globalization of economic activity seems to suggest that place—particularly the type of place represented by cities—no longer matters. All of these trends are still happening now, and they are becoming more intense.

I argue in this book that these trends are only half of the story of today's global and digital age. Alongside the well-documented spatial dispersal of economic activities and the increased digitizing of the sphere of consumption and entertainment are the growing spatial concentration of a wide range

1

of highly specialized professional activities, top-level management, and control operations, as well as, perhaps most unexpectedly, a multiplication of low-wage jobs and low-profit economic sectors. We might think more analytically of these trends as the development of novel forms of territorial centralization amid rapidly expanding economic and social networks with global span.

Given the generalized trends toward dispersal—whether at the metropolitan or global level—and given the widespread conviction that this is the future, what needs explaining is that at the same time centralized territorial nodes are growing. In this book, I examine why and how firms and markets that operate in multisited national and global settings require central places where the top-level work of running global systems gets done. I also show why information technologies and industries designed to span the globe require a vast physical infrastructure containing strategic nodes with hyper-concentrations of material facilities. Finally, I show how even the most advanced information industries, such as global finance and the specialized corporate legal and accounting services, have a production process that is partly place-bound.

Once these place-centered processes are brought into the analysis of the new global and electronic economy, funny things happen. It turns out to be not only the world of top-level transnational managers and professionals but also that of their secretaries and that of the janitors cleaning the buildings where the new professional class works. Further, it also turns out to be the world of a whole new workforce, increasingly made up of immigrant and minoritized citizens, who take on the functions once performed by the mother/wife of the older middle classes: the nannies, domestic cleaners, and dog walkers who service the households of the new professional class also hold jobs in the new globalized sectors of the economy. So do truck drivers and industrial service workers. Thus emerges an economic configuration very different from that suggested by the concept of *information economy*. We recover the material conditions, production sites, and place-boundedness that are also part of globalization and the information economy. To understand the new globalized economic sectors, we actually need detailed examinations of a broad range of activities, firms, markets, and physical infrastructures that go beyond the images of global electronic networks and the new globally circulating professional classes.

These types of detailed examinations allow us to see the actual role played by cities in a global economy. They help us understand why, when the new information technologies and telecommunications infrastructures were introduced on a large scale in all advanced industries beginning in the 1980s, we saw sharp growth in the central business districts of the leading cities and international business centers of the world—New York, Los Angeles, London, Tokyo, Paris, Frankfurt, São Paulo, Hong Kong, and Sydney, among others. For some, this took off in the 1980s, and for others, in the 1990s and into the new century. But all experienced some of their highest growth in decades, in terms of the actual area covered by state-of-the-art office districts; the related high-end shopping, hotel, and entertainment districts; and high-income residential neighborhoods and in the numbers of firms located and opening up in these downtown areas. These trends in major cities in the 1980s, 1990s, and onward go against what was expected according to models emphasizing territorial dispersal; this is especially true considering the high cost of locating in a major downtown area. Complicating understanding and often getting most of the attention from the media and commentators was the fact that even as the number of smaller, highly specialized and high-profit firms was growing in the downtowns of major cities, large banks and insurance firms and the administrative headquarters of large firms were often moving out. This suggests that the growth trends were part of a new type of economic configuration. Thus explaining the place of cities in terms of the departure of major corporate headquarters and large corporate firms and the growing dispersal trends was evidently missing a key new component of the story.

But this still leaves us with the question, If information technologies have not made cities obsolete, have they at least altered the economic function of cities—have cities lost some of their old functions and gained new ones we could not quite understand when these trends were taking off? And if this is so, what does it tell us about the importance of place and its far greater mix of diverse economic sectors and social groups than is suggested by the prevalent imagery of high-level corporate economic globalization and information flows? Is there a new and strategic role for major cities, a role linked to the formation of a truly global economic system, a role not sufficiently recognized by analysts and policymakers? And could it be that the reason this new and strategic role has not been sufficiently recognized is that economic globalization—what it actually takes to implement global markets and processes—is not only about massive dispersal of operations around the world and remaining connected no matter where one is located but also about thick places?

The notion of a global economy has become deeply entrenched in political and media circles all around the world. Yet its dominant images—the instantaneous transmission of money around the globe, the information economy, the neutralization of distance through telematics—are partial, and hence profoundly inadequate, representations of what globalization and the rise of information economies actually entail for the concrete life of cities.

Missing from this abstract model are the actual material processes, activities, and infrastructures crucial to the implementation of globalization. Overlooking the spatial dimension of economic globalization and overemphasizing the information dimensions both have served to distort the role played by major cities in the current phase of economic globalization.

A focus on cities almost inevitably brings with it recognition of the existence of multiple social groups, neighborhoods, contestations, claims, and inequalities. But this brings up its own questions. Where does the global function of major cities begin, and where does it end? How do we establish what segments of the thick and complex environment of cities are part of the global? These issues are difficult to measure and determine with precision. But that does not mean that we can overlook them and simply focus on the economic core of advanced firms and the households of top-level professionals. We need to enter the various worlds of work and social contexts and establish their articulations, if any, with the global functions that are partly structured in these cities. This requires using analytic tools and concepts that come from the scholarship on class and inequality, immigration, gendering, the politics of culture, and so on. These are scholarships not easily associated with the prevalent imagery about the information economy. At the same time, these kinds of inquiries also help us specify the question of globalization in more than its economic forms and contents. The help us specify the fact of multiple globalizations—economic, political, and cultural. Cities are good laboratories for these types of inquiries because they bring together vast mixes of people, institutions, and processes in ways that allow us to study them in great detail. Few if any other places contain such a mix of people and conditions and make their detailed study as possible.

One way of addressing the question of where the global begins and ends in this thick environment is to focus in detail on the shapes and contents of globalization rather than assuming it consists of global firms and global professionals.

Beginning in the late 1970s and taking off in the mid-1980s, there have been pronounced changes in the geography, composition, and institutional framework of the world economy. Although cross-border flows of capital, trade, information, and people have existed for centuries, the world economy has been repeatedly reconstituted over time. A key starting point for this book is the fact that in each historical period, the world economy has consisted of a distinct configuration of geographic areas, industries, and institutional arrangements. One of the most important changes in the current phase has been the increase in capital mobility at both the national and especially the transnational levels. This transnational mobility of capital has brought about specific forms of articulation among different geographic areas and transformations in the role played by these areas in the world economy. This trend in turn has produced several types of locations for international transactions, the most familiar of which are export processing zones and offshore banking centers; these began to be developed in the late 1960s, precisely a time when national states exercised strong regulatory powers over their economies. One question for us is, then, the extent to which major cities are yet another type of *location* for international transactions in today's world economy, although clearly one at a very high level of complexity compared with those zones and centers.

A key focus in studies on the global economy has been increased capital mobility, particularly in the shape of the changing geographic organization of manufacturing production and the rapidly expanding number of financial markets becoming part of global networks. These are critical dimensions, and they emphasize the dispersal of firms and markets worldwide. What such studies leave out is the fact that this dispersal itself generates a demand for specific types of production needed to ensure the management, control, and servicing of this new organization of manufacturing and finance. These new types of production range from the development of telecommunications to specialized services—legal, accounting, insurance—that are key inputs for any firm managing a global network of factories, offices, and service outlets, and for any financial market operating globally. The mobility of capital also generates the production of a broad array of innovations in these sectors. These types of service production have their own locational patterns; they tend toward high levels of agglomeration in cities with the needed resources and talent pools. Thus the fact itself that a manufacturing multinational firm produces its goods partly in export processing zones in 10, 20, or even 30 countries creates a demand for new types of accounting, legal, and insurance services. It is these increasingly specialized and complex services that can benefit from the many state-of-the-art firms and experienced professionals concentrated in cities.

We will want to ask whether a focus on the *production* of these service inputs illuminates the question of place in processes of economic globalization, particularly the kind of place represented by cities. In fact, specialized services for firms and financial transactions, as well as the complex markets connected to these economic sectors, are a layer of activity that has been central to the organization of major global processes beginning in the 1980s. To what extent is it useful to add the broader category of cities as key production sites for such services for firms to the list of recognized global spaces, that is, headquarters of transnational corporations, export processing zones, and offshore banking centers? These are all more narrowly defined locations compared with cities. But I show in this book that to further our understanding of major aspects of the world economy's organization and management we cannot confine our analysis to these narrow and self-evident "global" locations. We need to enter and explore the more complex space where multiple economies and work cultures come together to produce the complex organizational and management infrastructure necessary to handle the running of global operations. Further, we need to understand the new types of tensions, segmentations, and inequalities that are generated in this process and become visible in the space of the city.

However, this way of thinking about cities as a site for empirical research about economic, political, and cultural globalization has tended to fall between the cracks of existing scholarship. On the one hand, much of the research on cities focuses on internal social, economic, and political conditions, and it views cities as parts of national urban systems. International matters have typically been considered the preserve of nation-states, not of cities. On the other hand, the literature on international economic activities has traditionally focused on the activities of multinational corporations and banks and has seen the key to globalization in the *power* of multinational firms and the new telecommunications capabilities. This leaves no room for a possible role for cities. Finally, the scholarship on international relations has confined itself to a focus on states as the key actors in the global realm.

All of these approaches contain much useful and important empirical and analytical material. But they are not enough to allow us to understand cities as strategic global sites. Twenty years of empirical and theoretical struggles by a small but growing number of researchers from many parts of the world have now produced a novel type of scholarship that gets precisely at this issue. Usually referred to as the *world cities* or *global city* scholarship, it provides many of the materials examined and discussed in this book.

Including cities in the analysis adds three important dimensions to the study of globalization. First, it breaks down the nation-state into a variety of components and thereby allows us to establish whether and how some are articulated with global processes, and others, not at all. Second, it displaces our focus from the power of large corporations over governments and economies to the range of activities and organizational arrangements necessary for the implementation and maintenance of a global network of factories, service operations, and markets; these are all processes only partly encompassed by the activities of transnational corporations and banks. Third, it contributes to a focus on place and on the urban social and political order associated with these activities. Processes of economic globalization are thereby reconstituted as concrete production complexes situated in specific places containing a multiplicity of activities and interests, many unconnected to global processes. As with other production complexes—mines, factories, transport hubs—the narrowly economic aspects are only one, even if crucial, component. The organization of labor markets, their gendering, new inequalities, and local politics can variously be part of it all. Including these dimensions allows us to specify the microgeographies and politics unfolding within these places. Finally, focusing on cities allows us to specify a variety of transnational geographies that connect specific groups of cities—depending on economic activity, migration flows, and the like.

Bringing all of these elements together is a central thesis organizing this book: Since the 1980s, major transformations in the composition of the world economy, including the sharp growth of specialized services for firms and finance, have renewed the importance of major cities as sites for producing strategic global inputs. In the current phase of the world economy, it is precisely the combination of the global dispersal of factories, offices and service outlets, *and* global information integration—under conditions of continued concentration of economic ownership and control—that has contributed to a strategic role for certain major cities. These I call *global cities* (Sassen [1991] 2001), of which there are about 40 today in the world, covering a broad variety of specialized roles in today's global economy. Some of these, such as London, Amsterdam, Mumbai, and Shanghai, have been centers for world trade and banking for centuries. Others have not, notably São Paulo, Chicago, and Los Angeles. Today's global cities are (1) command points in the organization of the world economy; (2) key locations and marketplaces for the leading industries of the current period—finance and specialized services for firms; and (3) major sites of production, including the production of innovations, for these industries. Several cities also fulfill equivalent functions on the smaller geographic scales of both trans- and subnational regions. Furthermore, whether at the global or at the regional level, these cities must inevitably engage each other in fulfilling their functions, as the new forms of growth seen in these cities are a result of these networks of cities. There is no such entity as a single global city.

Once we focus on places, whether cities or other types of places, rather than whole national economies, we can easily take account of the fact that some places even in the richest countries are becoming poorer, or that a global city in a developing country can become richer even as the rest of the country becomes poorer. An analysis of places, rather than national indicators, produces a highly variable mosaic of results. Alongside these new global and regional hierarchies of cities is a vast territory that has become increasingly peripheral and is excluded from the major processes that fuel economic growth in the new global economy. Many formerly important manufacturing centers and port cities have lost functions and are in decline, not only in the less developed countries but also in the most advanced economies. This is yet another meaning of economic globalization. We can think of these developments as constituting new geographies of centrality that cut across the old divide of poor versus rich countries, or, as in my preferred usage in this book, the global South versus global North divide. But there are also new geographies of marginality cutting across the poor–rich country divide, as growing numbers of people in global cities of both the north and the south are now poorer and work in casual rather than unionized jobs.

The most powerful of these new geographies of centrality binds together the major international financial and business centers: New York, London, Tokyo, Paris, Frankfurt, Chicago, Zurich, Amsterdam, Sydney, Toronto, and Hong Kong, among others. But this geography now also includes cities such as Seoul, Singapore, São Paulo, Mexico City, Mumbai, and Buenos Aires. The intensity of transactions among these cities, particularly through financial markets, flows of services, and investment, has increased sharply, and so have the orders of magnitude involved. At the same time, there has been a sharpening inequality in the concentration of strategic resources and activities between each of these cities and others in their respective countries. For example, Paris now concentrates a larger share of leading economic sectors and wealth in France than it did as recently as 1980, whereas Marseilles, once a major economic center, has lost some of its share in France's economy. Frankfurt's financial center has gained in share sharply over the other financial centers in what is the rather decentralized political organization of Germany, which we might have expected to accommodate multiple equally strong financial centers. Some national capitals, for example, have lost central economic functions and power to the new global cities, which have taken over some of the coordination functions, markets, and production processes once concentrated in national capitals or in major regional centers. A case in point, São Paulo has gained immense strength as a business and financial center in Brazil over Rio de Janeiro—once the capital and most important city in the country—and over the once powerful axis represented by Rio and Brasilia, the current capital. This is one of the meanings, or consequences, of the formation of a globally integrated economic system.

These economic dynamics are partly constituted in social and cultural terms. For example, foreign or native migrant workforces supply the new types of professional households with nannies and cleaners; these same migrants also bring cultural practices that add to street life, and they bring political experiences that can help with union organizing. Further, these economic dynamics have often sharp and visible effects on urban space, notably the expansion of luxury housing and office districts at the cost of displacing lower income households and low-profit firms. The city brings together and makes legible the enormous variety of globalities that are emerging and the many different forms—social, cultural, spatial—they assume.

More generally, what is the impact of this type of economic growth on the broader social and economic order of these cities? Much earlier research on the impact of dynamic, high-growth manufacturing sectors in developed and developing countries shows that these sectors raised wages, reduced economic inequality, and contributed to the formation and expansion of a middle class. There is less research on the distributive outcomes of the new economic sectors that dominate global cities, partly because these are still young processes. But the available evidence does show much more inequality than that associated with dynamic manufacturing-based economies.

These various features of the globalized core in complex cities become legible when we emphasize the material conditions for, and the work of producing the specialized services that are a key component of all such cities. It means, as indicated earlier, bringing into the analysis nonprofessional workers and work cultures: for example, the truckers that deliver the software, not only the high-level professionals that use it. Such an emphasis is not typical in research on these specialized services; they are usually seen as a type of output—that is, the results of high-level technical expertise. Thus insufficient attention has been paid to the actual array of jobs, from high paying to low paying, involved in the production of even the most sophisticated and complex services. A focus on production displaces the emphasis from expertise to work. Services need to be produced, and the buildings that hold the workers need to be built and cleaned. The rapid growth of the financial industry and of highly specialized services generates not only high-level technical and administrative jobs but also low-wage unskilled jobs. This is one type of inequality we are seeing within cities, especially within global cities. Since it is also evident in global cities of developing and even poor countries, it feeds into the formation of new geographies of centrality that cut across the North–South divide discussed earlier.

This new urban economy is in many ways highly problematic, particularly in global cities where it assumes its sharpest forms given the large concentrations of high-profit firms and high-income households. The new growth sectors of specialized services and finance contain capabilities for profit making vastly superior to those of more traditional economic sectors. Many of these more traditional sectors remain essential for the operation of the urban economy, including the new globalized core, and for the daily needs of residents, but their survival is threatened in a situation in which finance and specialized services can earn superprofits. This sharp polarization in the profit-making capabilities of different sectors of the economy has always existed. But what we see happening today takes place on a higher order of magnitude, and it is engendering massive distortions in the operations of various markets, from housing to labor. We can see this effect, for example, in the unusually sharp increase in the beginning salaries of MBAs and lawyers in the corporate sector and in the falling or stagnating wages of low-skilled manual and clerical workers. We can see the same effect in the retreat of many real estate developers from the low- and medium-income housing market as the rapidly expanding demand for housing by the new highly paid professionals can deliver higher profits, as can the possibility of sharp overpricing of this housing supply. These trends are all evident in cities as diverse as New York and Dublin, Oslo and São Paulo, Shanghai and Istanbul.

The rapid development of an international property market has made this disparity even worse. It means that real estate prices at the center of New York City are more connected to prices in central London or Frankfurt than to the overall real estate market in New York's metropolitan area. In the 1980s, powerful institutional investors from Japan, for example, found it profitable to buy and sell property in Manhattan or central London. In the 1990s, this practice multiplied involving a rapidly growing number of cities around the world. German, Dutch, French, and U.S. firms invested heavily in properties in central London and in other major cities. Increasingly, the city itself became the object of investment. And even after the attacks of September 2001, New York City real estate has been bought by a growing number of foreign investors, partly due to the weak dollar, which made these acquisitions profitable. These practices generally force prices up because of the competition among very powerful and rich investors and buyers. Because much of the purpose is to sell at a profit rather than actually using the property, this further raises prices. How can a low- or medium-profit local commercial operation compete with such powerful investors for space and other resources, no matter how long and successful its record in the older economy?

The high profit-making capability of the new growth sectors rests partly on speculative activity. The extent of this dependence on speculation can be seen in the regular crises in many developed countries. Notable is the crisis in the late 1980s and early 1990s that followed the unusually high profits in finance and real estate in the 1980s. That real estate and financial crisis, however, seems to have left the basic dynamic of the sector untouched, and we saw prices and stock market values reach new highs by the mid-1990s—only to have yet another crisis in 1997–98, though by then most of the highly developed countries had learned how to protect themselves, and the price was largely paid by countries considered emerging markets for financial investments. This crisis was, once again, followed by enormous increases as the decade closed. These crises can thus be seen as a temporary adjustment to more reasonable (i.e., less speculative) profit levels. But the overall dynamic of polarization in profit levels in the urban economy remains in place across these various crises, as do the distortions in many markets.

The typical informed view of the global economy, cities, and the new growth sectors does not incorporate the multiple dimensions that this book focuses on. Elsewhere, I have argued that we could think of the dominant narrative or mainstream account of economic globalization as a narrative of eviction (Sassen 1996). In the dominant account, the key concepts of globalization, information economy, and high-level professional outputs all suggest that place no longer matters and that the only type of worker that matters is the highly educated one. That account favors (1) the capability for global transmission over the concentrations of material infrastructure that make transmission possible; (2) information outputs over the workers producing those outputs, from specialists to secretaries; and (3) the new transnational corporate culture over the multiplicity of cultural environments, including reterritorialized immigrant cultures within which many of the *other* jobs of the global information economy take place. In brief, the dominant narrative concerns itself with the upper circuits of capital, not the lower ones, and with the fact of hypermobility.

This narrow focus has the effect of excluding from the account the *place*-boundedness of significant components of the global information economy; it thereby also excludes a whole array of activities and types of workers from the story of globalization that are in their own way as vital to it as are international finance and global telecommunications. Failing to include these activities and workers ignores the variety of cultural contexts within which they exist, a diversity as present in processes of globalization as is the new international corporate culture. When we focus on place and production, we can see that globalization is a process involving not only the corporate economy and the new transnational corporate culture but also, for example, the immigrant economies and work cultures evident in global cities.

These new empirical trends and theoretical developments are making cities prominent once again for a small but growing number of social scientists and cultural theorists. Cities have reemerged not only as objects of study but also as a lens for research and theorization about a broad array of major social, cultural, economic, and political processes central to the current era:

(1) economic globalization and international migration, (2) the emergence of specialized services and finance as the leading growth sector in advanced economies, (3) new types of inequality, (4) the new politics of identity and culture, (5) new types of politically and ideologically radicalizing dynamics, and (6) the politics of space, notably the growing movement for claiming rights to the city. Many of these processes are not urban per se, but they have an urban moment; in many cases the urban moment has become increasingly important and/or capable of illuminating key features of the larger process involved. In this context, it is worth noting that we are also seeing the beginning of a repositioning of cities in policy arenas. Two instances in particular stand out. One is the programmatic effort at the World Bank to develop analyses that can show how important urban economic productivity is to macroeconomic performance; in the past, economic growth was measured simply in terms of national indicators. The other is the explicit effort by the leadership of a growing number of cities to bypass national states and gain direct access to global investment and tourism markets as well as to recruit firms, cultural projects (such as international festivals and science exhibitions), sports events, and conventions. The mayors of a growing number of cities worldwide have set up offices for foreign economic affairs in multiple countries and appear increasingly interested in dealing directly with mayors of other countries.

The subject of the city in a world economy is extremely broad. The literature on cities is enormous, but it focuses mostly on single cities and on domestic issues; further, international studies of cities tend to be comparative. What was lacking until recently a transnational perspective on the subject: that is to say, one that takes as its starting point a dynamic system or set of transactions that by their nature entail multiple locations involving more than one country. This contrasts with a comparative international approach, which focuses on two or more cities that may have no connections among each other.

This book focuses particularly on recent empirical and conceptual developments because they are an expression of major changes in urban and national economies and in modes of inquiry about cities. Such a choice is inevitably limited and certainly cannot account for the cases of many cities that may *not* have experienced any of these developments. Our focus on the urban impact of economic, political, and cultural globalization; the new inequalities among and within cities; and the new urban sociospatial order is justified by the major characteristics of the current historical period and the need for social scientists to address these changes.

Chapter 2 examines key characteristics of the global economy that matter for an understanding of globalization and cities. In many cities, these global presences are weak or nonexistent. But they are increasingly strong in a growing number of cities. Chapter 3 analyzes the new interurban inequalities, focusing on three key issues: (1) the impact of globalization, particularly the internationalization of production and the growth of tourism, on so-called primate urban systems in less developed countries; (2) the impact of economic globalization on so-called balanced urban systems; and (3) the possible formation of transnational urban systems. A rapidly growing research literature now finds sharp increases in the linkages binding the cities that function as production sites and marketplaces for global capital. Chapter 4 focuses on the new urban economy, where finance and specialized services have emerged as driving engines for profit making. Chapter 5 examines these issues in greater detail through a series of case studies of several cities at the turning point that led them into global city status. Chapter 6 focuses on the emergence of new urban social forms resulting from growing inequalities and segmentations in labor markets and urban space. The effort here is to understand whether the changes documented in this book are merely a quantitative transformation or also a qualitative one. Is it simply a matter of more poor and more inequality, or are we seeing a type of poverty and inequality that constitutes new social forms? Chapter 7 takes one particular case as a lens to get at a more detailed and focused account of the issues introduced in Chapter 6: women immigrants who increasingly constitute global care chains as they become the nannies, nurses, maids, and sex workers in global cities. Chapter 8 considers the larger social, cultural, and political dynamics that are becoming mobilized through the variety of processes examined in this book.

2

The Urban Impact
of Economic Globalization

Profound changes in the composition, geography, and institutional
framework of the world economy over the centuries have had major
implications for cities. In the 1800s, when the world economy consisted
largely of extracting natural resources and trade, cities were already servicing centers, typically developed alongside harbors; trading companies
depended on multiple industrial, banking, and other commercial services
located in cities. Many of the major cities in the colonial empires of Britain,
the Netherlands, France, Germany, Spain, and Portugal were international
gateways. Yet cities were not the key production sites for the leading industries in the 1800s; wealth production was centered in harbors, plantations,
factories, and mines.

Today's global economy still consists of international trade, agribusiness,
manufacturing, and extraction of natural resources, but these have all been
overshadowed both in value and in power by the development of vast global
financial markets as well as a proliferation of global markets for highly
specialized corporate services. In the 1980s, finance and services generally
emerged as the major components of international transactions: They service
all the other components of the global economy; thus as the latter grow, so
does the value of finance and services for firms. Further, finance has created
its own wealth-producing markets, as have some of the specialized services,
such as consulting services of various kinds. The shift to electronic financial

markets and the lifting of national country barriers to capital flows, both features taking off in the late 1980s, allowed finance to reach values that dwarfed those of other major components of the global economy. Thus, by the end of 2004, the value of global trade stood at US$11 trillion, compared with US$262 trillion for global finance—as measured through the value of traded derivatives. Foreign direct investment (FDI) grew three times faster in the 1980s than the export trade, and, by the mid-1980s, investment in services had become the main component in FDI flows, whereas before it had been in manufacturing and raw materials extraction—all trends that became even sharper in the 1990s. The crucial sites for financial and services transactions are financial markets, advanced corporate service firms, banks, and the headquarters of transnational corporations (TNCs). Today, it is these sites that lie at the heart of the global economy rather than mines, factories, and plantations. The most specialized and least routinized of these markets and firms are disproportionately concentrated in global cities. Indeed, they are the key components of the global city function.

Thus, one of the variables influencing the role of cities in the new global economy is the composition of international transactions. Although standard analyses of the world economy focus in great detail on this variable, they do not pick up on its spatial correlates and hence on the significance of cities in the global economy. It took the scholarship on global cities and world cities to arrive at this conceptualization.

In the first half of this chapter, I present a somewhat detailed account of the geography, composition, and institutional framework of the global economy today with an eye to capturing the implications for cities. In the second half, I focus on two types of strategic places for international financial and service transactions: global cities and offshore banking centers. Finally, I consider the impact of the collapse of the Pax Americana on the world economy and the subsequent shift in the geographical axis of international transactions.

The Global Economy Today

The emphasis here is on new investment patterns and the major features of the current period. The purpose is not to present an exhaustive account of all that constitutes the world economy today. It is rather to discuss what distinguishes the current period from the immediate past.

Geography

A key empirical feature of the world economy regardless of the century or the dominant empire is its geography. The geography of empire depends on multiple factors, ranging from the number of competing empires to the content of imperial transactions. When international flows consist of raw materials, agricultural products, or mining goods, the geography of transactions is in part determined by the location of natural resources. Historically, this has meant that a large number of countries in Africa, Latin America, and the Caribbean were key sites in this geography. When finance and specialized services became the dominant component of international transactions in the early 1980s, the role of many of these areas declined in importance and that of financial and service centers increased.

Compared with the 1950s, in the 1980s there was an increase in the values but a narrowing of the geography of the global economy. The result was a strengthened East–West axis with a sharp growth of investment and trade within what at the time was referred to as the *triad:* the United States, Western Europe, and Japan. In contrast, developing countries lost share in overall international investment in the 1980s even as absolute values rose; as a group, though not individually, these countries had regained their share by the mid-1990s but typically through novel articulations with the world economy.

The fact of a new geography of international transactions becomes evident in FDI flows—that is, investors acquiring a firm, wholly or in part, or building and setting up new firms in a foreign country (see UNCTAD 1993 for a full definition). Foreign direct investment flows are highly differentiated in their destination because they consist of a vast number of individual investments in particular firms and locations. They can be constituted through many different kinds of economic processes. In the 1980s and 1990s, the growth in FDI took place through the internationalization of production of goods and services, and of portfolio investment (buying firms). Overall, worldwide FDI inflows went from US$159.3 billion for the period 1986–91, to US$310.9 for the period 1992–97, then escalated to US$1.388 trillion in 2000, and began to fall after 2001 down to US$559.6 billion in 2003, though this was a significantly higher level than the total for the period 1992–97 (Exhibit 2.1). Tertiary sector shares grew consistently over this period, while primary sector shares fell.

The geography of FDI shows clearly that by far the largest share of FDI went and continues to go to developed countries, with an average annual growth of 24% from 1986 to 1990, reaching a value of US$129.6 billion in 1991, out of a total worldwide FDI inflow of US$159.3 billion, and jumping up to US$1.1 trillion in 2000 out of a world total of US$1.38 trillion (see Exhibit 2.1). On average, the share of developed countries has hovered around 70%, albeit with fluctuations across the years. There was sharp concentration in the destination of flows even among developed countries. Four countries tend to be the major recipient and capital-exporting countries

(United States, United Kingdom, France, and Germany); together they account for about half of world inflows and outflows. Financial concentration is also evident in a ranking of the top banks in the world, with only eight countries represented (Exhibit 2.2 and also Chapter 5)

The growth of investment flows into developing countries in the 1990s did not even come near the levels for developed countries, but they did represent a historic high—a fact that reflects the growing internationalization of economic activity generally (see Exhibit 2.1). From 1985 to 1990, FDI grew at an annual rate of 22%, compared with 3% from 1980 to 1984, and 13% from 1975 to 1979. Yet the share of worldwide flows going to developing countries as a whole fell from 26% to 17% between the early 1980s and the late 1980s, pointing to the strength of flows within the triad (United States, Western Europe, and Japan). From 1992 to 1997, the average share grew to 38% of world inflows, before falling again with the Asian financial crisis of 1997–98. After a low of 18% of world inflows, the share of developing countries was up to 30.7% in 2003. When the flows to developing countries are disaggregated for the 1980s and 1990s, it becomes clear that they went mostly into East, South, and Southeast Asia, where the annual growth rate on average was more than 37% a year in the 1980s and 1990s. These figures point to the emergence of this Asian region as a crucial transnational space for production. In the 1980s, it surpassed Latin America and the Caribbean for the first time ever as the largest host region for FDI in developing countries.

There was a time when Latin America was the single largest recipient region of FDI. But the 1980s marked the end of that phase. Between 1985 and 1989, Latin America's share of total flows to developing countries fell from 49% to 38%, and Southeast Asia's share rose from 37% to 48%. However, the absolute increase in FDI has been so sharp that, notwithstanding a falling share, Latin America actually experienced increases in the amount of FDI, especially toward the end of the 1980s and in the 1990s. But again, when the flows to Latin America are disaggregated, it's obvious that most investment went to a handful of countries, especially Brazil, Argentina, and Chile.

The other two major components of the global economy are trade and financial flows other than FDI. By its very nature, the geography of trade is less concentrated than that of direct foreign investment. Wherever there are buyers, sellers are likely to go. Finance, on the other hand, is enormously concentrated; it is described later in the book.

Composition

In the 1950s, the major international flow was world trade, especially of raw materials, other primary products, and resource-based manufacturing.

Exhibit 2.1 Inflows and Outflows of Foreign Direct Investment (FDI), 1986–2003 (US$ billions and percentage)

Year	Developed Countries		Developing Countries		Central and Eastern Europe		All Countries	
	Inflows	Outflows	Inflows	Outflows	Inflows	Outflows	Inflows	Outflows
Value (billions of US$)								
1986–1991	129.6	169.2	29.1	11.3	0.7	0.0	159.3	180.5
1992–1997	180.8	275.7	118.6	51.4	11.5	1.2	310.9	328.2
1998	472.6	631.5	194.1	53.4	24.3	2.3	690.9	687.2
1999	828.3	1014.3	231.9	75.5	26.5	2.5	1086.8	1092.2
2000	1108.0	1083.9	252.5	98.9	27.5	4.0	1388.0	1186.8
2001	571.5	658.1	219.7	59.9	26.4	3.5	817.6	721.5
2002	489.9	547.6	157.6	44.0	31.2	4.9	678.8	596.5
2003	366.6	569.6	172.0	35.6	21.0	7.0	559.6	612.2
Share in total (percentage)								
1986–1991	81.3	93.7	18.3	6.3	0.0*	0.00*	100.0	100.0
1992–1997	58.2	83.9	38.1	15.7	3.7	0.3	100.0	100.0
1998	68.4	91.9	28.1	7.8	3.5	0.3	100.0	100.0
1999	76.2	92.9	21.3	6.9	2.4	0.2	100.0	100.0
2000	79.8	91.3	18.2	8.3	2.0	0.3	100.0	100.0
2001	69.9	91.2	26.9	8.3	3.2	0.5	100.0	100.0
2002	72.2	91.8	23.2	7.4	4.6	0.8	100.0	100.0
2003	65.5	3.0	30.7	5.8	3.8	1.1	100.0	100.0

(Continued)

Exhibit 2.1 (Continued)

Year	Developed Countries		Developing Countries		Central and Eastern Europe		All Countries	
	Inflows	Outflows	Inflows	Outflows	Inflows	Outflows	Inflows	Outflows
Growth rate (percentage) 1998	161	129	64	4	111	92	122	109
1999	75	61	19	41	9	9	57	59
2000	34	7	9	31	4	60	28	9
2001	−48	−39	−13	−39	−4	−12	−41	−39
2002	−14	−17	−28	−27	18	40	−17	−17
2003	−25	4	9	−19	−33	43	−18	3

Note: Asterisk (*) denotes that the share in total FDI inflows and outflows was below 0.01 and 0.001, respectively.

Source: Calculations based on UNCTAD (1998:361–71; 2004:367–75).

Exhibit 2.2   Cities Ranked by Revenues of the World's Largest Commercial and Savings Banks, 2005 (US$ millions)

Rank	City	Number of Firms	Revenues	Profits
1	Paris	4	189,294	16,850
2	New York	2	165,207	21,512
3	London	3	140,822	22,264
4	Frankfurt	4	121,615	4,450
5	Brussels	3	120,211	7,796
6	Zurich	2	115,743	11,039
7	Edinburgh	2	107,506	13,868
8	Charlotte	2	91,391	19,357
9	Tokyo	3	86,055	6,808
10	Beijing	4	75,738	8,896
11 to 21		27	517,801	47,272
Total:	—	56	1,731,383	180,112

Source: Calculations based on "Global 500" (2005).

In the 1980s, the gap between the values mobilized through trade and those mobilized through financial flows began to widen sharply, a process that has continued since then. Thus, the global value of trade by 2004 stood at US$ 11 trillion; FDI stock, US$8 trillion; and internationally traded derivatives, US$262 trillion. Notwithstanding severe measurement problems, it is clear that the value reached by financial transactions dwarfs that of other flows. Finally, within FDI stock and flows, the tertiary sector raised its share over that of primary and secondary sector investments (Exhibit 2.3).

Many factors go into the composition of international transactions. For example, in the 1980s, (1) several developed countries became major capital exporters, most notably Japan; (2) the number of cross-border mergers and acquisitions grew sharply; and (3) the flow of services and transnational service corporations emerged as major components in the world economy. Services, which accounted for about 24% of worldwide stock in FDI in the early 1970s, had grown to 50% of stock and 60% of annual flows by the end of the 1980s. The single largest recipient of FDI in services in the 1980s was the European Community, yet another indication of a very distinct geography in world transactions (Exhibit 2.4). But investment in services also increased in absolute terms for developing countries. In the 1990s and into the early years of the twenty-first century, the second and third trends

(Text continues on page 26)

Exhibit 2.3 Sectoral Distribution of Foreign Direct Investment Stock for the Largest Developed Home Countries and the Largest Developed and Developing Host Countries, Select Years, 1970–1990 (US$ billions and percentage)

Group of Countries and Sectors	Billions of Dollars					Average Annual Growth Rate in Percentage					Share in Percentage				
	1970	1975	1980	1985	1990	1971–1975	1976–1980	1981–1985	1986–1990	1981–1990	1970	1975	1980	1985	1990
A. Outward stock															
Developed countries[a]															
Primary	29	58	88	115	160	14	8.7	5.5	6.8	6.2	22.7	25.3	18.5	18.5	11.2
Secondary	58	103	208	240	556	11.7	15.1	2.9	18.3	10.3	45.2	45	43.8	38.7	38.7
Tertiary	41	68	179	265	720	10.4	21.4	8.2	22.1	14.9	31.4	27.7	37.7	42.8	50.1
Total	129	229	475	620	1436	11.7	15.7	5.5	18.3	11.7	100	100	100	100	100
B. Inward stock															
Developed countries[b]															
Primary	12	17	18	39	94	4.7	5.9	16.7	19.2	18	16.2	12.1	6.7	9.2	9.1
Secondary	44	79	148	195	439	10.7	13.4	5.7	17.6	11.5	60.2	56.5	55.2	46.2	42.5
Tertiary	17	44	102	188	499	16.5	18.3	13	21.6	17.2	23.7	31.4	38.1	44.5	48.4
Total	73	140	268	422	1032	11.3	13.9	9.5	19.6	14.4	100	100	100	100	100

Group of Countries and Sectors	Billions of Dollars					Average Annual Growth Rate in Percentage					Share in Percentage				
	1970	1975	1980	1985	1990	1971–1975	1976–1980	1981–1985	1986–1990	1981–1990	1970	1975	1980	1985	1990
Developing countries/economies[c]															
Primary	—	7	17	31	46	—	19.4	12.8	8.2	10.5	—	20.6	22.7	24	21.9
Secondary	—	19	41	64	102	—	16.6	9.3	9.8	9.5	—	55.9	54.6	49.6	48.6
Tertiary	—	8	17	34	62	—	16.3	14.9	12.8	13.8	—	23.5	22.7	26.4	29.5
Total	—	34	75	129	210	—	17.1	11.4	10.2	10.8	—	100	100	100	100

Notes:

a. Australia, Canada, France, Federal Republic of Germany, Italy, Japan, Netherlands, United Kingdom, and United States; together these countries accounted for almost 90% of outward FDI stock in 1990. 1970 and 1971–1975 growth data exclude Australia and France.

b. Australia, Canada, France, Federal Republic of Germany, Italy, Japan, Netherlands, United Kingdom, Spain, and United States; together these countries accounted for approximately 72% of total inward FDI stock in 1990. 1970 and 1971–1975 growth data exclude Australia, France, and Spain.

c. Argentina, Brazil, Chile, China, Colombia, Hong Kong, Indonesia, Malaysia, Mexico, Nigeria, Philippines, Republic of Korea, Singapore, Taiwan Province of China, Thailand, and Venezuela. Together these countries accounted for 68% of total inward FDI in developing countries.

Source: UNCTAD (1993:62).

Exhibit 2.4   Foreign Direct Investment Flows by Sector, 1989–1991 and
2001–2002

	Inflows		Outflows	
	1989–1991	2001–2002	1989–1991	2001–2002
World:				
Primary	7.00%	9%	6%	7%
Manufacturing	39.00%	24%	39%	22%
Services	54.00%	67%	55%	71%
Developed Countries:				
Primary	6.00%	9%	6%	7%
Manufacturing	36.00%	18%	39%	22%
Services	58.00%	73%	55%	71%
Developing Countries:				
Primary	12.00%	10%	3%	1.80%
Manufacturing	53.00%	40%	58%	21%
Services	35.00%	50%	39%	77%

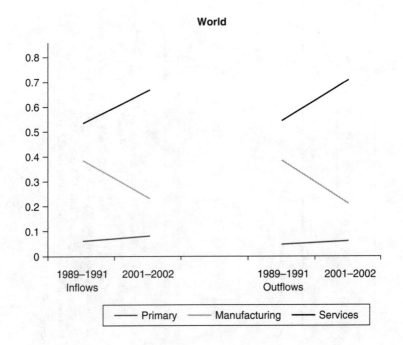

Developed Countries

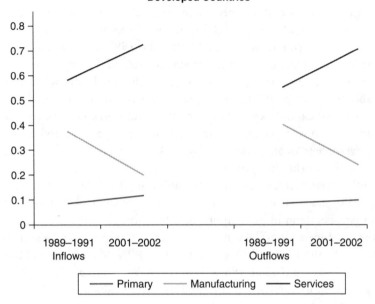

Developing Countries

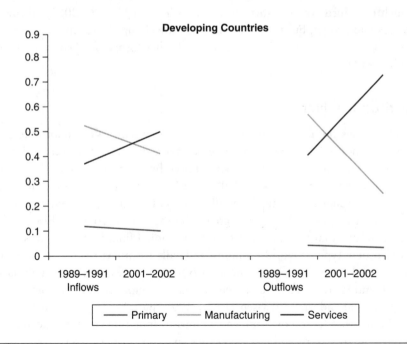

Source: UNCTAD (2004:263).

continued to shape the global economy. Services accounted for more than 70% of FDI inflows to developed countries by 2001–02. Mergers and acquisitions took off in the European Union and most recently in some of the most developed Asian countries, especially after the 1997–98 financial crisis. As for the first trend identified for the 1980s, the role of developed countries as the major capital exporters, it continues, including for Japan, which remains probably the leading exporter of capital; what is different is the absence of any new major capital exporters among the developed countries and the rise of China as a buyer (which we can think of as a type of capital export) of U.S. government debt, making it by 2005 the second leading owner of dollars in the world after Japan.

Another major transformation beginning in the 1980s and continuing today is the sharp growth in the numbers and economic weight of TNCs— firms that operate in more than one country through affiliates, subsidiaries, or other arrangements. The central role played by TNCs can be seen in the fact that U.S. and foreign TNCs accounted for 80% of international trade in the United States in the late 1980s (UNCTC 1991, chap. 3). By 1997, global sales generated by foreign affiliates of TNCs were valued at US$9.5 trillion, while worldwide exports of goods and services were at US$7.4 trillion, of which one-third was intrafirm trade (UNCTAD 1998). By 2003, all these figures had grown, but their relation was little changed, signaling the ongoing weight of TNCs and their affiliates and other forms of subcontracting in global trade.

Institutional Framework

How does the *world economy* cohere as a system? We cannot take the world economy for granted and assume that it exists simply because international transactions do. One question raised by the developments described earlier is whether today's global economic activities represent a mere quantitative change or actually entail a different international configuration, including changes in the regimes governing the world economy. Elsewhere, I have argued that the ascendance of international finance and services produces a new type of world economy and calls for novel regimes that often have sharply negative consequences for other industries, especially manufacturing, and for regional development insofar as regions tend to be dominated by particular industries (Sassen [1991] 2001, part 1). These are structural conditions that force powerful leaders into formulating certain conceptions about how to govern and how to ensure guarantees of contract.

One consequence of this new regime is that TNCs have become even more central to the organization and governance of the world economy, and new and vastly expanded older global markets are now an important element in the institutional framework. In addition to financing huge government deficits, the financial markets that exploded into growth in the 1980s served the needs of TNCs to a disproportionate extent. Transnational corporations also emerged as a source for financial flows to developing countries, both through direct inflows of FDI and indirectly, insofar as FDI stimulates other forms of financial flows. In some respects, TNCs replaced banks.[1] The bank crisis of 1982 sharply cut bank loans to developing countries to the point that the aggregate net flow of financial resources to developing countries was negative during much of the 1980s. For better or for worse, the TNC is now a strategic organizer of what we call the world economy.

Affiliates of TNCs and other contracting arrangements have become a key mechanism for organizing and governing the globalization of production and the delivery of services. The growth in their numbers has been sharp. From a world total of 174,900 in 1990, the number of affiliates reached about 927,000 by 2003. Partly reflecting the massive FDI flows among developed countries, the number of affiliates in developed countries grew from 81,800 in 1990 to 96,620 in 1996 and 102,560 in 2003. The United States, the United Kingdom, France, Germany, and Japan were the developed countries with the largest numbers. But by far the largest numbers of affiliates are in developing countries, because they are a mechanism for TNCs to enter the global South. Their number went from 71,300 in 1990 to 580,638 in 2003. Not surprisingly, the largest single concentration is in China, which accounted for 424,196 in 2002, up from about 16,000 as recently as 1989. A third area of sharp growth in the numbers of affiliates is Central and Eastern Europe, where the total went from 21,000 in 1990 to 243,750 in 2003 (Exhibit 2.5).

Global financial markets have emerged as yet another crucial institution for organizing and governing the world economy. The central role of financial markets, a key component of the world economy today, was in part brought about by the so-called third-world bank crisis formally declared in 1982. This was a crisis for the major transnational banks in the United States, with their massive loans to third-world countries and firms that were unable to repay. The crisis created a space into which moved small, highly competitive financial firms, far less subject to regulation than traditional banks, including transnational banks. This launched a whole new era in the 1980s in financial speculation, innovation, and levels of profitability. The result was a highly unstable period but one with almost inconceivably high levels of profits that fed a massive expansion in the volume of international financial transactions. Deregulation was another key mechanism facilitating

Exhibit 2.5   Number of Parent Transnational Corporations and Foreign
Affiliates, by Region and Country, Select Years, 1985–2003

	Year	Parent Corporations Based in Country	Foreign Affiliates Located in Country
All Developed Countries	1990	33,500	81,800
	1996	43,442	96,620
	2003	45,007	102,560
select countries:			
Australia	1992	1,306	695
	1997	485	2,371
	2001	682	2,352
Canada	1991	1,308	5,874
	1996	1,695	4,541
	1999	1,439	3,725
Fed. Rep. of Germany	1990	6,984	11,821
	1996	7,569	11,445
	2002	6,069	9,268
France	1990	2,056	6,870
	1996	2,078	9,351
	2002	1,267	10,713
Japan	1992	3,529	3,150
	1996	4,231	3,014
	2001	3,371	3,870
Sweden	1991	3,529	2,400
	1997	4,148	5,551
	2002	4,260	4,656
Switzerland	1985	3,000	2,900
	1995	4,506	5,774
United Kingdom	1991	1,500	2,900
	1996	1,059	2,609
	2003	2,607	13,176
United States	1990	3,000	14,900
	1995	3,379	18,901
	2000	3,235	15,712
All Developing Countries	1990	2,700	71,300
	1996	9,323	230,696
	2003	14,192	580,638
select countries:			
Brazil	1992	566	7,110
	1995	797	6,322
	1998	1225	8,050
China	1989	379	15,966
	1997	379	145,000
	2002	350	424,196

	Year	Parent Corporations Based in Country	Foreign Affiliates Located in Country
Colombia	1987	—	1,041
	1995	302	2,220
Hong Kong, China	1991	500	2,828
	1997	500	5,067
	2001	948	9,132
Indonesia	1988	—	1,064
	1995	313	3,472
Philippines	1987	—	1,952
	1995	—	14,802
Republic of Korea	1991	1,049	3,671
	1996	4,806	3,878
	2002	7,460	12,909
Singapore	1986	—	10,709
	1995	—	18,154
	2002	—	14,052
Central and Eastern Europe	1990	400	21,800
	1996	842	121,601
	2003	2313	243,750
World Total	1990	36,600	174,900
	1996	53,607	448,917
	2003	61,582	926,948

Source: Based on UNCTAD (1998:3–4; 2004:273–74).

this type of growth, centered in internationalization and speculation, as it opened up one country after another to these and other firms. Markets provided an institutional framework that organized these massive financial flows. Notwithstanding two financial crises, one in 1990–91 and the second in 1997–98, the end of the 1990s saw sharp growth in the value of financial transactions. And although the terrorist attacks of September 2001 in New York City created a temporary crisis, by the end of 2001, stock market capitalization had reached the levels it had had before September 2001. Considerable effort and resources have gone into the development of a framework for governing global finance, including the development of new institutional accounting and financial reporting standards, minimum capital requirements for banks, and efforts to institute greater transparency in corporate governance.

Trade has provided a third set of institutional framings. In 1993 the World Trade Organization (WTO) was set up to oversee cross-border trade. It has the power to adjudicate in cross-border disputes between countries and represents a potentially key institutional framework for the governance of the global economy. A second component in cross-border trade is the formation of transnational trading blocs. The three major blocs are the European Union (EU; which arose from the erstwhile European Economic Community), the Association of Southeast Asian Nations (ASEAN), and the North American Free Trade Agreement (NAFTA). But beyond these three massive blocs, there is a vast number of trade agreements both within and outside the framing of WTO. According to WTO, there were more than 70 regional trade agreements by the late 1990s and about 150 by 2004; given the role FDI can play in international trade, it is worth noting that by the mid-1990s 143 countries had adopted special regimes to attract FDI, up from 20 in 1982 (UNCTAD 1998, chap. 3). The specifics of each of the three major trading agreements and probably most of the other agreements vary sharply, but they all tend to feature the enhanced capability for capital to move across borders. Crucial to the design of the major blocs is the free movement of financial services as part of the international trade in services. Although trade has received far more attention, it is in many ways a less significant factor in changing the institutional apparatus of the world economy than is finance. There has long been considerable trade among the countries in each major bloc, and many import tariffs were already low for many goods in many countries. Beyond trade, the EU, NAFTA, and ASEAN blocs represent a further formalization of capital as a transnational entity, one that operates through TNCs and global trade.

These realignments have had pronounced consequences. The extremely high level of profitability in the financial industry, for example, has devalued manufacturing as production and a shift toward its value as a financial investment. This is illustrated by the rise of the notion of shareholder value: a shift in emphasis from production per se and on to securing good stock market valuations of a manufacturer's publicly listed shares. Second, much of the policy around deregulation has had the effect of making finance so profitable that it takes investment away from manufacturing. Third, finance also contains the possibility for superprofits by maximizing the circulation of and speculation in money—that is, multiplying buying and selling transactions over a given period of time with each such transaction a possible source of profit. Manufacturing does not have this option because capital for production is caught in much longer cycles (from six to nine months to produce a car or heavy equipment), and resale values are not where a company makes its profits. Fourth, beginning in the 1980s, a variety of instruments were created that made it possible to sell debts at a profit. A simple illustration is the bundling of a large number of home mortgages so as to reach certain value thresholds, no matter that these are negative values (debts), into instruments that can be sold many times over, even though the number of houses involved stays the same. *Securitization* is the general term used to describe this and other innovations that made it possible to transform various types of financial assets and debts into marketable instruments. This trend continues today with the invention of ever more complex and speculative instruments. Manufacturing as the production of goods does not have these options. The good is made and sold once; when the good enters the realm of circulation, it enters another set of industries, for example, trading firms and wholesalers, and the profits from subsequent sales accrue to these sectors.

These changes in the geography and composition of international transactions, and the framework through which these transactions are implemented, have contributed to the formation of new strategic sites in the world economy. This is the subject of the next section.

Strategic Places

Four types of places, above all others, symbolize the new forms of economic globalization: export processing zones, offshore banking centers, high-tech districts, and global cities. There are also many other locations where international transactions materialize. Harbors continue to be strategic in the world of growing international trade, and the major global harbors in the world contribute to a large demand for highly specialized legal, accounting, financial, and similar services. Massive industrial districts in major manufacturing export countries, such as the United States, Japan, and Germany, are in many ways strategic sites for international activity and specifically for production for export. None of these locations, however, captures the prototypical image of today's global economy the way the first four do.

Here, I do not examine export processing zones (e.g., Lim 1982) or high-tech districts (e.g., Saxenian 1996) in detail because their activities have a highly intermediated relationship to cities. These types of sites will reenter the analysis when I examine the role of manufacturing in the expansion of the specialized corporate services sector. My argument is, briefly, that if manufacturing is part of a corporate organization, the more it gets offshored, or, in the case of high-tech, the more global its markets and innovative its products, the more its umbrella corporation will need highly specialized legal, financial, accounting, and other such services to manage the manufacturing part. It suggests that from the perspective of a growth effect for the urban specialized services sector, where manufacturing is located matters less than whether it is part of a corporate organization.

Export processing zones, a less familiar entity than high-tech districts (made famous by California's Silicon Valley), deserve a brief description. Such zones tend to be located in low-wage countries where firms from developed countries can secure low wages for highly labor-intensive or high health-risk work. Labor-intensive manufacturing, processing, and assembling can be done at lower costs and with far less demanding environmental, workplace, and labor regulations than in home countries. What gets worked on typically is brought in from and reexported to the home countries of these firms. Developed countries had to implement a variety of legislative pieces to make this possible at a time when Keynesian tariffs and protections were the norm in developed countries. The central rationale for these zones is access to cheap labor for the labor-intensive stages of a firm's production process. Tax breaks and lenient workplace standards in the zones are additional incentives, whose granting also required legislative changes in the developing countries. These zones became a key mechanism in the internationalization of production that took off in the 1980s; but the first such zones were implemented in the late 1960s, partly as a response to the strength of labor unions at the time in developed countries and the emergence of strong legislatures willing to impose stricter environmental, workplace, and worker health standards. In addition to these zones, less formalized arrangements proliferated in the 1990s, which are usually referred to as *outsourcing*. The information on the explosion in the number of affiliates described earlier is one element in the infrastructure for outsourcing.

Now we turn to global cities and offshore banking centers, two sites of more direct concern to the analysis in this book.

Global Cities

Global cities are strategic sites for the management of the global economy and the production of the most advanced services and financial operations that have become key inputs for that work of managing global economic operations. The growth of international investment and trade and the need to finance and service such activities have fed the growth of these functions in major cities. The erosion of the role of the government in the world economy, which was much larger when trade was the dominant form of international transaction, has shifted some of the organizing and servicing work from governments to specialized service firms and global markets in services and finance. A second, much less noted, shift of functions to this specialized service sector concentrated in cities comes from the headquarters of global firms. The added complexity and uncertainties involved in running global operations and the need for highly specialized knowledge about the law, accounting, business cultures, and so on, of large numbers of countries has meant that a growing component of headquarter functions is now being outsourced to specialized corporate services firms. Therefore, today there are two sites for the production of headquarter functions of global firms: One is the headquarters proper, and the other is the specialized service sector disproportionately concentrated in major cities. Thus, when firms globalize their operations, they are not necessarily only exporting jobs, as is usually argued. They export certain jobs, for example, labor-intensive manufacturing and clerical work, but they actually may be adding jobs to their top headquarter functions. One way of putting it is to say that when Detroit lost many of its manufacturing jobs, New York City actually gained specialized service jobs, as the work of major auto manufacturing headquarters became increasingly complicated and required state-of-the-art legal, accounting, finance, and insurance advice, not to mention consulting of various kinds and new types of public relations efforts. Headquarters of firms that operate mostly globally tend to be located in global cities. But given the option to outsource the most complex and variable headquarter functions, headquarters can actually locate anywhere, a trend evident in the United States but less so in countries where there is only one major internationally connected city.

Here, I briefly examine these developments, first by presenting the concept of the global city and then some of the empirical evidence showing the concentration of major international markets and economic sectors in various cities.

Since the 1980s, the specific forms of the world economy have created particular organizational requirements that differ from those of the preceding phase, which had been dominated by large U.S. transnational corporations and banks seeking to develop markets for American products and bank accounts worldwide. The emergence of global markets for finance and specialized services, along with the growth of investment as a major type of international transaction, has created a demand for new types of organizational forms. These have contributed to the expansion in command functions and the demand for specialized services for firms, whether the firm is in agriculture, mining, transport, finance, or any other major sector. Much of this activity is not encompassed by the organizational form of the TNC or bank, even when these types of firms account for a disproportionate share of international flows. Nor is much of this activity encompassed by the power of transnationals, a power often invoked to explain the fact itself of economic globalization.

Of interest at this point are some of the hypotheses that launched the world city and global city analyses, especially those that examine the spatial and organizational forms of economic globalization and the actual work of running transnational economic operations. The aim of these hypotheses was to recover organizational forms other than that of the headquarters of powerful firms, which is the typical approach. Thus, these hypotheses also include particular types of places and work processes as part of the organizational framings for the current forms of economic globalization. In one of the first formulations that launched this new type of analysis, Friedmann and Wolff (1982) started from cities and emphasized the concentration of command and coordination functions of operations (see also Friedmann 1986). I proposed similar hypotheses but started from a somewhat different angle: The central proposition in the global city model (Sassen [1991] 2001) is that it is precisely the *combination* of geographic dispersal of economic activities with simultaneous system integration that gave cities a strategic role in the current phase of the world economy. Rather than becoming obsolete because of global geographic dispersal and integration made possible by information technologies, cities became strategic. In a very early formulation (Sassen-Koob 1982), I emphasized the growing need for long-distance management and how, ironically, this was going to generate all kinds of new professional jobs and firms, even though at the time most major cities in the United States and Europe were in severe economic and fiscal crisis. To the concentration of command and coordination functions emphasized by Friedmann and Wolff (1982) I added two additional functions: (1) Cities are postindustrial production sites for the leading industries of this period—finance and specialized services—and (2) cities are transnational marketplaces where firms and governments from all over the world can buy financial instruments and specialized services. These early formulations emerged long before this type of analysis exploded into a rapidly growing scholarship from the 1990s onward.[2]

The territorial dispersal of economic activity at the national and world scale implied by globalization has created new forms of territorial centralization. One critical and often overlooked fact is that this territorial dispersal is happening under conditions of ongoing concentration in ownership and control. Dispersal might have contributed to a parallel decentralization, even democratizing, of ownership and control. It did not. One way of getting at this empirically is to examine some of the figures on the growth of transnational enterprises and their affiliates. Exhibit 2.5 shows how vast is the number of TNC affiliates. This is dispersal along with ongoing central ownership and appropriation of profits. Further, the transactions among firms and their affiliates and other types of contracting account for a good share of global trade; this intrafirm trade is not strictly speaking *free* market trade, even though the imagery around the growth of global trade is centered on the expansion of free markets. Critical to understanding the place of cities in the global economy is that this is managed trade and hence requires the variety of management and command functions described here—there is not much of an invisible hand there. Thus, critical components of global trade actually contribute to some of the global city functions described earlier.

In the case of the financial industry, we see a similar dynamic of dispersal and global integration: a growth in the number of cities integrated in the global financial network and a simultaneous increased concentration of value managed at the top of the hierarchy of centers. We can identify two distinct phases. Up to the end of the 1982 third-world debt crisis, the large transnational banks dominated the financial markets in terms of both the volume and the nature of financial transactions. After 1982, this dominance was increasingly challenged by other financial institutions and the major innovations they produced. These challenges led to a transformation in the leading components of the financial industry, a proliferation of financial institutions, and the rapid internationalization of financial markets. The marketplace and the advantages of agglomeration—and hence, cities— assumed new significance beginning in the mid-1980s. These developments led simultaneously to (1) the incorporation of a multiplicity of worldwide markets into a global system that fed the growth of the industry after the 1982 debt crisis and (2) new forms of concentration, specifically the centralization of the industry in a network of leading financial centers. Hence, in the case of the financial industry, to focus only on the large transnational banks would exclude precisely those sectors of the industry where much of the new growth and production of innovations was launched in the 1980s and is continuing today. Also, it would leave out an examination of the wide range of activities, firms, and markets, many located in cities, that compose the financial industry beginning in the 1980s.

The geographic dispersal of plants, offices, and service outlets and the integration of a growing number of stock markets around the world could have been accompanied by a corresponding decentralization in control and central functions. But that has not happened.

If some of the evidence on financial flows is organized according to the places where the markets and firms are located, distinct patterns of concentration emerge. The evidence on the locational patterns of banks and securities houses points to sharp concentration. For example, the worldwide distribution of the 100 largest banks and 25 largest securities houses in 1991 shows that Japan, the United States, and the United Kingdom accounted for 39 and 23 of each, respectively (top of Exhibits 2.6 and 2.7). This pattern persisted throughout the late 1990s, notwithstanding multiple financial crises in the world and particularly in Japan, and only recently has it begun to slow (rest of Exhibits 2.6 and 2.7).

The full impact of deregulation and the growth of financial markets can be seen in the increases in value and in number of firms listed in all the major stock markets in the world (Exhibits 2.8 and 2.9). The market value of listings rose from US$2.8 trillion in 1990 to US$9.4 trillion in 1997 and US$12.9 trillion in 2004 in the New York Stock Exchange, and from US$1 trillion to US$2 trillion and $2.8 trillion in the London Exchange for those same years. Similar patterns, although at lower orders of magnitude, are evident in the other stock markets listed in Exhibits 2.8 and 2.9.

The concentration in the operational side of the financial industry is made evident by the fact that most of the stock transactions in the leading countries are concentrated in a few stock markets. The Tokyo exchange accounts for 90% of equities traded in Japan; New York accounts for about two-thirds of equities traded in the United States; and London accounts for most of the trading in the United Kingdom. There is, then, a disproportionate concentration of worldwide capitalization in a few cities and of national capitalization typically in one city in each country.

Certain aspects of the territorial dispersal of economic activity may have led to some dispersal of profits and ownership. Large firms, for example, have increased their subcontracting to smaller firms worldwide, and many national firms in the newly industrializing countries have grown rapidly, thanks to investment by foreign firms and access to world markets, often through arrangements with transnational firms. Yet this form of growth is ultimately part of a chain in which a limited number of corporations continue to control the end product and reap most of the profits associated with selling on the world market. Even industrial homeworkers in remote rural areas are now part of that chain (e.g., Beneria and Roldan 1987; Russell and Rath 2003).

Under these conditions, the territorial dispersal of economic activity creates a need for expanded central control and management if this dispersal is to occur along with continued economic concentration. This in turn has contributed to a sharp growth in central control and management functions, many of which get produced in cities, thereby feeding their strategic role in the world economy today.

Offshore Banking Centers

Offshore financial centers are another important spatial point in the worldwide circuits of financial flows. Such centers are, above all else, tax shelters, a response by private-sector actors to government regulation. The

Exhibit 2.6 United States, Japan, and United Kingdom: Share of World's 50 Largest Banks, 1991, 1997, and 2005 (US$ millions and percentage)

	1991				
	Number of Firms	Assets	% of Top 50	Capital	% of Top 50
Japan	27	6,572,416	40.7	975,192	40.6
United States	7	913,009	5.7	104,726	4.4
United Kingdom	5	791,652	4.9	56,750	2.4
Subtotal	39	8,277,077	51.3	1,136,668	47.4
Total for Top 50	50	16,143,353	100.0	2,400,439	100.0
	1997				
	Number of Firms	Assets	% of Top 50	Capital	% of Top 50
Japan	12	6,116,307	36.4	1,033,421	45.8
United States	6	1,794,821	10.7	242,000	10.7
United Kingdom	5	1,505,686	9.0	130,587	5.8
Subtotal	23	9,416,814	56.0	1,406,008	62.3
Total for Top 50	50	16,817,690	100.0	2,257,946	100.0
	2005				
	Number of Firms	Revenue	% of Top 50	Profits	% of Top 50
Japan	4	107,506	6.4	1,648	0.1
United States	7	321,142	19.1	54,928	31.9
United Kingdom	5	248,328	14.8	36,132	21.0
Subtotal	16	676,976	40.3	92,708	53.9
Germany	11	329,242	19.6	12,446	7.2
Total for Top 50	50	1,680,104	100.0	172,011	100.0

Note: 1997 data ranked by assets as determined by Dow Jones Global Indexes in association with WorldScope; figures are based on each company's 1997 fiscal-year results, except data on Japanese banks, which are based on fiscal 1998 results.

Source: Author's calculations based on "World Business" (1992; 1998) and "Global 500" (2005).

Exhibit 2.7   United States, Japan, and United Kingdom: Share of World's 25
Largest Security Firms, 1991 and 1997 (US$ millions and percentage)

	1991				
	Number of Firms	*Assets*	*% of Top 25*	*Capital*	*% of Top 25*
Japan	10	171,913	30.5	61,871	50.5
United States	11	340,558	60.4	52,430	42.8
United Kingdom	2	44,574	7.9	3,039	2.5
Subtotal	23	557,045	98.8	117,340	95.7
Total for Top 25	25	563,623	100.0	122,561	100.0
	1997				
	Number of Firms	*Assets*	*% of Top 25*	*Capital*	*% of Top 25*
Japan	6	236,712	11.9	36,827	14.1
United States	15	1,660,386	83.2	207,181	79.3
United Kingdom	2	41,396	2.1	9,501	3.6
Subtotal	23	1,938,494	97.1	253,509	97.1
Total for Top 25	25	1,995,782	100.0	261,180	100.0

Note: Ranked by capital as determined by Dow Jones Global Indexes; figures based on 1997
fiscal-year results.

Source: Based on "World Business" (1992; 1998).

implementation of offshore financial centers began in the 1970s, although
international tax shelters had existed in various incipient forms for a long
time before then. The 1970s marked a juncture—a growing gap between
economic internationalization and government control over the economy in
developed countries. Offshore banking centers emerged as one option to
avoid government control in a context of expanding internationalization.
They are, to a large extent, paper operations.

The Cayman Islands, for example, illustrate some of these issues (Roberts
1994). By 1997, they were ranked as the seventh largest international banking operation in the world and the fifth largest financial center after London,
Tokyo, New York, and Hong Kong, according to International Monetary
Fund (IMF) data (IMF 1999). They also were still the world's second largest
insurance location with gross capital of US$8 billion in 1997. The value of
deposits held in banks in the Cayman Islands grew from US$250 billion

Exhibit 2.8   Select Stock Exchanges by Market Size, 1990 and 1997
(US$ millions and number)

| | 1990 | | | |
| | Market Value | | Listed Companies (N) | |
City	Domestic	Domestic+Foreign	Domestic	Foreign
New York	2,692,123	2,819,778	1,678	96
Tokyo	3,416,495	—	1,627	125
London	921,583	1,037,531	2,006	553
Frankfurt	383,823	—	649	555
Paris	342,948	—	873	231
Zurich	172,709	—	234	245
Toronto	233,752	585,637	1,127	66
Amsterdam	153,144	—	323	240
Milan	133,506	—	229	—
Sydney	120,888	170,212	1,089	33
Hong Kong	126,921	—	284	15
Singapore	196,868	—	163	166
Taiwan	110,454	—	199	—
Seoul	122,937	—	669	—

| | 1997 | | | |
| | Market Value | | Listed Companies (N) | |
City	Domestic	Domestic+Foreign	Domestic	Foreign
New York	6,595,209	9,413,109	2,691	356
Tokyo	2,321,928	—	1,805	60
London	2,049,459	1,879,137	2,465	526
Frankfurt	855,689	—	700	1,996
Paris	696,765	—	727	172
Zurich	578,232	—	216	212
Toronto	586,698	917,484	1,362	58
Amsterdam	570,943	—	332	179
Milan	352,323	—	209	4
Sydney	337,777	578,059	1,149	70
Hong Kong	413,670	—	638	20
Singapore	332,825	—	303	181
Taiwan	314,668	—	404	—
Seoul	74,624	—	776	—

Note: For Australia 1997, the number of listed companies is from 1996; when only domestic is listed, it represents the total market value.

Source: Based on Meridian Securities Markets (1998).

Exhibit 2.9 Stock Exchanges by Capitalization for Top 12 Markets, 2002–2004 (US$ millions)

Stock Market	2004 Market Capitalization	2004 Percentage of Members Capitalization	2003 Market Capitalization	2003 Percentage of Members Capitalization	2002 Market Capitalization	2002 Percentage of Members Capitalization
NYSE	12,707.60	34.20	11,329.00	36.20	9,015.30	39.50
NASDAQ	3,532.90	9.50	2,844.20	9.10	1,994.50	8.70
Tokyo	3,557.70	9.60	2,953.10	9.40	2,069.30	9.10
London	2,865.20	7.70	2,460.10	7.90	1,856.20	8.10
Euronext	2,441.30	6.60	2,076.40	6.60	1,538.70	6.70
Osaka	2,287.00	6.20	1,951.50	6.20	1,491.90	6.50
Deutsche Borse	1,194.50	3.20	1,079.00	3.40	686	3.00
Toronto	1,177.50	2.80	888.7	2.80	570.2	2.50
Spanish Exchange	940.7	2.50	726.2	2.30	461.6	2.00
Swiss Exchange	826.	2.20	727.1	2.30	547	2.40
Hong Kong	861.5	2.30	714.6	2.30	463.1	2.00
Italy	789.6	2.10	614.8	2.00	477.1	2.10
Percentage of Capitalization for Top 12[a]		89.30		90.50		92.70

Note: a. Compiled from World Federation of Exchanges (2003:83; 2004:50), year-end figures with calculations of percentages added.

in 1990 to US$640 billion in 1997. Its 593 banks in 1997 included 47 of the world's top 50 banks. But even though that tiny country supposedly has well over 500 banks from all around the world, only 69 banks have offices there, and only 6 are "real" banks for cashing and depositing money and other transactions. Many of the others exist only as folders in a cabinet (Walter 1989; Roberts 1994).

These offshore centers are located in many parts of the world. The majority of Asian offshore centers are located in Singapore and Hong Kong; Labuan (Malaysia) and Macau are also significant centers. In the Middle East, Bahrain took over from Beirut in 1975 as the main offshore banking center, with Dubai close behind. In the South Pacific, major centers are located in Australia and New Zealand, and smaller offshore clusters are in Vanuatu, the Cook Islands, Nauru, and Samoa. In the Indian Ocean, centers cluster in the Seychelles and in Mauritius. In Europe, Switzerland tops the list, and Luxembourg is a major center; others are Cyprus, Madeira, Malta, the Isle of Man, and the Channel Islands. Several small places are struggling to compete with established centers: Gibraltar, Monaco, Liechtenstein, and Andorra. The Caribbean has Bermuda, the Cayman Islands, Bahamas, Turks and Caicos, and the British Virgin Islands.

Why do offshore banking centers exist? This question is especially pertinent given the massive deregulation of major financial markets beginning in the 1980s and the establishment of de facto "free international financial zones" in several major cities in highly developed countries. The best example of such free international zones for financial activity is the Euromarket, which started in the 1960s and is much expanded today, with London at the center of the Euromarket system. Other examples, as of 1981, were international banking facilities in the United States, mostly in New York City, that allowed U.S. banks to establish special adjunct facilities to accept deposits from foreign entities free of reserve requirements and interest rate limitations. Tokyo, finally, saw the development of a facility in 1986 that allowed transactions in the Asian dollar market to be carried out in that city; this meant that Tokyo got some of the capital being transacted in Hong Kong, Singapore, and Bahrain—all Asian dollar centers.

Compared with the major international centers, offshore banking centers offer certain types of additional flexibility: secrecy, openness to *hot* money and to certain quasi-legitimate options not quite allowed in the deregulated markets of major financial centers, and tax minimization strategies for international corporations. Thus, offshore centers are used not only for Euromarket transactions but also for various accounting operations aimed at tax avoidance or minimization.

In principle, the Euromarkets of London are part of the offshore markets. They were set up to avoid the system for regulating exchange rates and balance-of-payments imbalances contained in the Bretton Woods agreement of 1945. The Bretton Woods agreement set up a legal framework for the regulation of international transactions, such as foreign currency operations, for countries or banks wanting to operate internationally. Euromarkets were initially Eurodollar markets, where banks from the United States and other countries could do dollar transactions and avoid U.S. regulations. Over the last decade, Euromarkets have expanded to include other currencies.

In finance, *offshore* does not always mean overseas or foreign; basically, the term means that less regulation takes place than *onshore*—the latter describing firms and markets not covered by this special legislation (Roberts 1994). The onshore and offshore markets compete with each other. Deregulation in the 1980s brought a lot of offshore capital back into onshore markets, especially in New York and London—a not insignificant factor in convincing governments in these countries to proceed with deregulation of the financial markets in the 1980s. London's much-noted "big bang" and the less-noted "petit bang" in Paris are instances of such a process of deregulation of financial markets.

The Euromarkets are significant in international finance. According to the Bank for International Settlements, the Eurocurrency markets grew from US\$9 billion in 1964 to US\$57 billion in 1970, US\$661 billion in 1981 to US\$ 17 trillion in 2004 (BIS 2005). The oil crisis was important in feeding this growth. In the 1980s, much growth came through Eurobonds and Eurosecurities—bonds and securities traded offshore, that is, outside the standard regulatory framework. Securitization was crucial to launch the new financial era by making liquid what had been illiquid forms of debt. Since the launch of the euro in January 1999, Euromarkets have changed and grown sharply, with the current value of outstanding international debt in both euro and legacy currencies reaching US\$1.6 trillion in 1998 (IMF 1999, part 2) to 2.3 trillion in 2005 (BIS 2005).

Offshore banking centers basically grew out of tax havens in the 1970s, which is one of the ways in which they differ from the Euromarkets. Some offshore centers today are mere tax havens, whereas some old tax havens have become full-fledged offshore banking centers; many offshore centers specialize in certain branches of banking, insurance, and other financial transactions. There is a clustering of small offshore banking centers within the time zone of each of the three major financial centers (New York City, London, and Tokyo); these marginal offshore centers do some servicing of business being transacted in the major centers and within that time zone. But not all offshore activity is related to major centers, nor is location offshore totally determined by time zones.

In brief, offshore banking centers represent a highly specialized location for certain types of international financial transactions. They are also buffer zones in case the governments of the leading financial centers in the world should decide to re-regulate the financial markets. On the broader scale of operations, however, they represent a fraction of the financial capital markets now concentrated in global cities.

Conclusion: After the Pax Americana

The world economy has never been a planetary event; it has always had more or less clearly defined boundaries. Moreover, although most major industries were involved throughout, the cluster of industries that dominated any given period changed over time, contributing to distinct structurations of the world economy. Finally, the institutional framework through which the world economy coheres has also varied sharply, from the earlier empires through the quasi-empire of the Pax Americana—the period of U.S. political, economic, and military dominance—and its decay in the 1970s.

It is in this decaying Pax Americana, with the rebuilt economies of Western Europe and Japan reentering the international markets, that we see emerging a new phase of the world economy. There is considerable agreement among specialists that in the mid-1970s new patterns in the world economy became evident. First, the geographical axis of international transactions changed from North–South to East–West. In this process, significant parts of Africa and Latin America became unhinged from their hitherto strong ties with world markets in commodities and raw materials. Second was a sharp increase in the weight of FDI in services and the role played by international financial markets. Third was the breakdown of the Bretton Woods agreement, which had established the institutional framework under which the world economy had operated since the end of World War II. This breakdown was clearly linked to the decline of the United States as the single dominant economic power in the world. Japanese and European multinationals and banks became major competitors with U.S. firms. The financial crises in Asia in the 1990s once again strengthened the role of the North-Atlantic system in the global economy. But the rise of China, the massive indebtedness of the United States, and its growing dependence on Japan and China for financing that debt, point to the possibility of a final blow to the remnants of the Pax Americana that once provided a U.S.-centered global order.

This does not mean that U.S. global firms are suffering. While there is disagreement on this point, I argue that a key feature of the current phase of globalization is that global firms, whether American, European, or Asian, are increasingly exiting the old arrangements that connected them to their respective nation-states through protectionisms of various sorts and strong-hand politics by their governments aimed at protecting their national firms whenever possible. These arrangements were a critical part of the Pax Americana, with the United States playing a key role in enabling its firms to dominate the world economy. By the end of the 1990s, the global economy had become largely structured in terms of global markets and multiple protections for global firms in all the countries that had deregulated their economies to become part of the global economy. Though the U.S. government remains the major military and economic power in the world, its government is in a far more dubious position: It continues to extract exceptions for itself and major U.S. global firms, even as the tax share of corporations continues to decline and many industries are declining fast.

These realignments are the background for understanding the position of different types of cities in the current organization of the world economy. A limited but growing number of major cities are the sites for the major financial markets and leading specialized services needed to manage global operations. And a large number of other major cities have lost their role as leading export centers for manufacturing, precisely because of the worldwide dispersal of factories. This shift in roles among major cities in the new world economy will be the focus of Chapter 3.

Notes

1. Foreign direct investments by transnationals may be financed through transnational banks or the international capital markets. In the mid-1980s, the share of the latter began to grow sharply (see Sassen [1991] 2001, chap. 4).

2. For one of the best examinations of the evolution of several distinct strands in urban research since the 1980s, see Paddison's Introduction in the *Handbook of Urban Studies* (Paddison 2001).

3

National and Transnational Urban Systems

The trends described in Chapter 2 point to the emergence of a new kind of urban system, one operating at the global and transnational regional levels (Taylor 2004; Marcatullio and Io 2001). This is a system in which cities are crucial nodes for the international coordination and servicing of firms, markets, and even whole economies that are increasingly transnational. This global map of the organizational side of the world economy needs to be distinguished from the global map of the consumption of globally distributed goods and services. And it needs to be distinguished from the global map of foreign direct investment; the fact of a few foreign direct investment projects does not necessarily make a city part of the organizational map. First, the foreign direct investment and, especially, the consumption map are far wider and more diffuse than the organizational map, which is strategic. Second, these cities also emerge as strategic places in an emergent transnational political and cultural geography. The number of cities constituting the organizational map and these novel political and cultural geographies grew sharply during the 1990s, because the global economy expanded vastly as more and more countries, often under pressure, adopted the deregulatory and privatizing policies required for joining the global corporate system.

Most cities, however, including most large cities, are not part of these new transnational urban systems. Typically, urban systems are coterminous with nation-states, and most cities exist within these national geographies.

Correspondingly, with rare exceptions (Chase-Dunn 1984; GaWC [Globalization; and World Cities Study Group and Network] 1998; Sassen [1991] 2001; Walters 1985; Timberlake 1985), studies of city systems have until recently assumed that the nation-state is the unit of analysis. Although this is still the most common view, there is a growing scholarship that allows for the possibility that intercity networks can cross national borders directly, bypassing national states as these have reduced older gatekeeping functions on cross-border economic flows. This novel focus is partly a function of actual changes in the international sphere, notably the formation of global economic processes discussed in Chapter 2, and the accompanying deregulation and opening up of national systems.

In this chapter, I ask, What is the impact of economic globalization on national urban systems? Does the globalization of major industries, from auto manufacturing to finance, have distinct effects on different types of national urban systems? I focus on the effects of the shift to services and economic globalization on balanced and primate urban systems, the two major types of urban systems that have been identified in the research literature on cities. Western European nations have typically been regarded as a good example of balanced urban systems; and Latin American nations, as a good example of primate systems—that is, inordinate concentrations of population and major economic activities in one city, typically the national capital. The most recent research signals some sharp changes in these two regions. Later in this chapter, I turn to the emergence of transnational urban systems.

Impacts on Primate Systems: The Case of Latin America and the Caribbean

Many regions in the world—Latin America, the Caribbean, large parts of Asia, and (to some extent) Africa—have long been characterized by urban primacy as an older scholarship has established (Abreu et al. 1989; Dogan and Kasarda 1988; Feldbauer et al. 1993; Hardoy 1975; Lee 1989; Linn 1983; Lozano and Duarte 1991; Stren and White 1989). Exhibit 3.1 shows some of the main cities in Latin America I discuss here; while many are primate cities, which are also national capitals, some are neither. Primate cities account for a disproportionate share of population, employment, and gross national product (GNP), a fact illustrated by the figures presented in Exhibit 3.2. For example, in 1970, greater São Paulo accounted for 36% of national domestic product (NDP) and 48% of net industrial product in Brazil, a country with several major economic regions. Santo Domingo accounted for 56% of industrial growth and 70% of commercial and banking transactions

Exhibit 3.1   Select Cities in Latin America and the Caribbean, 2005

in the Dominican Republic in 1981. And Lima accounted for 43% of gross domestic product (GDP) in Peru in 1980.

Primacy is not simply a matter of absolute size, nor is large size a marker of primacy. Santo Domengo or Lima (Exhibit 3.2), both primate cities, are not necessarily among the largest in the world. Primacy is a relative condition that holds within a national urban system. Some of the largest urban

Exhibit 3.2 Some Indicators of the Estimated Economic Importance of Select Urban Areas Worldwide, Various Years, 1970–1981 (in percentages)

Urban Area	Year	Population	Employment	Public Revenues	Public Expenditures	Output Measure
Brazil						
Greater São Paulo	1970	8.6	—	—	—	36.0 of NDP
						48.0 of net industrial product
China						
Shanghai	1980	1.2	—	—	—	12.5 of gross industrial product
Dominican Republic						
Santa Domingo	1981	24.0				70.0 of commercial and banking transactions
						56.0 of industrial growth
Ecuador						
Guayaquil[a]		13.0	—	—	—	30.0 of GDP
Haiti						
All urban	1976	24.2	15.6			57.6 of national income
Port-au-Prince	—	15.0	7.7	47.2	82.7[b]	38.7 of national income
Other urban	—	9.2	7.9	—	—	18.9 of national income
India						
All urban	1970–71	19.9	17.7[c]	—	—	38.9 of NDP
Kenya						
All urban	1976	11.9	—	—	—	30.3 of income
Nairobi	—	5.2	—	—	—	20.0 of income
Other urban	—	6.7	—	—	—	10.3 of income

Urban Area	Year	Population	Employment	Public Revenues	Public Expenditures	Output Measure
Mexico						
All urban	1970	60.0			(29.0)[d]	79.7 of personal income
Federal District	—	14.2				33.6 of personal income
Pakistan						
Karachi	1974–75	6.1				16.1 of GDP
Peru						
Lima	1980	28.0				43.0 of GDP
Philippines						
Metro Manila	1970	12.0	—	45		25.0 of GDP
Thailand						
Metro Bangkok	1972	10.9	14.0[e]		30.5[f]	37.4 of GDP
Turkey						
All urban	1981	47.0	42			70.0 of GNP
Tunisia						
Tunis	1975	16.0	17.2	—	—	

Notes:
a. Guayas Province.
b. Current expenditures only.
c. Workers.
d. Federal public investment only.
e. 1970 data.
f. 1969 data.
Source: Friedrich Kahnert, "Improving Urban Employment and Labor Productivity," May 1987, World Bank Discussion Paper No. 10. Reprinted with permission.

agglomerations in the world do not necessarily entail primacy: New York, for example, is among the 20 largest cities in the world, but it is not a primate city, given the multipolar nature of the urban system in the United States. Furthermore, primacy is not an exclusive trait of developing countries, even though its most extreme forms are to be found in the developing world: Tokyo and London are primate cities. Finally, the emergence of so-called megacities may or may not be associated with primacy. The 20 largest urban agglomerations by 2003 (and the foreseeable future) include some cities that are not necessarily primate, such as New York, Los Angeles, Tianjin, Osaka, Calcutta, and Shanghai, and others that can be characterized as having low levels of primacy, such as Paris and Buenos Aires (see Exhibit A.3).

Primacy and megacity status are clearly fed by urban population growth, a process that is expected to continue. But they combine in multiple patterns; there is no single model. The evidence worldwide points to the ongoing urbanization of the population, especially in developing countries. As in the developed countries, one component of urban growth in those countries is the suburbanization of growing sectors of the population. The figures in Exhibit 3.3 show rates of urban growth in select developing countries for the period that saw the beginning of today's sharp urbanization of the world's population. The higher the level of development, the higher the urbanization rate is likely to be. Thus, a country like Argentina had an urbanization rate of 90.1% by 2003, which is quite similar to that of highly developed countries, although it is to some extent a function of the primacy of Buenos Aires in the national urban system. In contrast, Algeria's urbanization rate of 59% and Kenya's 39% differ sharply from the urbanization level in developed countries. Finally, there are countries such as India and China that have vast urban agglomerations, notwithstanding their very low rate of urbanization; they are, clearly, among the most populous countries in the world. As a result, the information conveyed by an indicator such as the urbanization rate in these countries differs from that of countries with more average population sizes.

On the subject of primacy, the literature about Latin America shows considerable convergence in the identification of major patterns, along with multiple interpretations of these patterns. Many studies in the late 1970s and early 1980s found sharper primacy rather than the emergence of the more balanced national urban systems forecast by *modernization* theory (for critical evaluations, see Edel 1986; El-Shakhs 1972; Roberts 1976; Smith 1985; Walters 1985). The disintegration of rural economies, including the displacement of small landholders by expanding large-scale commercial agriculture, and the continuing inequalities in the spatial distribution of institutional resources are generally recognized as key factors strengthening

Exhibit 3.3 Urban Growth Patterns in Select Developing Countries, Select Periods, 1980–2030 (numbers and percentage)

| Country | Per Capita GNP Level 2003 (US$)[a] | Size of Population (in 000's)[b] | | | | Percentage of Urban Population[b] | | Average Rate of Growth[c] | | | | | |
| | | 2003 | | 2030 | | | | Urban Pop. (%) | | | Rural Pop. (%) | | |
		Urban	Rural	Urban	Rural	2003	2030	1980–1985	1995–2000	2000–2005	1980–1985	1995–2000	2000–2005
Argentina	3,372	34,642	3,786	45,568	3,043	90.1	93.7	1.88	1.39	2.00	-0.87	-0.88	-1.10
Mexico	6,052	78,100	25,357	110,770	22,821	75.5	82.9	3.36	2.39	1.80	0.34	-0.07	0.40
Colombia	1,779	33,808	10,414	51,860	8,982	76.5	85.2	3.11	2.29	2.20	0.28	-0.07	-0.50
Brazil	2,759	148,270	30,201	202,686	19,392	83.1	91.3	3.71	2.28	2.00	-1.27	-1.00	-2.40
Algeria	2,092	18,711	13,089	32,032	12,087	58.8	72.6	3.71	3.85	2.60	2.51	1.25	0.30
Morocco	1,431	17,564	13,002	30,824	11,680	57.5	72.5	4.28	3.42	2.80	1.40	0.50	0.10
Malaysia	4,247	15,611	8,814	27,324	7,867	63.9	77.6	4.51	3.32	3.00	1.06	0.15	0.10
Senegal	644	5,008	5,086	11,350	5,577	49.6	67.1	3.34	4.26	3.90	2.11	1.52	1.00
Cote d'Ivoire	826	7,464	9,167	14,054	9,204	44.9	60.4	6.63	5.24	2.60	2.54	2.26	0.80
Nigeria	471	57,907	66,102	134,398	72,298	46.7	65.0	6.07	5.33	4.40	2.22	2.02	1.00
Kenya	449	12,593	19,394	25,807	15,334	39.4	62.7	8.06	6.72	4.40	3.17	2.78	-0.40
India	564	301,260	764,202	586,052	830,525	28.3	41.4	3.91	3.96	2.30	1.65	0.93	1.20
Indonesia	946	100,294	119,859	187,846	89,721	45.6	67.7	4.60	3.62	3.90	1.13	0.14	-0.90
China[d]	1,086	503,740	800,456	877,623	572,898	38.6	60.5	1.44	2.95	3.20	1.18	0.58	-0.80

Sources:

a. World Bank (2005).

b. United Nations Department for Economic and Social Affairs, Policy Analysis (2003).

c. United Nations Department for International Economic and Social Affairs (1988; 2003).

d. Excluding Hong Kong SAR and Macao SAR.

primacy (Kowarick, Campos, and de Mello 1991; PREALC [Regional Employment Program for Latin America and the Caribbean] 1987).

Less widely known and documented is that in the 1980s there was a deceleration in primacy in several, although not all, countries in Latin America. This trend will not eliminate the growth of megacities, but it is worth discussing in some detail because it resulted in part from specific aspects of economic globalization—concrete ways in which global processes implant themselves in particular localities. The overall shift in growth strategies toward export-oriented development and large-scale tourism enclaves created growth poles that emerged as alternatives to the primate cities for rural to urban migrations (Gilbert 1996; Landell-Mills, Agarwala, and Please 1989; Portes and Lungo 1992a, 1992b; Roberts and Portes 2006).[1] This shift was substantially promoted by the expansion of world markets for commodities and the foreign direct investments of transnational corporations, both in turn often stimulated by World Bank and IMF programs.

One of the best sources of information on the emergence of these patterns in the 1980s is a large, collective, multicity study directed by Portes and Lungo (1992a, 1992b) that focused on the Caribbean region, including Central America.[2] The Caribbean has a long history of urban primacy. Portes and Lungo studied the urban systems of Costa Rica, the Dominican Republic, Guatemala, Haiti, and Jamaica, countries that clearly reflect the immense variety of cultures and languages in this region. These countries represent a wide range of colonization patterns, ethnic compositions, economic development, and political stability. In the 1980s, export-oriented development, a cornerstone of the Caribbean Basin Initiative, and the intense promotion of tourism began to draw workers and firms. Expanded suburbanization has also had the effect of decentralizing population in the primate cities of the Caribbean, while adding to the larger metropolitan areas of these cities. The effect of these trends can be seen clearly in Jamaica, for example, where the primacy index declined from 7.2 in 1960 to 2.2 in 1990, largely as a result of the development of the tourist industry on the northern coast of the island, the revival of bauxite production for export in the interior, and the growth of satellite cities at the edges of the broader Kingston metropolitan area. (See McMichall 2003 generally on development.)

In some Caribbean countries, however, the new growth poles have had the opposite effect. Thus, in Costa Rica, a country with a far more balanced urban system, the promotion of export manufacturing and tourism has tended to concentrate activities in the metropolitan area of the primate city of San José and its immediate surrounding cities, such as Cartago. Finally, in the case of Guatemala, export manufacturing and tourism are far less developed, largely because of the extremely violent political situation until the 1990s (Jonas 1992). Development of export-oriented growth remains centered in agriculture. Guatemala has one of the highest levels of urban primacy in Latin America because alternative growth poles have been rare. Only in the 1990s did efforts to develop export agriculture promote some growth in intermediate cities, with coffee and cotton centers growing more rapidly than the capital, Guatemala City.

At the same time, deregulation and the associated sharp growth of foreign direct investment since the early 1990s (Exhibit 3.4) has further strengthened the role of the major Latin American business centers, particularly Mexico City, São Paulo, and Buenos Aires. Buenos Aires has had sharp ups and downs—a sharp downturn in 2001, due to Argentina's massive crisis, and a resurgence in 2005. As shown in Chapter 2, privatization has been a key component of this growth. Foreign direct investment, via privatization and other channels, has been associated with deregulation of financial markets and other key economic institutions. Thus the central role played by the stock market and other financial markets in these increasingly complex investment processes has raised the economic importance of the major cities where these institutions are concentrated. Because the bulk of the value of investment in privatized enterprises and other, often related, investments has

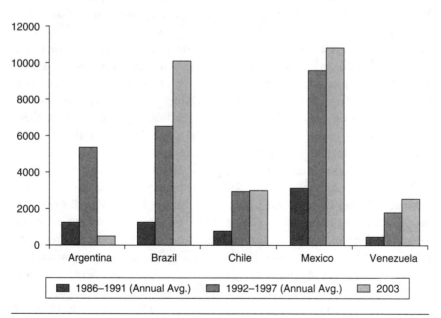

Exhibit 3.4   Foreign Direct Investment in Select Latin American Countries, 1986–2003 (US$ millions)

Source: UNCTAD (1998:364–65; 2004:367–71).

been in Mexico, Argentina, and Brazil, the impact of vast capital inflows is particularly felt in the corporate and financial sectors in their primate cities—Mexico City, Buenos Aires, and São Paulo.[3] We see in these cities the emergence of conditions that resemble patterns evident in major Western cities: highly dynamic financial markets and specialized service sectors; the overvalorization of the output, firms, and workers in these sectors; and the devalorization of the rest of the economic system (Schiffer Ramos 2002; Parnreiter 2002; Ciccolella and Mignaqui 2002). This is a subject I return to in Chapter 4.

In brief, economic globalization has had a range of impacts on cities and urban systems in Latin America and the Caribbean. In some cases, it has contributed to the development of new growth poles outside the major urban agglomerations. In others, it has actually raised the weight of primate urban agglomerations, in that the new growth poles were developed in these areas. A third case is that represented by the major business and financial centers in the region, several of which saw a sharp strengthening in their linkages with global markets and with the major international business centers in the developed world.

Production zones, centers for tourism, and major business and financial centers are three types of sites for the implantation of global processes. Beyond these sites is a vast terrain containing cities, towns, and villages that are either increasingly unhinged from this new international growth dynamic or are part of the low-profit end of long chains of production (for one of the most detailed accounts, see the larger project summarized in Beneria 1989). The character of the articulation or dissociation is not simply a question of city size, since there exist long subcontracting chains connecting workers in small villages to the world markets. It is, rather, a question of how these emergent transnational economic systems are articulated, how they connect specific localities in less developed countries with markets and localities in highly developed countries (see, e.g., Gereffi, Humphrey, and Sturgeon 2005; Gereffi and Korzeniewicz 1994; Beneria 1989; Bonacich et al. 1994; Bose and Acosta-Belen 1995; Chaney and Castro 1993; Ward 1991). The implantation of global processes seems to have contributed to sharpening the separation between cities, or sectors within cities, that are articulated with the global economy and those that are not. This is a new type of interurban inequality, one not predicated on old hierarchies of city size. The new inequality differs from the long-standing forms of inequality present in cities and national urban systems because of the extent to which it results from the *implantation* of a global dynamic, be it the internationalization of production and finance or international tourism.

Impacts on Balanced Urban Systems: The Case of Europe

One of the most interesting findings of a major multiyear, multicountry study on cities in Europe, sponsored by the European Economic Community (EEC), was the renewed demographic and economic importance of Europe's large cities in the 1980s. (For a summary, see European Institute of Urban Affairs 1992; Kunzmann and Wegener 1991; see also Eurocities 1989; INURA 2003; Kazepov 2005). In the 1960s and 1970s, most, if not all, of these large cities had experienced declines in population and in economic activity, whereas smaller cities experienced growth in both dimensions. We saw a similar pattern in the United States, where this process took the form of suburbanization.

Many analysts, both in Europe and in the United States, asserted that central cities, with the exception of old historical centers with cultural importance, had lost much of their use to people and to the economy. The widespread growth of small cities in Europe in those two earlier decades was seen as a strong indication of how balanced the urban systems of Western European nations were and continue to be. And, indeed, compared with almost any other major continental region, Western European nations had and continue to have the most balanced urban systems in the world. Nonetheless, it is now clear that beginning in the 1980s and continuing today, major cities in Europe have gained population and experienced significant economic growth (Exhibit 3.5a). The exceptions were some of Europe's large cities in more peripheral areas: There were continuing losses in Marseilles, Naples, and England's old industrial cities, Manchester and Birmingham. But some of these cities have also seen new population and economic gains as of the late 1990s (see Kazepov 2005). At the same time, compared with the 1960s, the sharpest growth has occurred in the larger metropolitan areas (Exhibit 3.5b). Smaller cities slowed down, often markedly, in the 1980s, and continue to do so today. Indeed, there is now an emergent field of research focused on "shrinking cities" in older industrial areas of Europe. Exhibit 3.6 shows some of the major cities in Europe.

These trends can be interpreted in several ways. On one hand, these could be mild demographic shifts that leave the characteristics of the urban system basically unaltered, that is, urban systems remain balanced at the levels of the nation and of Western Europe as a whole. On the other hand, the trends could indicate a renewed importance of major cities because the economic changes evident in all developed countries have organizational and spatial

(Text continues on page 59)

Exhibit 3.5a Population Change in Select European Cities, Select Periods, 1970–2005 (percentages)

Core City[a]	1970–1975		1975–1980		1980–1985		1985–1990		1990–1995		1995–2000		2000–2005[b]	
	Core	Ring	Core	Ring	Core	Ring	Core	Ring	Core	Ring	Core	Ring	Core	Ring
Hamburg	-0.77	0.85	-0.91	0.36	-0.77	0.06	0.24	0.06	0.65	—	0.33	—	0.13	—
Frankfurt	—	—	—	—	-1.01	-0.04	1.62	0.11	—	—	—	—	—	—
Dortmund	-0.41	0.08	-0.79	-0.27	-1.15	-0.56	0.54	0.37	—	—	—	—	—	—
Berlin	-0.47	-0.25	-0.02	-0.07	0.21	0.03	2.19	0.09	0.18	—	0.05	—	0.02	—
Paris	-1.48	1.93	-0.69	0.66	-1.02	0.78	1.01	2.06	0.38	—	0.38	—	0.33	—
Lyons	-1.79	4.25	-1.23	-1.18	0.07	-0.04	0.07	1.21	0.74	—	0.74	—	0.67	—
Marseilles	0.27	4.47	-0.48	2.91	-1.10	1.57	-1.10	2.84	0.39	—	0.39	—	0.39	—
Milan	-0.14	1.06	-1.17	1.07	-2.02	0.6	-1.03	0.35	-1.05	—	-0.86	—	-0.86	—
Amsterdam	-1.84	1.51	-1.11	0.81	-1.18	0.57	0.34	0.47	0.9	—	0.46	—	0.53	—
Rotterdam	-1.99	1.1	-1.38	0.81	-0.28	0.56	0.22	0.28	0.57	—	0.29	—	0.34	—
Brussels	-1.99	0.48	-1.38	0.15	-0.95	0.02	-0.17	0.04	-0.04	—	0.04	—	1.31	—
London	-1.89	-0.37	-1.6	-0.14	-0.38	-0.06	0.56	-0.32	-0.03	—	-0.03	—	-0.03	—
Birmingham	-0.3	0.35	-1.01	-0.66	-0.33	0	-0.37	0.06	-0.25	—	-0.25	—	-0.25	—

Core City[a]	1970–1975		1975–1980		1980–1985		1985–1990		1990–1995		1995–2000		2000–2005[b]	
	Core	Ring	Core	Ring	Core	Ring	Core	Ring	Core	Ring	Core	Ring	Core	Ring
Glasgow	-3.38	-1.47	-1.84	-0.11	-1.06	-0.17	-1.41	-0.32	—	—	—	—	—	—
Dublin	-0.41	—	-0.41	—	-1.61	—	—	—	0.65	—	0.87	—	0.88	—
Copenhagen	-2.28	2	-1.47	0.46	-0.59	-0.12	-0.72	0.14	0.3	—	-4.61	—	0.23	—
Thessaloniki	2.06	—	1.44	—	0.93	0.54	—	—	0.66	—	0.67	—	0.67	—
Athens	1.09	—	-0.16	—	-1.43	1.45	—	—	0.34	—	0.37	—	0.37	—
Madrid	0.45	8.28	-0.2	8.19	-0.63	3.16	0.28	0.07	0.51	—	0.43	—	0.43	—
Barcelona	-0.07	3.4	0.13	2.27	-0.58	0.71	0.04	-0.04	0.62	—	0.21	—	0.21	—
Valencia	1.44	1.47	1.11	1.73	-0.41	1.26	0.6	-0.48	—	—	—	—	—	—
Seville	1.24	-0.02	1.81	1.23	0.16	1.19	0.75	0.52	—	—	—	—	—	—

Notes:

a. Core City refers to cities in growth or dynamic regions in Western Europe.

b. Estimated.

Source: Data for 1970–1990 taken from European Institute of Urban Affairs (1992:56); data for 1990–2005 taken from United Nations Department for International Economic and Social Affairs (2003, table A.14).

Exhibit 3.5b   Population Change in Select European Cities, 1965–2004
(percentages)

	Metropolitan		
Core City	Area	Core	Ring
Amsterdam	8.4	−17.7	34.5
Antwerp	20.7	−36.7	39.2
Athens	63.5	14.6	87.9
Barcelona	73.1	−8.8	330.9
Berlin	1.9	4.5	−9.1
Birmingham	2.5	−13.4	14.0
Brussels	26.6	−17.0	30.6
Copenhagen	10.4	−28.9	51.6
Dublin	45.5	−7.8	232.7
Dusseldorf	25.3	−18.9	115.3
Frankfurt	30.8	−7.8	66.4
Glasgow	−0.8	−35.6	41.2
Hamburg	12.7	−7.0	94.8
Helsinki	68.5	17.4	221.4
Köln	22.1	13.2	33.1
Leeds	12.5	−17.5	30.7
Lille	32.1	−4.1	42.6
Lisbon	73.1	−29.7	238.6
Liverpool	−10.1	−34.7	9.1
London	7.8	−12.9	14.6
Lyon	64.9	−22.6	169.7
Madrid	97.6	20.0	1618.4
Manchester	−3.2	−38.2	7.2
Mannheim	34.1	-4.6	48.9
Marseille	74.3	2.6	680.4
Milan	36.6	−21.6	123.8
Munich	26.3	4.5	104.9
Naples	78.5	−14.5	289.4
Newcastle	16.9	−27.9	30.0
Nuremburg	50.8	5.4	152.2
Paris	39.7	−24.1	74.0
Porto	38.0	−13.2	72.7
Rhine-Ruhr	12.0	−18.8	17.0
Rome	29.4	13.2	265.6
Rotterdam	31.2	−18.2	161.2
Seville	57.3	54.6	61.2
Stockholm	42.7	−5.3	143.7
Stuttgart	83.3	−8.6	159.5
Turin	14.8	−17.0	162.1
Valencia	111.8	46.1	325.8
Vienna	−9.9	6.6	−24.7
Zurich	70.6	−22.7	220.0

Source: Demographia (2005).

Exhibit 3.6   Select Cities in Europe, 2005

implications for such cities. The EEC study mentioned earlier found that the second of these interpretations fits the data gathered for 24 cities in Europe for the 1980s. The evidence shows clearly that the period 1985 to 1990 marks the crucial turnaround from negative to positive population growth in the urban core after consistent losses in the preceding periods (see Exhibit 3.5; see also Eurocities 1989; Kazepov 2005; for critical accounts of the contents of this growth, see Hitz et al. 1995; INURA 2003; Bodnar 2000). Finally, the evidence also signals that the new organizational and compositional features of the economy of core cities can accommodate high economic growth with little, if any, and even negative, population growth (see also Sassen [1991] 2001, chaps. 8–9).

The organizational and spatial implications of the new economic trends assume distinct forms in various urban systems. Some cities become part of transnational networks, whereas others become unhinged from the main centers of economic growth in their regions or countries. A review of the EEC report, as well as other major studies on cities in Europe, suggests that there are at least three tendencies in the reconfiguration of urban systems in Western Europe that began in the 1980s. First, several sub-European regional systems have emerged (CEMAT [European Conference of Ministers Responsible for Regional Planning] 1988; Kunzmann and Wegener 1991; Rhine-Ruhr 2005). Second, within the territory of the EEC and several immediately adjacent countries (Austria, Denmark, and Greece) in the 1980s, the new European Union in the 1990s, and the enlarged union as of 2004, a limited number of cities have strengthened their role in an emergent European urban system. Finally, a few of these cities are also part of an urban system that operates at the global level (Exhibit 3.7)

National European urban systems are also being affected by these developments. The traditional national urban networks are changing. Cities that were once dominant in their countries may lose that importance, while cities in border regions or transportation hubs may gain a new importance. Furthermore, the new European global cities may capture some of the business, demands for specialized services, and investments that previously went to national capitals or major provincial cities. Cities at the periphery will feel the widening gap with the newly defined and positioned geography of centrality.

Cities in peripheral regions and old port cities began to lose ground in the 1970s and 1980s in their national urban systems as a result of the new hierarchies (Castells 1989; Hausserman and Siebel 1987; Parkinson, Foley, and Judd 1989; Roncayolo 1990; Siebel 1984; van den Berg et al. 1982; Vidal et al. 1990). By the late 1980s, it had become clear that many cities were increasingly disconnected from the major European urban systems. Some of these peripheralized cities with outmoded industrial bases have reemerged with new functions and as part of new networks in the 1990s—for example, Lille in France as a major transportation hub, including the Eurostar transport system, and Glasgow in the United Kingdom as a major tourism and cultural destination. Others have lost politico-economic functions and are unlikely to regain them in the foreseeable future. Yet others are becoming centers for tourism or places for second homes; for example, a growing number of high-income Germans and English have bought country houses—indeed, whole "castles"—in rural Ireland, inducing other continental Europeans to do the same. In an ironic twist, much of the beauty and current value of the Irish countryside—whole regions untouched by

Exhibit 3.7 Location of Top Banking, Industrial, and Commercial Firms by City, Select Years, 1960–2005

City, Country[a]	2005[b]	1997[c]	1990[c]	1980[c]	1970[c]	1960[c]
Tokyo, Japan	10 (1)[d]	18 (5)	12 (2)	6	5 (1)	1
New York, USA	7 (2)	12 (1)	7 (5)	10 (4)	25 (8)	29 (8)
Paris, France	8 (1)	11 (1)	5	7 (2)	0	0
Osaka, Japan	1	7 (3)	2 (1)	1	1	0
Detroit, USA	1 (1)	4 (2)	2 (2)	2 (2)	3 (3)	5 (2)
London, UK	4 (1)	3 (1)	7 (2)	8 (3)	7 (3)	7 (3)
Chicago, USA	1	3	2	4 (2)	5	6 (2)
Munich, Germany	4 (1)	3	2	1	1	1
Amsterdam, Netherlands	1 (1)	3	0	0	0	0
Seoul, South Korea	2	3	0	0	0	0

Notes:

a. After ranking cities according to the number holding the world's 100 largest corporation headquarters (in 1999), the list was trimmed to the top 40 cities, of which 10 are listed in the table above.

b. Author's calculations based on "Global 500" (2005).

c. Short and Kim (1999:26).

d. The figure in parentheses gives the number of the world's top 20 corporations for that city.

61

industrialization—is a legacy of poverty; it may now be undermined by Ireland's rapid growth, much of it centered in high-tech manufacturing. The requirement for becoming transnational centers for tourism and second homes is that these sites cannot pursue industrial development and need to preserve high levels of environmental quality. Further, changes in military defense policies resulting from the fall of the Soviet Union and its recomposition into a series of smaller nation-states will cause decline in cities that were once crucial production centers or control centers for national security systems. Smaller port cities, or large ones that have not upgraded and modernized their infrastructures, will be at a great disadvantage in competing with the large, modernized port cities in Europe. Marseilles was once a great port, strategically located on the Mediterranean; today, it has been left behind by Rotterdam and a few other major European ports that constitute a cluster of state-of-the-art ports. Nothing in the near future seems to secure the revitalization of old industrial centers on the basis of the industries that once were their economic core. The most difficult cases are small- and medium-size cities in somewhat isolated or peripheral areas dependent on coal and steel industries. They are likely to have degraded their environments and hence do not even have the option of becoming tourist centers.

The shifts that took off in the 1980s were sufficiently dramatic to engage a whole series of scholars into painting new urban scenarios for Europe. Kunzmann and Wegener (1991) asserted that the dominance of large cities would continue in part because they would be more competitive in getting both European and non-European investors' preferences for the larger high-tech industrial and service cities (see also Deecke, Kruger, and Lapple 1993). Furthermore, according to some researchers, this spatial polarization would deepen because of the development of high-speed transport infrastructure and communications corridors, which tend to connect major centers or highly specialized centers essential to the advanced economic system (Castells and Hall 1994; Graham and Marvin 1996; Masser, Sviden, and Wegener 1990). Much of this forecasting is turning out to be correct. We see massive concentrations of resources in some cities (e.g., Rutherford 2004; Abrahamson 2004). But today, a growing number of small, somewhat peripheral cities in Europe are literally shrinking: Their built environment is severely underutilized and in some cases fully abandoned (see, e.g., Giesecke 2005). However, an old mining and steel city such as Lille is now one of Western Europe's major transportation and communications hubs. This has radically changed this once-dying industrial city; further, using internationally known architects to do much of the critical building has also made Lille a cultural destination of sorts, a wonderful turn of events for what was once a place of factories and coal mines.

A process of recentralization may be occurring in certain cities that have been somewhat peripheral. Some of the smaller cities in Europe (such as Aachen, Strasbourg, Nice, Liege, and Arnheim) are likely to benefit from the single European market insofar as they can expand their hinterland and function as a nexus to a broader European region. Changes in Eastern Europe are likely to strengthen the role of Western European cities that used to have extensive interregional linkages before World War II—notably Hamburg, Copenhagen, and Nuremberg—which in turn may have the effect of weakening the position of other peripheral cities in those regions. Cities bordering Eastern Europe may assume new roles or recapture old ones; Vienna and Berlin are emerging as international business platforms for the whole central European region.[4]

Finally, major Eastern European cities such as Budapest, Prague, and Warsaw may regain some of their prewar importance. Budapest is a good example: Toward the late 1980s, it emerged as the leading international business center for the Eastern European region, a role illustrated by the fact that Hungary has since consistently been a major recipient of foreign direct investment in Eastern Europe (see Exhibit 3.8) (Bodnar 2000). Although the

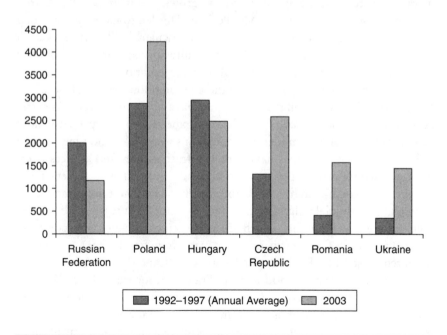

Exhibit 3.8   Foreign Direct Investment in Select Central and Eastern European Countries, 1986–2003 (US$ millions)

Source: UNCTAD (2004:371).

absolute investment levels were lower than those in the Russian Federation (with its vastly larger territory and economy than Hungary), in relative terms, these figures represent a sharper internationalization than in the former Soviet Union. Western European and non-European firms seeking to do business in Eastern Europe established offices in Budapest to launch operations for a large transnational Central European region. By the early 1990s, Budapest had a rather glamorous Western-looking international business enclave that offered the requisite comforts, hotels, restaurants, and business services to an extent that most other major Eastern European cities did not have at the time.

Immigration has become a major factor in demographic and labor-force growth in many European cities and, especially from the late 1990s on, an increasingly polarizing political issue. An initial scholarship that engaged the new migration phase that took off in the 1980s recognized that this was a feature that was there to remain (Balbo and Manconi 1990; Blaschke and Germershausen 1989; Brown 1984; Canevari 1991; Cohen 1987; Gillette and Sayad 1984; SOPEMI [Systeme d'Observation Permanente pour les Migrations] 1999–2005; Tribalat et al. 1991).[5] Cities that function as gateways into Europe were expected to receive growing immigration flows from Eastern Europe, Africa, and the Middle East. This led to increasingly strong political divisions as many of these cities, particularly old port cities such as Marseilles, Palermo, and Naples, were already experiencing economic decline and were seen as unable to absorb the additional labor and costs (for critical examinations of some of these assumptions, see Pugliese 2002; Mingione 1991). Although these cities may have functioned largely as entrepôts, with variable shares of immigrants expected to move on to more dynamic cities, resident immigrant populations also took root. One concern in these cities has been that having their infrastructures and services overburdened would further peripheralize these gateway cities in the emerging European urban hierarchy connecting leading cities in Europe and contribute to sociospatial polarization. However, some of Europe's global cities, such as Paris and Frankfurt, which are at the center of major transportation networks and are final destinations for many immigrants, have recognized the often major benefits associated with significant shares of immigrants in their populations and workforces. In Frankfurt, for example, 28% of the workforce is foreign born, including significant shares of top-level professionals. In other cases, it is older imperial geographies that have made certain cities key destinations, with often positive disposition towards immigrants. Thus, Berlin, an emerging global city in a variety of highly specialized sectors (culture, new media, software design), is also a preferred destination of many new migrations, as is Vienna. In the past, Berlin and

Vienna were centers of vast regional migration systems, and they seem to be recapturing that old role. The enlarging of the European Union in 2004 has created a new perimeter for Europe with growing concerns that the Eastern edge cities in that perimeter will have to take on control and gateway functions for which they are not fully equipped or prepared. Elsewhere (Sassen 1999; 2004), I have argued that Europe has had immigration for centuries, with sharp up and down cycles of positive and negative dispositions toward immigrants, and has always wound up with significant levels of integration—as is suggested by, for example, a third of France's native born population having a foreign-born ancestor two or three generations back, a figure that goes up to 40% in the case of a city such as Vienna. I return to immigration issues in some of the later chapters.

There are, then, a multiplicity of economic and demographic geographies of centers and margins in Europe at this time. A central urban hierarchy connects major cities, many of which in turn play key roles in the wider global system of cities: Paris, London, Frankfurt, Amsterdam, Zurich, Madrid, and Milan. Somewhat less oriented to the global economy is a major network of European financial/cultural/service capitals, such as Edinburgh, Berlin, Dublin, Rome, Stockholm, Prague, and Warsaw—some with only one, and others with several of these functions, which articulate the European region. And then there are several geographies of margins: the East–West divide and the North–South divide across Europe, as well as new micro-divisions. In Eastern Europe, certain cities and regions are rather attractive for European and non-European investment, whereas others will increasingly fall behind (notably, those in the former Yugoslavia and Albania). A similar differentiation exists in the south of Europe: Madrid, Barcelona, and Milan are gaining in the new European hierarchy; Naples and Marseilles are not.

Transnational Urban Systems

A rapidly growing and highly specialized research literature began to focus in the 1980s on different types of economic linkages binding cities across national borders (Friedmann and Wolff 1982; Castells 1989; Daniels 1991; GaWC 1998; Graham and Marvin 1996; Leyshon, Daniels, and Thrift 1987; Noyelle and Dutka 1988; Sassen-Koob 1982; 1984; Sassen 1988).

Today, this has emerged as a major issue of interest to a variety of disciplines (Taylor 2004), even though the data are partial and often problematic. Prime examples of such linkages are the multinational networks of affiliates and subsidiaries typical of major firms in manufacturing and specialized services (see Exhibits 2.5 and 4.7). The internationalization and deregulation of various financial markets is yet another, very recent development that binds cities across borders (see Exhibits 2.8, 2.9, 3.9, 3.10, 3.11, and several exhibits in Chapter 4).[6] An increasing number of stock markets around the world now participate in a global equities market. There are also a growing number of less directly economic linkages, notable among which are a variety of initiatives launched by urban governments that amount to a type of foreign policy by and for cities. In this context, the long-standing tradition of designating sister cities (Zelinsky 1991) has recently been reactivated, taking on a whole new meaning in the case of cities eager to operate internationally without going through their national governments (Eurocities 1989; Sassen 2002; Urban Age 2005).

Some of the most detailed data on transnational linkages binding cities come from studies on corporate service firms. These firms have developed vast multinational networks containing special geographic and institutional linkages that make it possible for client firms—transnational firms and banks—to use a growing array of service offerings from the same supplier (Bryson and Daniels 2005; Daniels 1991; Ernst 2005). There is good evidence that the development of transnational corporate service firms was associated with the needs of transnational firms for global servicing capabilities (Ernst 2005; Sassen [1991] 2001, chap. 5). One of the best data sets on the global networks of affiliates of leading firms in finance, accounting, law, and advertising is the Globalization and World Cities Study Group and Network, usually referred to (including in this book) as GaWC. Recent GaWC research shows that the network of affiliates in banking/finance and law firms closely follows the relative importance of world cities in those two sectors (Exhibits 3.9a and 3.9b). The transnational banking/finance or law firm, therefore, can offer global finance and legal services to a specific segment of potential customers worldwide. And so can the global communications firms. Global integration of affiliates and markets requires making use of advanced information and telecommunications technology that can come to account for a significant share of costs—not only operational costs but also, and perhaps most important, research and development costs for new products or advances on existing products. Exhibit 3.10 shows the probability that firms with offices in one of the listed cities will have a branch office or affiliate in another city.

The need for scale economies on all these fronts helps explain the recent increase in mergers and acquisitions, which has consolidated the position of a few very large firms in many of these industries and has further strengthened cross-border linkages between the key locations that concentrate the needed telecommunications facilities. These few firms can now control a significant share of national and international markets. The rapid increase in foreign direct investment in services is strongly linked with the high level of concentration in many of these industries and a strong tendency toward increasing market share among the larger firms. This is particularly true

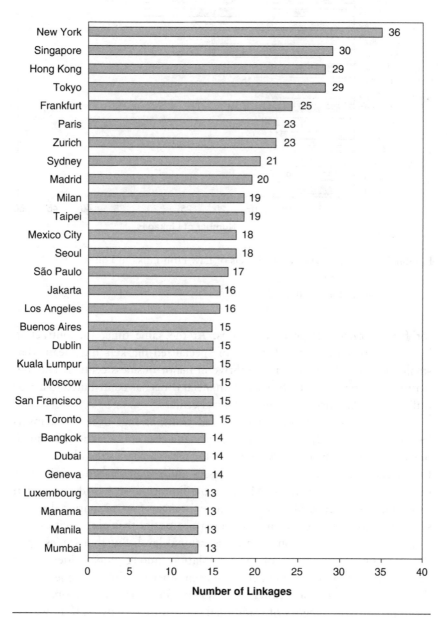

Exhibit 3.9a   Cities with Major Levels of Banking/Finance Links to London (number of firms, 1998)

Source: Taylor, Walker, and Beaverstock (2000).

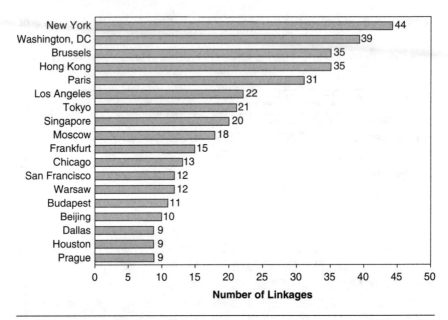

Exhibit 3.9b   Cities with Major Levels of Law Firm Links to London (number of firms, 1998)

Source: Taylor, Walker, and Beaverstock (2000).

for firms servicing large corporations. At the same time, subcontracting by larger firms and a proliferation of specialized markets has meant that small independent firms can also thrive in major business centers. The link between international law firms and financial firms has contributed to a centralization of law firms in major financial centers.

Whether these links have engendered transnational urban systems is less clear and is partly a question of theory and conceptualization. So much of social science is profoundly rooted in the nation-state as the ultimate unit for analysis that conceptualizing processes and systems as transnational is bound to create controversy. Much of the literature on world and global cities does not necessarily proclaim the existence of a transnational urban system: In its narrowest form, this literature posits that global cities perform central place functions at a transnational level. But that leaves open the question of the nature of the articulation among global cities. If we accept that they basically compete with each other for global business, then they do not constitute a transnational system. Studying several global cities then falls into the category of traditional comparative analysis. If, however, we posit that in addition to competing with each other, global cities are also the sites for transnational processes with multiple locations (Taylor 2004),

Exhibit 3.10 Intrafirm Service Networks among Top Business Centers, 1998 (probabilities in percentages)

Linkage from	Linkage to									
	Chicago	Frankfurt	Hong Kong	London	Los Angeles	Milan	New York	Paris	Singapore	Tokyo
Chicago	—	89	89	100	91	79	100	89	83	100
Frankfurt	67	—	93	100	72	87	100	95	94	95
Hong Kong	60	82	—	100	80	80	100	85	92	90
London	59	77	87	—	78	78	98	83	83	86
Los Angeles	67	73	89	100	—	70	97	84	81	89
Milan	59	88	93	100	67	—	100	88	91	93
New York	59	77	87	98	77	77	—	79	83	85
Paris	64	85	90	100	80	81	97	—	90	90
Singapore	60	87	98	100	78	83	100	92	—	95
Tokyo	64	84	93	100	83	81	100	87	88	—

Note: The table is an asymmetric matrix showing probabilities of connections between cities; each cell contains the percentage probability that a firm in City X will have an office in City Y.

Source: Taylor, Walker, and Beaverstock (2000)

Exhibit 3.11   Top 5 Global Command Centers Based on Corporations, Banks, Telecommunications, and Insurance Agencies, 2005

Rank	City[a]	Corporations	Banks	Telecommunications	Insurance Agencies
1	Tokyo	56	3	2	6
2	Paris	26	4	2	3
3	London	23	3	0	5
4	New York	22	2	1	4
5	Beijing	12	4	2	1

Note:

a. Cities with the most high-revenue multinational corporations.

Source: Calculations based on "Global 500" (2005).

then we can begin to explore the possibility of a systemic dynamic binding these cities.

Elsewhere (Sassen [1991] 2001, chaps. 1 and 7; 2002), I have argued that in addition to the central place functions performed by these cities at the global level as posited by Hall (1966), Friedmann and Wolff (1982), and Sassen-Koob (1982), these cities relate to one another in distinct systemic ways. For example, already in the 1980s, when the notion of global multisited systems was barely developed, I found that the interactions among New York, London, and Tokyo, particularly in terms of finance, services, and investment, consisted partly of a series of processes that could be thought of as "chains of production" and international divisions of labor. Thus, in the case of global finance in the mid-1980s, I argued that Tokyo functioned as the main exporter of the raw material we call money, while New York was the leading financial processing and innovation center in the world. Many of the new financial instruments were invented in New York; and money, either in its raw form or in the form of debt, was transformed into instruments aimed at maximizing the returns on that money. London, the world's major banking entrepôt, had the network to centralize and concentrate small amounts of capital available in a large number of smaller financial markets around the world, partly as a function of its older network for the administration of the British Empire (Exhibit 3.11). More recently, I have replicated this type of analysis focusing on the specialized advantage of major global cities, for example, New York's, and Chicago's financial centers (Sassen 2002, chap. 1).

These are examples suggesting that cities do not simply compete with each other for the same business. There is an economic system that rests on the distinct types of locations and specializations each city represents. Furthermore, it seems likely that the strengthening of transnational ties among the leading financial and business centers is accompanied by a weakening of the linkages between each of these cities and its hinterland and national urban system (Sassen [1991] 2001). Cities such as Detroit, Liverpool, Manchester, Marseilles, the cities of the Ruhr, and now Nagoya and Osaka have been affected by the territorial decentralization of many of their key manufacturing industries at the domestic and international level. But this same process of decentralization has contributed to the growth of service industries that produce the specialized inputs to run spatially dispersed production processes and global markets for inputs and outputs. In a representative case, General Motors, whose main offices are in Detroit, also has a headquarters in Manhattan, which does all the specialized national and global financial and public relations work this vast multinational firm requires. Such specialized inputs—international legal and accounting services, management consulting, and financial services—are heavily concentrated in business and financial centers rather than in manufacturing cities. In brief, the manufacturing jobs that Detroit began to lose in the 1970s and 1980s fed a growing demand for specialized corporate services in New York City to coordinate and manage a now globally distributed auto manufacturing system.

Global Cities and Diasporic Networks

A particular type of transnational urban system is slowly emerging from a variety of networks concerned with transboundary issues such as immigration, asylum, international women's agendas, antiglobalization struggles, and many others. These types of networks have proliferated rapidly since the late 1980s and increasingly intensified their transactions. Although these networks are not necessarily urban in their orientation or genesis, their geography of operations is partly inserted in a large number of cities. The new network technologies, especially the Internet, ironically have strengthened the urban map of these transboundary networks. It does not have to be that way, but at this time cities and the networks that bind them function as an anchor and an enabler of cross-border transactions and struggles. Global cities especially already have multiple intercity transactions and immigrants from many different parts of the world. These same developments and conditions also facilitate the globalizing of terrorist and trafficking networks.

Global cities and the new strategic geographies that connect them and partly bypass national states are becoming a factor in the development of globalized diasporic networks. This is a development from the ground up, connecting a diaspora's multiple groups distributed across various places. In so doing, these networks multiply the transversal transactions among these groups and destabilize the exclusive orientation to the homeland typical of the older radial pattern (Axel 2002). Furthermore, even a partial reorientation away from national homeland politics can ease these groups' transactions in each city with that city's other diasporas and nondiasporic groups involved in diverse types of transnational activities and imaginaries (Bartlett 2006). In such developments, in turn, lies the possibility that at least some of these networks and groups can become part of the infrastructure for global civil society rather than being confined to deeply nationalistic projects. These dynamics can then be seen as producing a shift toward globalizing diasporas by enabling transversal connections among the members of a given worldwide diaspora, and by intensifying the transactions among diverse diasporic and nondiasporic groups within a given city.

Cities are thick enabling environments for these types of activities, even when the networks themselves are not urban per se. In this regard, these cities enable the experience of participation in global nonstate networks. One might say that global civil society gets enacted partly in the microspaces of daily life rather than on some putative global stage. Groups can experience themselves as part of a globalized diaspora even when they are in a place where there might be few conationals, and thus the term *diaspora* hardly applies. In the case of global cities, there is the added dimension of the global corporate economy and its networks and infrastructures enabling cross-border transactions and partially denationalizing urban space.

Both globalization and the international human rights regime have contributed to create operational and legal openings for nonstate actors to enter international arenas once exclusive to national states. Various, often as yet very minor developments signal that the state is no longer the exclusive subject for international law or the only actor in international relations. Other actors—from NGOs (nongovernmental organizations) and first-nation peoples to immigrants and refugees who become subjects of adjudication in human rights decisions—are increasingly emerging as subjects of international law and actors in international relations. Therefore, these nonstate actors can gain visibility as individuals and as collectivities, and they can come out of the invisibility of aggregate membership in a nation-state exclusively represented by the state.

The nexus in this configuration is that the weakening of the exclusive formal authority of states over national territory facilitates the ascendance of sub- and transnational spaces and actors in politico-civic processes. The *national* as container of social process and power is cracked enabling the emergence of a geography of politics and civics that links subnational spaces. Cities are foremost in this new geography. The density of political and civic cultures in large cities and their daily practices roots, implants, and localizes global civil society in people's lives. Insofar as the global economic system can be shown to be partly embedded in specific types of places and partly constituted through highly specialized cross-border networks connecting today's global cities, one research task to help understand how this all intersects with immigrants and diasporas is, then, to find out about the specific contents and institutional locations of this multiscalar globalization, the subject of this book. Further, it means understanding how the emergence of global imaginaries changes the meaning of processes that may be much older than the current phase of globalization, but that today are inscribed by the latter. Thus, immigrant and diasporic communities are much older than today's globalization. But that does not mean that they are not altered by various specific forms of globalization today.

As discussed in preceding chapters and again later in Chapter 7, recapturing the geography of places involved in economic political globalization allows us to recapture people, workers, communities, and the many different political projects in and of these communities (e.g., Mele 1999; Espinoza 1999). The global city can be seen as one strategic research site about these processes and the many forms through which global processes become localized in specific arrangements. This localizing includes a broad range of processes: the new, *very*-high-income, gentrified urban neighborhoods of the transnational professional class and rich exiles, and the work lives of the foreign nannies and maids in those same neighborhoods and of the poor refugees concentrated in asylum housing. Although the formation of the network of global cities is largely driven by corporate economic globalization, multiple political and cultural processes have localized in these complex, partly denationalized environments. This is an old history for cities, but it has received a whole new life through the formation of today's networks of global cities.

The next subsection briefly addresses some general issues of an emergent global politics centered on local struggles and actors.

A Politics of Places on Global Circuits

The space constituted by the worldwide grid of global cities, a space with new economic and political potentialities, is perhaps one of the most strategic spaces for the formation of transnational identities and communities. This is a space that is both place-centered, in that it is embedded in particular and strategic cities, and transterritorial because it connects sites that are not geographically proximate yet are intensely connected to each other. It is not only the transmigration of capital that takes place in this global grid but also that of people, both rich (i.e., the new transnational professional workforce) and poor (i.e., most migrant workers). It is also a space for the transmigration of cultural forms and the reterritorialization of local subcultures.

An important question is whether it is also a space for a new politics, one going beyond the politics of culture and identity, though likely to be embedded partly in these. The politics of diasporic groups may be grounded in shared identities, but these politics do not necessarily conform to the politics of identity in our Western societies. The possibility of transnational identity formation among politicized diasporic groups is an interesting question, given a history of homeland orientation. It is one of the questions running through this book, particularly because global cities are enabling environments in this regard. One of the most radical forms assumed today by the linkage of people to territory is the loosening of selfhood from traditional sources of identity, such as the nation or the village. This unmooring in the process of identity formation engenders new notions of community of membership and of entitlement.

Immigration is one major process through which a new transnational political economy is being constituted, largely embedded in major cities because most immigrants are concentrated in major cities. It is one of the constitutive processes of globalization today, even though not recognized or represented as such in mainstream accounts of the global economy. Immigration becomes part of a massive demographic transition in these cities with a growing presence of women, native minorities, and immigrants in the population of more and more cities. Global capital and immigrants are two major examples, each a unified crossboder actor (or aggregate of actors) who find themselves in contestation with each other inside global cities.

Insofar as immigration is one of the forces shaping diasporas, these current features of immigration can be expected, first, to at least partly transnationalize diasporas, moving them away from an exclusive orientation to the homeland; and second, to urbanize at least some of their contestatory politics, moving them away from an exclusive focus on national states—either their homeland state or the state that has robbed them of having a homeland state. In the case of high-level professional diasporic groups, the dynamics are not dissimilar, and indeed the tendency to form global networks is strong.

These two major types of actors—global corporate capital and the mix of disadvantaged and minoritized people—find in the global city a strategic site for their economic and political operations. The leading sectors of corporate capital are now global in their organization and operations. And many of the disadvantaged workers in global cities are women, immigrants, and people of color—including diasporic groups in each of these—all people whose sense of membership is not adequately captured in terms of the national, and, in the case of diasporas especially, the national as constructed in the host country. Indeed, these groups often evince cross-border solidarities around issues of substance.

There is an interesting correspondence between great concentrations of corporate power and large concentrations of *others*. Large cities in both the global South and global North are the terrain where a multiplicity of globalization processes assume concrete, localized forms. A focus on cities allows us to capture, further, not only the upper but also the lower circuits of globalization. These localized forms are, in good part, what globalization is about, pointing to the possibility of a new politics of traditionally disadvantaged and excluded actors operating in this new transnational economic geography. This politics arises out of actual participation as workers in the global economy but under conditions of disadvantage and lack of recognition—whether factory workers in export-processing zones or cleaners on Wall Street.

The cross-border network of global cities is a space where we are seeing the formation of new types of global politics of place. These vary considerably: They may involve contesting corporate globalization or involve homeland politics. The demonstrations by the antiglobalization network have signaled the potential for developing a politics centered on places understood as locations on global networks. Some of the new globalizing diasporas have become intensive and effective users of the Internet to engage in these global politics of place. This is a place-specific politics with global span. It is a type of political work deeply embedded in people's actions and activities, made possible partly by the existence of global digital linkages. Further, it is a form of political and institution-building work centered in cities and networks of cities and in nonformal political actors. We see here the potential transformation of a whole range of local conditions or institutional domains (such as the household, community, neighborhood, school, and health care clinics) into localities situated on global networks (Sassen 2004b). From being lived or experienced as nonpolitical, or domestic, these places are transformed into microenvironments with global span. *Microenvironments with global span* are small local entities in which technical connectivity creates a variety of links with similar entities in other neighborhoods—whethers located in the same city, or other cities in the same country or abroad. A community of practice can emerge that creates multiple lateral, horizontal communications, collaborations, solidarities, and supports. This can enable local political or nonpolitical actors to enter into cross-border politics (e.g., Warkentin 2001; Hajnal 2002).

The space of the city is a far more concrete space for politics than that of the national state system. It becomes a place where nonformal political actors can be part of the political scene in a way that is much easier than at the national level. Nationally, politics needs to run through existing formal systems: whether the electoral political system or the judiciary (taking state agencies to court). Nonformal political actors are rendered invisible in the space of national politics. The city accommodates a broad range of political activities—squatting, demonstrations against police brutality, fighting for the rights of immigrants and the homeless, the politics of culture and identity, gay and lesbian politics, and the homeland politics that many diasporic groups engage in. Much of this becomes visible on the street. Much of urban politics is concrete, enacted by people rather than dependent on massive media technologies. Street-level politics make possible the formation of new types of political subjects that do not have to go through the formal political system. These conditions can be critical for highly politicized diasporic groups and in the context of globalization and Internet access, can easily lead to the globalizing of a diaspora. The city also enables the operations of illegal networks.

The mix of focused activism and local or global networks creates conditions for the emergence of transnational identities. The possibility of identifying with larger communities of practice or membership can bring about the partial unmooring of identities and thereby facilitate the globalizing of a diaspora. It can weaken the radial structure (with the homeland at the center of the distribution of the groups of a given diaspora). Although this does not necessarily neutralize attachments to a country or national cause, it does shift this attachment to include translocal communities of practice and/or membership.

Beyond the impact on immigrants and diasporas, these various conditions are a crucial building block for a global civil society that can incorporate both the micropractices and microobjectives of people's political passions. The possibility of transnational identities emerging as a consequence of micropolitics is crucial for strengthening global civil society; the risk of nationalism and fundamentalism is, clearly, present in these dynamics as well.

Conclusion: Urban Growth and Its Multiple Meanings

Major recent developments in urban systems point to several trends. In the developing world, we see the continuing growth of megacities and primacy, as well as the emergence of new growth poles resulting from the internationalization of production and the development of tourism. In some cases, these new growth poles emerge as new destinations for migrants and thereby contribute to a deceleration in primacy; in other cases, when they are located in a primate city's area, they have the opposite effect.

In the developed world, and particularly in Western Europe, we see the renewed strength of major cities that appear to concentrate a significant and often disproportionate share of economic activity in leading sectors. In the 1970s, many of the major cities in highly developed countries were losing population and economic activity. Much was said at the time about the irreversible decline of these cities. But beginning in the mid-1980s, there has been a resurgence that results in good part from the intersection of two major trends in all advanced economies: (1) the shift to services, including importantly services for firms, such as finance and corporate services, and (2) the increasing transnationalization of economic activity. This transnationalization can operate at the regional, continental, or global level. These two trends are interlinked. The spatial implication is a strong tendency toward agglomeration of the pertinent activities in major cities. A fact typically overlooked in much of today's commentary about cities is that this dynamic of urban growth is based largely on the locational needs or preferences of firms and does not necessarily compensate for population losses to suburbanization. Urban growth in less developed countries, by contrast, results largely from population growth, especially in-migration. However, beneath the megacity syndrome, we now also see, as of the 1990s, the two trends mentioned earlier in emergent global cities; in the case of very large cities, these trends are easy to overlook, and the focus is often confined to the megacity syndrome.

The transnationalization of economic activity has raised the intensity and volume of transaction among cities; whether this has contributed to the formation of transnational urban systems is a question that requires more research. The growth of global markets for finance and specialized services, the need for transnational servicing networks in response to sharp increases in international investment, the reduced role of the government in the regulation of international economic activity and the corresponding ascendance of other institutional arenas, notably global markets and corporate headquarters—all these point to the existence of transnational economic arrangements with multiple urban locations in more than one country. Here is the formation, at least incipiently, of a transnational urban system.

The pronounced orientation to the world markets evident in such cities raises questions about the articulation with their hinterlands and nation-states. Cities typically have been and still are deeply embedded in the economies of their region, often reflecting the characteristics of the latter.

But cities that are strategic sites in the global economy tend, in part, to disconnect from their region. This phenomenon also conflicts with a key proposition in traditional scholarship about urban systems—namely, that these systems promote the territorial integration of regional and national economies.

Two tendencies contributing to new forms of inequality among cities are visible in the geography and characteristics of urban systems. On one hand, there is growing transnational articulation among an increasing number of cities. This is evident at both a regional transnational level and the global level; in some cases, there are overlapping geographies of articulation or overlapping hierarchies that operate at more than one level; that is, there are cities such as Paris or London that belong to a national urban system or hierarchy, transnational European system, and global system. On the other hand, cities and areas outside these hierarchies tend to become peripheralized.

A second major trend is for powerless groups in global cities to become active in transnational activities, producing a whole series of new, and newly invigorated, intercity networks. Although economic transactions among cities many have launched the formation of emergent transnational urban systems, a proliferation of people networks began to emerge in the late 1980s and have grown rapidly since then. Generally, those networks with a key basing point in cities originate from two types of conditions. One is immigration and diasporic politics. Although these have long existed across the centuries and the world, the new information technologies have made a significant difference in the intensity and simultaneity of transactions they make possible and in the multiplication of transversal linkages, beyond the radial pattern centered in the homeland. The second type originates from a variety of activist and information sharing networks concerned largely with localized politico-social struggles: It produces a kind of horizontal globality anchored in localities. Even individuals and organizations that are not mobile—too poor or persecuted, or simply not interested in traveling—can become part of these new global networks. The marking condition is the recurrence of certain issues—environmental, political, social—in many localities across the world.

Notes

1. See also the special case of border cities such as Tijuana, which have exploded in growth because of the internationalization of production in the Mexico–U.S. border region and have become major destinations for migrants (Sanchez and Alegria 1992). Another type of case is represented by the new export

manufacturing zones in China that have drawn large numbers of migrants from many regions of the country (Sklair 1985; Solinger 1999:277–90; Chen 2005). For one of the best accounts of boder cities see Herzog 1990.

2. This region is here defined as consisting of the island nations between the Florida peninsula and the north coast of South America, and the independent countries of the Central American isthmus; it excludes the large nations bordering on the Caribbean Sea.

3. There are several new excellent global city analyses of these cities (e.g., Ciccolella and Mignaqui 2002; Schiffer Ramos 2002; see various chapters in Gugler 2006 and in Amen et al. 2006).

4. The strengthening of Berlin, both through reunification and regaining the role of capital, may alter some of the power relations among Budapest, Vienna, and Berlin. Indeed, Berlin could become a major international business center for Central Europe after the recent 2004 enlargement, with possibly corresponding reductions in the roles of Budapest and Vienna. However, these three cities may create a regional transnational urban system for the whole region—a multinodal urban center of gravity, in which both competition and a division of functions have the effect of strengthening the overall international business capability of the region.

5. This is not an exceptional situation. All developed countries in the world now have immigrant workers. Even Japan, a country known for its anti-immigration stance, became a destination for migrant workers in the late 1980s, a role that has continued since, albeit with ups and downs and a changing nationality composition in the flows (AMPO 1988; Asian Women's Association 1988; Iyotani 1998; Iyotani, Sakai and de Bary 2005; Morita and Sassen 1994; Sassen 1998, chap. 4; [1991] 2001, chap. 9).

6. See also the section, "Why Do We Need Financial Centers in the Global Digital Era?" in Chapter 5.

4

The New Urban Economy:
The Intersection of Global
Processes and Place

How are the management, financing, and servicing processes of internationalization actually constituted in cities that function as regional or global nodes in the world economy? And what are the actual components of the larger work of running the global operations of firms and markets that get done in these cities?

The answers to these two questions help us understand the new or sharply expanded role of a particular kind of city in the phase of the world economy that took off in the mid-1980s. At the heart of this development lie two intersecting processes critical to the current phase. The first process is the sharp growth in the globalization of economic activity (discussed in Chapter 2) and the concomitant increases in the scale and the complexity of international transactions, which in turn feeds the growth of top-level multinational headquarters' functions and of advanced corporate services. Although globalization raises their scale and complexity, these operations are also evident at smaller geographic scales and lower orders of complexity, as is the case with firms that operate regionally or nationally. Also these firms run increasingly dispersed operations, albeit not global, as they set up chains and/or buy up the traditional single-owner shops that sell flowers, food, or fuel, or run chains of hotels and a growing range of service facilities. Though operating in simpler contexts, these firms also need to centralize their control, management, and specialized servicing functions. National and regional market firms need not negotiate the complexities of international borders and the regulations and accounting rules of different countries, but they do create a growing demand for corporate services of all kinds, feeding economic growth in second-order cities as well.

The second process we need to consider is the growing service intensity in the organization of all industries (Sassen [1991] 2001, chap. 5). This development has contributed to a massive growth in the demand for services (legal, accounting, insurance, etc.) by firms in all industries, from mining and manufacturing to finance and consumer industries. Cities are key sites for the production of services for firms. Hence, the increase in service intensity in the organization of all industries has had a significant growth effect on cities beginning in the 1980s. This growth in services for firms is evident in cities at different levels of a nation's urban system. Some of these cities cater to regional or subnational markets, others cater to national markets, and yet others cater to global markets. In this context, the specific effect of globalization is a question of scale and added complexity. The key process from the perspective of the urban economy is the growing demand for services by firms in all industries and across market scale—global, national, or regional.

As a result of these two intersecting processes, we see in cities the formation of a new urban economic core of high-level management and specialized service activities that comes to replace the older, typically manufacturing-oriented office core. In the case of cities that are major international business centers, the scale, power, and profit levels of this new core suggest the formation of a new urban economy, in at least two regards. First, even though these cities have long been centers for business and finance, since the mid-1980s there have been dramatic changes in the structure of the business and financial sectors, as well as sharp increases in the overall magnitude of these sectors and their weight in the urban economy. Second, the ascendance of the new finance and services complex engenders a new economic regime; that is, although this sector may account for only a fraction of the economy of a city, it imposes itself on that larger economy. Most notably, the possibility for superprofits in finance has the effect of devalorizing manufacturing because manufacturing cannot generate the superprofits typical in much financial activity.

This does not mean that everything in the economy of these cities has changed. On the contrary, these cities still show a great deal of continuity and many similarities with cities that are not global nodes. Rather, the implantation of global processes and markets has meant that the internationalized sector of the economy has expanded sharply and has imposed a new valorization dynamic—that is, a new set of criteria for valuing or pricing various economic activities and outcomes. This has had devastating effects on large sectors of the urban economy. High prices and profit levels in the internationalized sector and its ancillary activities, such as top-of-the-line restaurants and hotels, have made it increasingly difficult for other sectors to compete for space and investments. Many of these other sectors have experienced considerable downgrading and/or displacement; for example, neighborhood shops tailored to local needs have been replaced by upscale boutiques and restaurants catering to the new high-income urban elite.

Although at a different order of magnitude, these trends also took off in the early 1990s in a number of major cities in the developing world that have become integrated into various world markets: São Paulo, Buenos Aires, Bangkok, Taipei, and Mexico City are a few examples. Also in these cities, the new urban core was fed by the deregulation of financial markets, the ascendance of finance and specialized services, and integration into the world markets. The opening of stock markets to foreign investors and the privatization of what were once public-sector firms have been crucial institutional arenas for this articulation. Given the vast size of some of these cities, the impact of this new core on their larger urban area is not always as evident as in central London or Frankfurt, but the transformation is still very real.

In this chapter, I examine the characteristics of this new dominant sector in the urban economy of global cities. I begin with a discussion of producer services (services for firms), the core sector of the new urban economy, and the conditions shaping the growth and locational patterns of these services. I then turn to the formation of a new producer-services complex in major cities, using the coordination and planning requirements of large transnational corporations as a working example of some of these developments. I also examine the locational patterns of major headquarters as a way to understand their significance for cities and, vice versa, the significance of cities for headquarters. I conclude with a look at the impact on the urban economy of the international financial and real-estate crisis beginning at the end of the 1980s, and the impact of the September 2001 attacks on the financial sector in New York City.

Producer Services

The expansion of producer services is a central feature of growth in today's advanced urban economies and, to a lesser degree, in national economies as well. The critical period for the rise of producer services in the developed countries was the 1980s, and their rise can in fact function as a lens on the underlying structural transformations in the economy. The concern here is to capture this shift rather than to track the evolution of producer services since then.

In country after country, the 1980s saw a decline or slowdown in manufacturing alongside sharp growth in producer services. Elsewhere, I have posited that the fundamental reason for this growth lies in the increased service intensity in the organization of all industries (Sassen [1991] 2001: 166–68). Whether in manufacturing or in warehousing, firms are using more legal, financial, advertising, consulting, and accounting services. These services can be seen as part of the supply capacity of an economy because they facilitate adjustments to changing economic circumstances (Marshall et al. 1986:16). They are a mechanism that organizes and adjudicates economic exchange for a fee (Thrift 1987) and are part of a broader intermediary space of economic activity.

Producer services are services for firms, from the most sophisticated to the most elementary ones. They include financial, legal, and general management matters; innovation; development; design; administration; personnel; production technology; maintenance; transport; communications; wholesale distribution; advertising; cleaning services for firms; security; and storage. Central components of the producer-services category are a range of industries with mixed business and consumer markets. They are insurance, banking, financial services, real estate, legal services, accounting, and professional associations.[1]

Although disproportionately concentrated in the largest cities, producer services are actually growing at faster rates at the national level in most developed economies. The crucial process feeding the growth of producer services is the increasing use of service inputs by firms in all industries. Consumption of services has also risen in households, either directly (such as the growing use of accountants to prepare tax returns) or indirectly via the reorganization of consumer industries (buying flowers or dinner from franchises or chains rather than from self-standing and privately owned "mom-and-pop" shops). Services directly bought by consumers tend to be available, often through mere outlets, wherever population is concentrated. In that regard, they are far less geographically concentrated than producer services, especially those catering to top firms. The demand for specialized services by households, from accounting to architects, may be a key factor contributing to the growth of these mixed-market services at the national level.

National employment trends for the crucial period of the shift (Exhibit 4.1) clearly show that some of the mixed-market producer services (usually categorized as "mostly producer services") make up the fastest growing sector in most developed economies even though they account for a small share of total jobs. Generally, these trends continue today. Total employment in the United States grew from 137 million in 1970 to 226.4 million in 2005, but mostly producer services more than quadrupled, from 6.3 to 28.8 million, with the largest single increase in miscellaneous business services, followed by financial activities. In contrast, manufacturing dropped from 17.8 to 14.3 million. The other major growth sectors were the social services (health, education), which grew from 4.5 to 17.4 million, and personal services (leisure, hospitality), from 4.7 to 12.8 million—significant levels but not nearly the rate of producer services. Distributive services also showed strong growth, from 14.1 to 25.5 million.

Parallel patterns are emerging in other developed economies. Total employment in Japan grew from 52.1 million in 1970 to 64.2 million in 2005, but the mostly producer services almost tripled from 2.5 to 7.2 million, while social services grew from 5.4 to 8.5 million. In France, total employment went from 20.6 million in 1970 to 24.7 million in 2003. From 1992 to 2003, producer and personal services doubled, while social and distributive services showed strong growth, too. Manufacturing fell from 4.2 to 43.7 million. By 2003, 69.9% of employment was in the services sector. In the United Kingdom, total employment grew from 23.4 million in 1970 to 29.2 million in 2003. Manufacturing lost half of its jobs, going from 9 to 4 million in 2003. But as in other developed economies, the mostly producer services grew exponentially, fivefold from 1.2 million in 1970 to 6.2 million in 2003, and social services grew from 4.2 to nearly 9 million. By 2003, 74% of employment was in the services sector. Finally, in Canada, total employment grew from 8.4 million in 1971 to 15.9 million in 2004. The mostly producer services grew more than sixfold from 0.5 to 3.3 million; miscellaneous business services accounted for two-thirds of this growth. From 1985 to 2004, business services alone grew from 0.6 to 1.6 million. All other service sectors also grew strongly, while manufacturing remained at 2.2 million, albeit with ups and downs throughout the period.

A focus on cities reveals the same trends, only with far greater intensity in the critical period of the shift in the mid-1980s, when producer services became the most dynamic, fastest-growing sector in many cities. Particularly notable here is the United Kingdom, where overall employment actually fell and manufacturing suffered severe losses. Yet in only three years, between 1984 and 1987, producer services in Central London raised their share from 31% to 37% of all employment, reaching 40% by 1989 (Frost and Spence 1992). Both relative and absolute declines occurred in Central London in all other major employment sectors. Similar developments took place in New York City: In 1987, at the height of the 1980s boom, producer services accounted for 37.7% of private-sector jobs. There were high growth rates in many of the producer services during the period when economic restructuring was consolidated in New York City: From 1977 to 1985, employment in legal services grew by 62%; in business services, by 42%; and in banking, by 23%. In contrast, employment fell by 22% in manufacturing and by 20% in transport.

Accompanying these sharp growth rates in producer services was an increase in the level of employment specialization in business and financial services in major cities throughout the 1980s. For example, more than 90% of jobs in finance, insurance, and real estate (FIRE) in New York City were located in Manhattan, as were 85% of business service jobs. By 1990, after large-scale suburbanization of households and firms, the finance and business services in the New York metropolitan area were more concentrated in Manhattan than they had been in the mid-1950s (Harris 1991).[2]

In the 1990s, the mostly producer services began to grow faster at the national level than in major cities. This is commonly interpreted as cities losing producer-services jobs to larger metropolitan areas and small towns. I interpret the data differently: The fact of growth nationwide is an indicator of the growing importance of producer services for all sectors of the economy (see Sassen [1991] 2001, chap. 5). If we consider only those components of producer services that may be described as information industries, we can see a steady growth in jobs across the United States. But the incidence of these industries does not decline in major cities. New York City posted a significantly higher concentration than any other major American city. From 1970 to 2000, employment in professional and business services grew from 24.2% of jobs in New York City to 37.2%, from 24.1 to 33.2% in Los Angeles, and from 19.2% to 33.5% in Chicago. All three cities show a higher incidence than the U.S. average, which grew from 15.1% to 17.6%.

Beginning in the mid-1980s, a general trend developed toward a high concentration of finance and certain producer services in the downtowns of major international financial centers around the world. From Toronto and Sydney to Frankfurt and Zurich, there is growing specialization in financial districts everywhere. This trend is also evident in the multipolar urban system of the United States: Against all odds, New York City has kept its place at the top in terms of concentration in banking and finance (Exhibits 4.2 through 4.6).

These cities emerged as important producers of services for firms, including for export to the rest of their national economies and worldwide. There is a strong tendency toward hierarchy and specialization. New York and London are the leading producers and exporters of accounting, advertising,

(Text continues on page 92)

Exhibit 4.1 National Employment Trends in Three Developed Economies, 1970 and 1991 (in millions)

	Japan		Germany		United States	
	1970	1990	1970	1987	1970	1991
I. Extractive	10,309	4,448	2,313	1,103	3,504	4,123
Agriculture	10,087	4,383	1,991	866	2,868	3,390
Mining	222	66	323	237	636	733
II. Transformative	17,772	20,795	12,481	10,835	25,310	28,824
Construction	3,943	5,906	2,033	1,908	4,634	7,087
Utilities	288	345	215	274	811	1,303
Manufacturing	13,541	14,544	10,234	8,654	19,864	20,434
Food	1,086	1,391	964	778	1,456	1,784
Textiles	1,427	714	635	307	968	688
Metal	2,103	1,985	1,243	1,168	2,391	1,992
Machinery	2,596	3,620	2,517	1,311	3,921	4,349
Chemical	666	679	634	736	1,189	1,525
Misc. mfg.	5,664	6,155	4,240	4,353	9,940	10,096
III. Distributive Services	11,689	14,987	4,748	4,765	17,190	24,079
Transportation	2,636	3,097	1,443	1,574	3,013	4,170
Communication	577	598	—	—	1,132	1,598
Wholesale	3,159	4,377	1,125	873	3,100	4,640
Retail	5,316	6,916	2,179	2,318	9,946	13,671
IV. Producer Services	2,522	5,945	1,187	1,977	6,298	16,350
Banking	729	1,181	438	658	1,658	3,286
Insurance	376	783	244	257	1,406	2,419
Real estate	274	707	92	109	789	2,081
Engineering	268	509	163	198	333	833

(Continued)

Exhibit 4.1 (Continued)

	Japan		Germany		United States	
	1970	1990	1970	1987	1970	1991
Accounting	93	188	—	—	303	660
Misc. bus. serv.	741	2,493	250	754	1,401	5,797
Legal services	42	85	—	—	409	1,274
V. Social Services	5,359	8,855	4,155	6,550	16,888	29,839
Medical, health serv.	211	943	815	1,465	1,846	5,259
Hospital	923	1,328	—	—	2,836	4,839
Education	1,537	2,757	802	1,314	6,546	9,366
Welfare, relig. serv.	381	847	245	410	908	3,154
Nonprofit org.	524	656	112	56	330	468
Postal service	—	—	—	—	732	852
Government	1,759	2,092	2,053	2,545	3,484	5,639
Misc. social services	23	232	128	760	206	262
VI. Personal Services	4,441	6,296	1,610	1,687	7,696	13,659
Domestic serv.	153	80	116	56	1,272	1,000
Hotel	463	677	730	731	731	1,813
Eating, drinking places	1,585	2,538	—	—	2,479	5,744
Repair services	480	614	271	297	1,056	1,670
Laundry	239	349	120	62	587	470
Barber, beauty shops	565	650	234	258	728	876
Entertainment	425	822	119	248	632	1,570
Misc. personal serv.	532	567	19	35	211	516
All Other Services	19	366	—	—	—	—
Total	52,110	61,734	26,494	26,908	76,805	116,877

Source: Based on Castells and Aoyama (1994).

88

Exhibit 4.2   Cities Ranked by Assets of the World's Top 100 Largest Publicly Listed Financial Companies, 2003 (US$ millions)

Rank	City	Assets	Percentage of Top 100
1	New York	6,503,764	15.53
2	Tokyo	4,640,834	11.08
3	Paris	3,799,065	9.07
4	London	3,599,982	8.60
5	Zurich	2,474,926	5.91
6	Munich	2,238,616	5.35
7	Frankfurt	1,997,733	4.77
8	Amsterdam	1,686,464	4.03
9	Edinburgh	1,544,645	3.69
10	Brussels	1,383,624	3.30
11	Toronto	1,082,111	2.58
12	Washington, DC*	1,009,569	2.41
13	Stockholm	821,879	1.96
14	McLean, VA*	803,449	1.92
15	Milan	627,724	1.50
16	Osaka	514,090	1.23
17	Rome	488,853	1.17
18	Melbourne	445,715	1.06
19	Madrid	443,010	1.06
20	Winston-Salem, NC*	401,032	0.96
21	Sydney	396,318	0.95
22	San Francisco*	387,798	0.93
23	Bilbao*	361,608	0.86
24	Antwerp*	326,951	0.78
25	Newark, NJ*	321,274	0.77
26	Ottawa*	310,551	0.74
27	Copenhagen*	308,456	0.74
28	The Hague*	294,646	0.70
29	Seoul	290,253	0.69
30	OTHERS	2,368,506	5.66
	TOTAL	41,873,446	100.00

Notes: Asterisk (*) denotes a city with only one headquarters of a top 100 company.

Ranked by assets as determined by the *Wall Street Journal* Market Data Group and FactSet Research Systems, Inc.

Figures are based on each company's fiscal 2003 results (2004 for Japanese firms).

Source: Based on "World Business" (2004).

Exhibit 4.3   Cities Ranked by Assets of the World's Top 25 Largest Securities
Firms, 1997 (US$ millions)

Rank	City	Assets	Percentage of Top 25
	Total for Top 25	1,995,782	—
1	New York, NY	1,586,737	79.50
2	Tokyo	236,712	11.86
3	Zurich	55,215	2.77
4	London	41,396	2.07
5	San Francisco, CA	28,786	1.44
6	St. Louis, MO	28,514	1.43
7	Baltimore, MD	16,349	0.82
8	Toronto	2,073	0.10

Note: Ranked by capital as determined by Dow Jones Global Indexes; figures based on 1997
fiscal-year results.

Source: Based on "World Business" (1989; 1998).

Exhibit 4.4a   Top 5 U.S. Cities Ranked by Assets of the World's Top 100
Largest Public Financial Companies, 2005 (US$ millions)

City	Assets	Percentage of World's Top 100
New York, NY	6,503,764	15.53
Washington, DC	1,009,569	2.41
McLean, VA	803,449	1.92
Winston-Salem, NC	401,032	0.96
San Francisco, CA	387,798	0.93
Total of Above Cities	9,105,612	21.75
World Total	41,873,446	100.0

Source: Calculations based on "World Business" (2004).

Exhibit 4.4b   Top 5 U.S. Cities Ranked by Revenues of the World's Top 50 Commercial and Savings Banks, 2005 (US$ millions)

City	Assets	Percentage of World's Top 50
New York, NY	165,207	15.53
Charlotte, NC	91,391	2.41
San Francisco, CA	33,876	1.92
Seattle, WA	15,962	0.96
Minneapolis, MN	14,706	0.93
Total of Above Cities	321,142	21.7
World Total	1,731,382	100.0

Source: Calculations based on "Global 500" (2005).

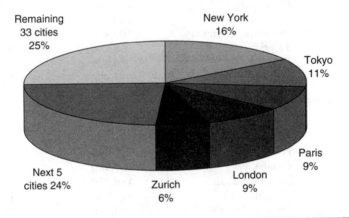

Exhibit 4.5   Cities Ranked by Assets of the World's Top 100 Largest Publicly Listed Financial Companies, 2003 (US$ millions)

Notes: Ranked by assets as determined by the *Wall Street Journal* Market Data Group and FactSet Research Systems, Inc.

Figures are based on each company's fiscal 2003 results (2004 for Japanese firms).

Source: Calculations based on "World Business" (2004).

Exhibit 4.6   Cities Ranked by Assets of the World's 50 Largest Insurers, 2005

Rank	City	Assets	Percentage of Top 50
Total for Top 50		8,324,240	100.00
Total for US		2,760,140	33.16
Top 20 Cities in the World (ranked by assets)			
1	Munich	1,374,460	16.51
2	New York	1,251,180	15.03
3	London	938,180	11.27
4	Paris	759,880	9.13
5	Zurich	553,280	6.64
6	Toronto	388,110	4.66
7	Newark, NJ	381,940	4.59
8	Tokyo	352,370	4.23
9	Trieste	317,660	3.81
10	The Hague	311,160	3.74
11	Hartford, CT	259,740	3.12
12	Omaha, NE	181,860	2.18
13	Northbrook, IL	149,730	1.80
14	Columbus, OH	116,880	1.40
15	Philadelphia, PA	110,380	1.33
16	St. Paul, MN	109,680	1.32
17	Hamilton, Bermuda	103,470	1.24
18	Taipei	68,840	0.83
19	Dorking	60,020	0.72
20	Sydney	55,400	0.67
Top 10 Cities in the United States			
1	New York	1,251,180	15.03
2	Newark, NJ	381,940	4.59
3	Hartford, CT	259,740	3.12
4	Omaha, NE	181,860	2.18
5	Northbrook, IL	149,730	1.80
6	Columbus, OH	116,880	1.40
7	Philadelphia, PA	110,380	1.33
8	St. Paul, MN	109,680	1.32
9	Columbus, GA	52,910	0.64
10	Warren, NJ	43,130	0.52

Note: Calculations based on "The Forbes Global 2000" (2005).

management consulting, international legal, and other business services. In fact, New York, London, Tokyo, Paris, and Zurich accounted for 50.2% of the world's top 100 largest public financial company assets in 2003 (see

Exhibit 4.2), and also accounted for 46.3% of the world's top 50 largest insurer assets in the same year (see Exhibit 4.6) They are the most important international markets for these services, with New York the world's largest source of service exports. By the late 1980s, Tokyo emerged as an important center for the international trade in services, going beyond its initial restricted role of exporting only the services required by its large international trading houses. Beginning early on, Japanese firms gained a significant share of the world market in certain producer services, namely, construction and engineering, but not in others, such as advertising and international legal services (Rimmer 1988). For instance, in the late 1970s, the United States accounted for 60 of the top 200 international construction contractors and Japan, for 10 (Rimmer 1988). By 1985, in a sharp reversal, each accounted for 34 (see Sassen [1991] 2001:174–75).

There are also tendencies toward specialization among different cities within a country. In the United States, New York is more narrowly specialized as a financial, business, and cultural center; thus, it leads in banking, securities, manufacturing administration, accounting, and advertising. Washington, DC, leads in legal services, computing and data processing, management and public relations, research and development, and membership organizations; at the same time, some of the legal activity concentrated in Washington, DC, is actually serving New York businesses that have to go through legal and regulatory procedures, lobbying, and so on. Such services are bound to be found in the national capital, and many are oriented to the national economy and to noneconomic purposes. Furthermore, in another contrast with New York City, much of the specialized activity in Washington is aimed not at the world economy but at the national economy in sectors such as medical and health research. Thus, adequate understanding requires we specify the composition of a city's producer-services complex and whether it is oriented to world markets and integration into the global economy or whether it responds largely to domestic demand.[3]

It is important to recognize that manufacturing remains a crucial sector in all of these economies, even when it may have ceased to be a dominant sector in major cities. Indeed, several scholars have argued that the producer-services sector could not exist without manufacturing (Cohen and Zysman 1987; Markusen and Gwiasda 1991). In this context, it has been argued, for example, that the weakening of the manufacturing sector in the broader New York region is a threat to the city's status as a leading financial- and producer-services center (Markusen and Gwiasda 1991). A key proposition for this argument is that producer services depend on a strong manufacturing sector for growth. There is considerable debate around this issue (Drennan 1992; Noyelle and Dutka 1988; Sassen [1991] 2001). Drennan (1992), the leading analyst of the producer-services sector in

New York City, argues that a strong finance- and producer-services sector is possible in that city, notwithstanding decline in its industrial base and that these sectors are so strongly integrated into the world markets that articulation with their hinterland—that is, integration with their regions— becomes secondary.

In a variant on both positions (Sassen [1991] 2001), I argue that manufacturing is one factor feeding the growth of the producer-services sector, but that it does so whether located in the area in question or overseas. Even though manufacturing—and mining and agriculture, for that matter—feeds growth in the demand for producer services, its actual location is of secondary importance for global-level service firms. Thus, whether manufacturing plants are located offshore or within a country is irrelevant as long as they are part of a multinational corporation likely to buy the services from top-level firms. Second, the territorial dispersal of plants, especially if international, actually raises the demand for producer services (see the section on "Global Cities" in Chapter 2). This is yet another meaning, or consequence, of globalization: The growth of producer service firms headquartered in New York or London or Paris can be fed by manufacturing located anywhere in the world as long as it is part of a multinational corporate network. Third, a good part of the producer-services sector is fed by financial and business transactions that have nothing to do with manufacturing, as in many of the global financial markets, or for which manufacturing is incidental, as in much merger and acquisition activity (which is centered on buying and selling firms no matter what they do).

Some of the employment figures for New York and London, two cities that experienced heavy losses in manufacturing and sharp gains in producer services, illustrate this point. The sharp shift takes place in the 1970s and 1980s. Thus New York lost 34% of its manufacturing jobs from 1969 to 1989 in a national economy that overall lost only 2% of such jobs and that actually saw manufacturing growth in many areas. The British economy lost 32% of its manufacturing jobs from 1971 to 1989, and the London region lost 47% of such jobs (Fainstein, Gordon, and Harloe 1992; Buck, Drennan, and Newton 1992). Yet both cities had sharp growth in producer services and raised the shares of those jobs in each city's total employment. Furthermore, consider the different conditions in each city's larger region: London's region had a 2% employment decline compared with a 22% job growth rate in the larger New York region. This divergence shows that the finance and producer-services complex in each city rests on a growth dynamic that is somewhat independent of the broader regional economy—a sharp change from the past, when a city was presumed to be deeply articulated with its hinterland.

The Formation of a New Production Complex

According to standard conceptions about information industries, the rapid growth and disproportionate concentration of many of the producer services in central cities should not have happened. This is especially so for advanced corporate services, because they are thoroughly embedded in the most advanced information technologies; they would seem to has locational options that bypass the high costs and congestion typical of major cities. But cities offer agglomeration economies and highly innovative environments. Some of these services are produced in-house by firms, but a large share are outsourced to specialized service firms. The growing complexity, diversity, and specialization of the services these firms require makes it more efficient to buy them from specialized firms rather than hiring in-house full-time professionals. The growing demand for these services has enabled a freestanding specialized service sector to become economically viable in cities.

The work of producing these services benefits from proximity to other specialized services, especially in the leading and most innovative sectors of these industries. Complexity and innovation often require highly specialized inputs from several industries. The production of a financial instrument, for example, requires inputs from accounting, advertising, legal services, economic consulting, public relations, software innovations, design, and printing. In this regard, these are highly networked firms. These particular characteristics of production explain the centralization of management and servicing functions that has fueled the economic boom in major cities beginning in the mid-1980s.

The commonly heard explanation that high-level professionals require face-to-face interactions needs to be refined in several ways. Producer services, unlike other types of services, are not necessarily dependent on spatial proximity to buyers—that is, firms served. Rather, economies occur in such specialized firms when they locate close to others that produce key inputs or whose proximity makes possible joint production of certain service offerings. The accounting firm can service its clients at a distance, but producing that service depends on proximity to specialists, from lawyers to programmers. My interpretation is that so-called face-to-face communication is actually a production process that requires multiple simultaneous inputs and feedbacks. At the current stage of technical development, having immediate and simultaneous access to the pertinent experts is still the most effective way to operate, especially when dealing with a highly complex product. Moreover, concentration arises out of the needs and expectations of the people likely to be employed in these new high-skill jobs who tend to be attracted to the amenities and lifestyles that large urban centers can offer.

A critical variable in the most advanced and specialized segments of the sector is speed. Time replaces weight as a force for agglomeration. In the past, the weight of inputs from iron ore to unprocessed agricultural products was a major constraint that encouraged agglomeration in sites where the heaviest inputs were located. Today, the combination of added complexity and acceleration of economic transactions has created new forces for agglomeration; that is, if there were no time pressures and little complexity, the client could conceivably make use of a widely dispersed array of cooperating specialized firms. And this is often the case in routine operations. Where time is of the essence, however, as it is today in many of the leading sectors of these industries, the benefits of agglomeration in the production of specialized services are still extremely high—to the point where whatever the costs of urban agglomeration, the concentration of multiple state-of-the-art specialized service firms has become an indispensable arrangement. Central here has been the general acceleration of all transactions, especially in finance (where minutes and seconds count), the stock markets, the foreign-currency markets, the futures markets, and so on. Speed in these types of sectors puts a premium not just on competence among lawyers, accountants, financiers, and so on, but on the knowledge that emerges from the interactions among talented and experienced professionals.

This combination of constraints and advantages has promoted the formation of a producer-services complex in all major cities. The producer-services complex is intimately connected to the world of corporate headquarters, leading to the formation of a joint headquarters–corporate-services complex. But, the two need to be distinguished. Although headquarters still tend to be disproportionately concentrated in cities, many have moved out during the last two decades. Headquarters can indeed be located outside cities, but they need a producer-services *complex* somewhere in order to gain access to the needed specialized services and financing. Headquarters of firms with very high overseas activity or in highly innovative and complex lines of business still tend to locate in major cities. In brief: On the one hand, firms in more routinized lines of activity, with predominantly regional or national markets, appear to be increasingly free to move or install their headquarters outside cities. On the other hand, firms in highly competitive and innovative lines of activity and/or with a strong world-market orientation appear to benefit from being located at the center of major international business centers, no matter how high the costs.

Both types of firms, however, need access to a corporate-services complex; access to individual firms is not enough. Where this complex is located is increasingly unimportant from the perspective of many, though not all, headquarters. However, from the perspective of producer-services firms, such a specialized complex is most likely to be in a city, rather than, for example, in a suburban office park. The latter will be the site for producer-services firms but not for a services complex. And only such a complex is capable of handling the most advanced and complicated corporate needs.

These issues are examined in the next two sections. The first discusses how the spatial dispersal of economic activities engenders an increased demand for specialized services; the transnational corporation is one of the major agents in this process. The second section examines whether and, if so, under what conditions corporate headquarters need cities.

The Servicing of Transnational Corporations

The territorial dispersal of multiestablishment firms, whether at the regional, national, or global level, has been one important factor in the sharp rise of producer services. Firms running multiple plants, offices, and service outlets must coordinate planning, internal administration, distribution, marketing, and other central headquarters activities. As large corporations move into the production and sale of final consumer services, a wide range of management functions previously performed by independently owned consumer-service firms are moved to the central headquarters of the new corporate chains. Regional, national, or global chains of motels, food outlets, and flower shops require vast centralized administrative and servicing structures. A parallel pattern of expansion of central high-level planning and control operations takes place in governments, brought about partly by the technical developments that make this expansion possible and partly by the growing complexity of regulatory and administrative tasks. Thus, governments are also buying more outside consulting services of all sorts and outsourcing what were once government jobs.

Formally, the development of the modern corporation and its massive participation in world markets and foreign countries have made planning, internal administration, product development, and research increasingly important and complex. Diversification of product lines, mergers, and transnationalization of economic activities all require highly specialized skills. A firm with several geographically dispersed manufacturing plants contributes to the development of new types of planning in production and distribution surrounding the firm. The development of multisite manufacturing, service, and banking has created an expanded demand for a wide range of specialized service activities to manage and control global networks of factories, service outlets, and branch offices. Although to some extent these activities can be carried out in-house, a large share is not. Together, headquarters and the producer services deliver the components of what might be called *global control capability*. High levels of specialization, the possibility of externalizing the production of some of these services, and the growing demand by large and small firms and increasingly also governments are all conditions that have both resulted from and made possible the development of a market for freestanding producer-services firms.

This in turn means that small firms can buy components of that global control capability, such as management consulting or international legal advice, as can firms and governments from anywhere in the world. This accessibility contributes to the formation of marketplaces for such services in major cities. Thus, although the large corporation is undoubtedly a key agent inducing the development of this capability and is its prime beneficiary, it is not the sole user.

A brief examination of the territorial dispersal entailed by transnational operations of large enterprises illustrates some of the points raised here. Exhibits 4.7a and 4.7b show the portion of assets, sales, and workers that the 25 largest nonfinancial transnational corporations of the world have outside their home countries. Chapter 2 introduced data about the number of transnational corporations (TNCs) and their affiliates worldwide (Exhibit 2.5). Calculations using the information in Exhibits 4.7a and 4.7b show that the share of foreign sales in the top 25 largest nonfinancial transnational corporations in the world grew from 37% to 58% between 1990 and 1996. The share of foreign employment to total employment in the top corporations held steady at approximately 50%, a considerable figure given that the average workforce of these TNCs was 175,000 employees. Exhibit 4.9 shows the disproportionate concentration of the origins of the top TNCs ranked by foreign assets, in two parts of the world—the European Union, with 39 TNCs, and the United States, with 30. Together, these two regions account for two-thirds of the central managements of these firms.

These figures show a vast operation dispersed over a multiplicity of locations. Operations as extensive as these feed the expansion of central management, coordination, control, and servicing functions. Some of these functions are performed in the headquarters; others are bought or contracted for, thereby feeding the growth of the producer-services complex.

Corporate Headquarters and Cities

It is very common in the general literature and in some more scholarly accounts to use the concentration of major headquarters as an indication of a city's status as an international business center. The loss of these types of

(Text continues on page 107)

Exhibit 4.7a The 25 Largest Nonfinancial Transnational Corporations, Ranked by Foreign Assets, 1990 (US$ billions and number of employees)

Rank	Corporation	Country	Industry[a]	Assets		Sales		Employment	
				Foreign	Total	Foreign	Total	Foreign	Total
1	Royal Dutch Shell	United Kingdom/Netherlands	Petroleum refining	69.2[b]	106.4	47.1[b]	106.5	99,000	137,000
2	Ford	United States	Motor vehicles and parts	55.2	173.7	47.3	97.7	188,904	370,383
3	GM	United States	Motor vehicles and parts	52.6	180.2	37.3	122	251,130	767,200
4	Exxon	United States	Petroleum refining	51.6	87.7	90.5	115.8	65,000	104,000
5	IBM	United States	Computers	45.7	87.6	41.9	69	167,868	373,816
6	British Petroleum	United Kingdom	Petroleum refining	31.6	59.3	43.3	59.3	87,200	118,050
7	Asea Brown Boveri	Switzerland	Industrial and farm equipment	26.9	30.2	25.6[d]	26.7	200,177	215,154
8	Nestlé	Switzerland	Food	—[c]	28	35.8	36.5	192,070	199,021
9	Philips Electronics	Netherlands	Electronics	23.3	30.6	28.8[d]	30.8	217,149	272,800
10	Mobil	United States	Petroleum refining	22.3	41.7	44.3	57.8	27,593	67,300
11	Unilever	United Kingdom/Netherlands	Food	—[c]	24.7	16.7[b]	39.6	261,000	304,000
12	Matsushita Electric	Japan	Electronics	—[c]	62	21	46.8	67,000	210,848
13	Fiat	Italy	Motor vehicles and parts	19.5	66.3	20.7[d]	47.5	66,712	303,238
14	Siemens	Germany	Electronics	—[c]	43.1	14.7[d]	39.2	143,000	373,000
15	Sony	Japan	Electronics	—[c]	32.6	12.7	20.9	62,100	112,900
16	Volkswagen	Germany	Motor vehicles and parts	—[c]	42	25.5[d]	42.1	95,934	268,744

(Continued)

Exhibit 4.7a (Continued)

Rank	Corporation	Country	Industry[a]	Assets		Sales		Employment	
				Foreign	Total	Foreign	Total	Foreign	Total
17	Elf Aquitaine	France	Petroleum refining	17	42.6	11.4[d]	32.4	33,957	90,000
18	Mitsubishi	Japan	Trading	16.7	73.8	45.5	129.3	—	32,417
19	GE	United States	Electronics	16.5	153.9	8.3	57.7	62,580	298,000
20	Du Pont	United States	Chemicals	16	38.9	17.5	37.8	36,400	124,900
21	Alcatel Alsthom	France	Electronics	15.3	38.2	13	26.6	112,966	205,500
22	Mitsui	Japan	Trading	15	60.8	48.1	136.2	—	9,094
23	News Corporation	Australia	Publishing and printing	14.6	20.7	4.6	5.7	—	38,432
24	Bayer	Germany	Chemicals	14.2	25.4	20.3	25.9	80,000	171,000
25	B.A.T. Industries	United Kingdom	Tobacco	—[c]	48.1	16.5[d]	22.9	—	217,373

Notes:

a. Industry classification of companies follows that in the *Fortune* Global 500 list in *Fortune*, July 29, 1991, and the Fortune Global Service 500 list in *Fortune*, August 26, 1991.

In the *Fortune* classification, companies are included in the industry or service that represents the greatest volume of their sales; industry groups are based on categories established by the United States Office of Management and Budget. Several companies, however, are highly diversified.

b. Excludes other European countries.

c. Data for foreign assets not available; ranking is according to foreign assets estimated by the Transnational Corporations and Management Division on the basis of the ratio of foreign to total employment, foreign to total fixed assets, or other similar ratios.

d. Includes export sales which are not separately reported.

Source: Based on UNCTAD, Programme on Transnational Corporations, company annual financial statements, Worldscope company accounts database, unpublished sources from companies, The Industrial Institute for Economic and Social Research (2005) in Stockholm, Sweden, and Stopford (1992). The Worldscope database uses standardized data definitions to adjust for differences in accounting terminology. Data for United States companies with fiscal year-end up to February 10, 1991, as well as for non-United States companies with fiscal year-end until January 15, 1991, are classified as 1990 data.

Exhibit 4.7b The 25 Largest Nonfinancial Transnational Corporations Ranked by Foreign Assets, 1996 (US$ billions and number of employees)

Ranking by: Foreign Transnatl. Assets	Index[a]	Corporation	Country	Industry[b]	Assets Foreign	Assets Total	Sales Foreign	Sales Total	Employment Foreign	Employment Total
1	83	General Electric	United States	Electronics	82.8	272.4	21.1	79.2	84,000	239,000
2	32	Shell, Royal Dutch[c]	United Kingdom/Netherlands	Petroleum expl./ref./dist.	82.1	124.1	71.1	128.3	79,000	101,000
3	75	Ford Motor Company	United States	Automotive	79.1	258	65.8	147	—[e]	371,702
4	22	Exxon Corporation	United States	Petroleum expl./ref./dist.	55.6	95.5	102	117	—[e]	79,000
5	85	General Motors	United States	Automotive	55.4	222.1	50	158	221,313	647,000
6	52	IBM	United States	Computers	21.4	81.1	46.6	75.9	121,655	240,615
7	79	Toyota	Japan	Automotive	39.2	113.4	51.7	109.3	34,837	150,736
8	49	Volkswagen Group	Germany	Automotive	—[d]	60.8	41	64.4	123,042	260,811
9	71	Mitsubishi Corporation	Japan	Diversified	—[d]	77.9	50.2	127.4	3,819	8,794
10	38	Mobil Corporation	United States	Petroleum expl./ref./dist.	31.3	46.4	53.1	80.4	22,900	43,000
11	3	Nestlé SA	Switzerland	Food	30.9	34	42	42.8	206,125	212,687
12	2	Asea Brown Boveri (ABB)	Switzerland/Sweden	Electrical equipment	—[d]	30.9	32.9	33.8	203,541	214,894
13	47	Elf Aquitaine SA	France	Petroleum expl./ref./dist.	29.3	47.5	26.6	44.8	41,600	85,400
14	14	Bayer AG	Germany	Chemicals	29.1	32	25.8	31.4	94,375	142,200
15	34	Hoechst AS	Germany	Chemicals	28	35.5	18.4	33.8	93,708	147,862
16	57	Nissan Motor Co., Ltd.	Japan	Automotive	27	58.1	29.2	53.8	—[e]	135,331
17	74	FIAT Spa	Italy	Automotive	26.9	70.6	19.8	51.3	90,390	237,865

(Continued)

Table 4.7b (Continued)

Ranking by: Foreign Transnatl. assets	index[a]	Corporation	Country	Industry[b]	Assets Foreign	Assets Total	Sales Foreign	Sales Total	Employment Foreign	Employment Total
18	8	Unilever[f]	Netherlands/United Kingdom	Food	26.4	31	45	52.2	273,000	304,000
19	70	Daimler Benz AG	Germany	Automotive	—[d]	65.7	44.4	70.6	67,208	290,029
20	11	Philips Electronics N.V.	Netherlands	Electronics	24.5	31.7	38.9	40.9	21,600	262,500
21	9	Roche Holding AG	Switzerland	Pharmaceuticals	24.5	29.5	12.6	12.9	39,074	48,972
22	56	Siemens AG	Germany	Electronics	24.4	56.3	38.4	62.6	176,000	379,000
23	36	Alacatel Alsthom Cie	France	Electronics	23.5	48.4	24.6	31.6	112,820	190,600
24	40	Sony Corporation	Japan	Electronics	23.5	45.8	32.8	45.7	95,000	163,000
25	19	Total SA	France	Petroleum expl./ref./dist.	—[d]	30.3	25.8	34	—[e]	57,555

Notes:

a. The index of transnationality is calculated as the average of three ratios: foreign assets to total assets, foreign sales to total sales, and foreign employment to total employment.

b. Industry classification for companies follows the United States Standard Industrial Classification as used by the United States Securities and Exchange Commission.

c. Foreign sales are outside Europe whereas foreign employment is outside United Kingdom and the Netherlands.

d. Data on foreign assets are either suppressed to avoid disclosure or they are not available. In case of nonavailability, they are estimated on the basis of the ratio of foreign to total foreign to total assets or similar ratios.

e. Data on foreign employment are either suppressed to avoid disclosure or they are not available. In case of nonavailability, they are estimated on the basis of the ratio of foreign to total foreign to total assets or similar ratios.

f. Foreign assets, sales, and employment are outside of the United Kingdom and the Netherlands.

g. Foreign assets, sales, and employment are outside of the United Kingdom and Australia.

Source: UNCTAD/Erasmus University (1998:36–38).

Exhibit 4.7c The 25 Largest Nonfinancial Transnational Corporations Ranked by Foreign Assets, 2002 (US$ billions and number of employees)

Ranking by: Foreign Assets	Transnatl. Index[a]	Corporation	Country	Industry[b]	Assets		Sales		Employment	
					Foreign	Total	Foreign	Total	Foreign	Total
1	84	General Electric	United States	Electrical and electronic equipment	229.0	575.2	45.4	131.7	150,000	315,000
2	12	Vodafone Group Plc	United Kingdom	Telecommunications	207.6	232.9	33.6	42.3	56,667	66,667
3	67	Ford Motor Company	United States	Motor vehicles	165.0	295.2	54.5	163.4	188,453	350,321
4	16	British Petroleum Company Plc	United Kingdom	Petroleum expl./ref./dist.	126.1	159.1	146.0	180.2	97,400	116,300
5	95	General Motors	United States	Motor vehicles	107.9	370.8	48.0	186.8	101,000	350,000
6	45	Royal Dutch/Shell Group	United Kingdom/ Netherlands	Petroleum expl./ref./dist.	94.4	145.4	114.3	179.4	65,000	111,000
7	73	Toyota Motor Corporation	Japan	Motor vehicles	79.4	167.3	72.8	127.1	85,057	264,096
8	22	Total Fina Elf	France	Petroleum expl./ref./dist.	79.0	89.5	77.5	97.0	68,554	121,469
9	65	France Telecom	France	Telecommunications	73.5	111.7	18.2	44.1	102,016	243,573

(Continued)

Exhibit 4.7c (Continued)

Ranking by: Foreign Transnatl. Assets	Index[a]	Corporation	Country	Industry[b]	Assets Foreign	Assets Total	Sales Foreign	Sales Total	Employment Foreign	Employment Total
10	41	ExxonMobile Corporation	United States	Petroleum expl./ref./dist.	60.8	94.9	141.3	200.9	56,000	92,000
11	53	Volkswagen Group	Germany	Motor vehicles	57.1	114.2	59.7	82.2	157,887	324,892
12	86	E.On	Germany	Electricity, gas, and water	52.3	118.5	13.1	35.1	42,063	107,856
13	78	RWE Group	Germany	Electricity, gas, and water	50.7	105.1	17.6	44.1	55,563	131,765
14	40	Vivendi Universal	France	Media	49.7	72.7	30.0	55.0	45,772	61,815
15	50	ChevronTexaco Corp	United States	Petroleum expl./ref./dist.	48.5	77.4	55.1	98.7	37,038	66,038
16	29	Hutchinson Whampoa Limited	Hong Kong, China	Diversified	48.0	63.3	8.1	14.2	124,942	154,813
17	—	Siemens AG	Germany	Electrical and electronic equipment	47.5	76.5	50.7	77.2	251,340	426,000
18	94	Électricité de France	France	Electricity, gas, and water	47.4	151.8	12.6	45.7	50,437	171,995
19	66	Fiat Spa	Italy	Motor vehicles	46.2	97.0	24.6	52.6	98,703	186,492
20	31	Honda Motor Co	Japan	Motor vehicles	43.6	63.8	49.2	65.4	42,885	63,310
21	9	News Corporation	Australia	Media	40.3	45.2	16.0	17.4	31,220	35,000

| Ranking by: | | | | | Assets | | Sales | | Employment | |
Foreign Assets	Transnatl. Index[a]	Corporation	Country	Industry[b]	Foreign	Total	Foreign	Total	Foreign	Total
22	6	Roche Group	Switzerland	Pharmaceuticals	40.2	46.2	18.8	19.2	61,090	69,659
23	19	Suez	France	Electricity, gas, and water	38.7	44.8	34.2	43.6	138,200	198,750
24	58	BMW AG	Germany	Motor vehicles	37.6	58.2	30.2	40.0	20,120	96,263
25	64	Eni Group	Italy	Petroleum expl./ref./dist.	37.0	69.0	22.8	45.3	36,973	80,655

Notes:

a. The index of transnationality is calculated as the average of three ratios: foreign assets to total assets, foreign sales to total sales, and foreign employment to total employment.

b. Industry classification for companies follows the United States Standard Industrial Classification as used by the United States Securities and Exchange Commission.

c. Foreign sales are outside Europe whereas foreign employment is outside the United Kingdom and the Netherlands.

d. Data on foreign assets are either suppressed to avoid disclosure or they are not available. In case of nonavailability, they are estimated on the basis of the ratio of foreign to total assets or similar ratios.

e. Data on foreign employment are either suppressed to avoid disclosure or they are not available. In case of nonavailability, they are estimated on the basis of the ratio of foreign to total foreign to total assets or similar ratios.

f. Foreign assets, sales, and employment are outside of the United Kingdom and the Netherlands.

g. Foreign assets, sales, and employment are outside of the United Kingdom and Australia.

Source: UNCTAD (2004:276).

Exhibit 4.8 Distribution of Outward Affiliates of Major Investing Countries by Sector, Various Years, 1980–1990 (number and percentage)

Country	Year		All	Sectors		
				Primary	Manufacturing	Services
Germany, Federal Republic of[a]	1984	Number	14,657	558	4,936	9,163
		Percentage	100	4	34	63
	1990	Number	19,352	422	5,729	13,201
		Percentage	100	2	30	68
Japan[b]	1980	Number	3,567	194	1,587	1,786
		Percentage	100	5	44	50
	1990	Number	7,986	194	3,408	4,384
		Percentage	100	2	43	55
United States[c]	1982	Number	18,339	995	7,005	10,339
		Percentage	100	5	38	56
	1989	Number	18,899	785	7,552	10,562
		Percentage	100	4	40	56

Notes:

a. Includes only affiliates whose balance sheet total exceeds DM 500,000.

b. Includes only nonbank affiliates that responded to a questionnaire on FDI and that continued their foreign operations.

c. Includes only affiliates whose assets, sales, or income exceeded $3 million.

Sources: UNCTAD (1992); Japan Ministry of International Trade and Industry (2005); U.S. Department of Commerce (1985; 1992).

Exhibit 4.9   Geographical Concentration of TNCs by Foreign Assets, Foreign
Sales, Foreign Employment, and Number of Entries, 1996
(percentage of total and number)

Region/Economy	Foreign Assets	Foreign Sales	Foreign Employment	Number of Entities
European Union	37	38	46	39
France	9	8	9	11
Germany	12	11	12	9
Netherlands	8	8	10	3
United Kingdom	12	12	15	11
Japan	16	26	10	18
United States	33	27	20	30
Total value (US$ billions and number)	1,475.0	2,147.9	4,447,732	100

Source: UNCTAD (1997:35).

headquarters is then interpreted as a decline in the city's status. In fact, using
such headquarters' concentration as an index is an increasingly problematic measure, given the way in which corporations are classified, the locational options telecommunications offer corporations, and the analysis
developed earlier about a trend toward outsourcing the functions of corporate headquarters.

A number of variables determine which headquarters concentrate in
major international financial and business centers. First, how we measure or
simply count headquarters makes a difference. Frequently, the key measure
is the size of the firm in terms of employment and overall revenue. Using this
measure, some of the largest firms in the world are still manufacturing firms,
and many of these have their main headquarters in proximity to their major
factory complex, which is unlikely to be in a large city because of space constraints. Such firms *are* likely, however, to have secondary headquarters for
highly specialized functions in major cities. Furthermore, many manufacturing firms are oriented to the national market and do not need to be located
in a city's national business center. Thus, the much-publicized departure of
major headquarters from New York City in the 1960s and 1970s involved
these types of firms, as did the large numbers of departures from Chicago in
the 1990s. A quick look at the Fortune 500 list of the largest U.S. firms

shows that many have left large cities. If, however, instead of size, the measure is the share of total firm revenue coming from international sales, many firms that are not on the Fortune 500 list come into play. In the case of New York, for example, the results change dramatically: In 1990, 40% of U.S. firms with half their revenue from international sales had their headquarters in New York City. Further, while moving away from major metropolitan areas has become the general trend for firms in a broad range of economic sectors, two of the largest components of producer services—the high-tech industry and financial services—continue to concentrate in large cities. "In this instance, profound deregulation has encouraged firm consolidation and market expansion. In response, the now-larger companies have chosen to locate their headquarters in larger metropolitan areas" (Klier and Testa 2002). Klier and Testa's calculations regarding the headquarters of large U.S. corporations (employing more than 2,500 worldwide) also show that in 2000 New York still was home to 14% of these companies, and the top five U.S. metro areas combined accounted for 33% of such firms.

Second, the nature of the urban system in a country is a factor in the geographic distribution of headquarters. Sharp urban primacy tends to entail a disproportionate concentration of headquarters in the primate city no matter what measure one uses. Third, different economic histories and business traditions may combine to produce different results. Finally, headquarters concentration may be linked to a specific economic phase. For example, unlike New York's loss of top Fortune 500 headquarters, Tokyo has gained these types of headquarters. Osaka and Nagoya, the two other major economic centers in Japan, lost headquarters to Tokyo. This change seems to be linked to the combination of the increasing internationalization of the Japanese economy and the ongoing role of government regulation on cross-border transactions. Firms need easy access to government regulators. As a result, there was an increase in central headquarters command and servicing functions in Tokyo.

In brief, understanding the meaning of headquarters concentration requires disaggregation across several variables. Although headquarters are still disproportionately concentrated in major cities, the patterns that became evident in the mid-1980s and continue today do represent a change.

The discussion about producer services, the producer-services complex, and the locational patterns of headquarters point to two significant developments since the 1980s. One is the growing service intensity in the organization of the economy; and the other, the emergence of a producer-services complex that, although strongly geared toward the corporate sector, is far more likely to remain concentrated in urban centers than are the headquarters it serves.

Impacts of Major Crises on Global City Functions: The Case of New York City

There have been multiple economic and financial crises since the new economic patterns took off in the 1980s. The subject of the rise of the producer-services complex inevitably brings up the financial and real estate crisis of the late 1980s and early 1990s, since so much of the highly speculative character of the 1980s was engineered by financial, legal, accounting, and other kindred experts in the major international business centers, and the growth of these activities also contributed to the sharp growth and internationalization of real estate development. These developments also bring up the vulnerabilities associated with sharp agglomeration of key activities, as became brutally evident with the terrorist attacks in New York City in September 2001. I turn to these next.

New York City after October 1987

The high level of speculation and profitability that fed growth in the 1980s was clearly unsustainable. The financial crisis of the late 1980s raises two possibilities. One is that it was a true crisis of the economic system; the other, that it was rather a sharp readjustment to more sustainable levels of speculation and profitability. New York was the first of the major international financial centers to experience massive losses in the new economic phase that took off in the 1980s. Its post-1987 evolution may provide some useful insights into the interaction between crisis and readjustment in the dominant sector.

In the securities industry, an area that suffered some of the sharpest job losses after the 1987 stock market crisis, New York City soon reemerged as a major center. Ten years later, it still housed 11 of the world's 25 largest securities firms and accounted for 79% of the combined assets of these firms. City firms and their overseas affiliates that had acted as advisers for almost 80% of the value of all international mergers and acquisitions at the height of the financial boom in the mid-1980s remained strong in the financial boom of the mid-1990s. Because the securities industry is almost completely export oriented, it turned out to be less sensitive to crises in the U.S. economy and in New York City specifically. For example, focusing on some of the fastest growing subsectors during a period of regular growth—just before the 1997–98 financial crisis—from 1993 to 1996, employment in securities and commodities grew by 25%; in investment offices, by 36%; and in a variety of services not elsewhere classified, by 254%. However, employment in banking, one of the core sectors in the city, did not quite recover, with employment falling by 20% (Sassen [1991] 2001, Table 6.18). It is worthwhile to look at the composition of losses. Employment fell from 169,000 in 1989 to 157,000 in 1991. Most of this loss (more than 10,000 jobs) was in domestic, not international, banking; further, some of these losses were the result of the massive restructuring within the industry, including mergers among large domestic banks. Thus the job losses were not so much an effect of the crisis as part of the restructuring of the banking function in the city.

Even after the financial crisis of 1997–98, New York City continued to function as an important international center and continued to be dominated by financial and related industries. According to many analysts, the 1987 crisis was a much-needed adjustment to the excesses of the 1980s. The 1997–98 crisis had far less of an impact on New York City (and London) than did the 1987 crisis. Within the United States, New York City remained the banking and financial capital of the country, leading in total assets, number of banks, and volume in various markets (currency, options trading, merchant banking). Worldwide, it remained the leading financial center along with London. Further, foreign banking was a growth sector in New York City throughout the 1990s and remains central to the city's role as a leading financial center for the world. So, even as Japanese and European banks were surpassing U.S. banks in size (see Exhibit 2.2), they had offices in New York City. Indeed, in 1990, New York City surpassed London in its number of international bank offices. Ten years after one of the most dramatic financial crises to hit them, London and New York City remained the leading banking and financial centers in the world.

Notwithstanding reductions in the domestic banking industry and major crises in several industry branches, at the beginning of the twenty-first century, New York remained a major platform for international operations. What emerges from these developments is that New York City retained its central role as a financial center but with a far greater participation by foreign firms making loans, selling financial services, and assisting in mergers and acquisitions. The same was and is still the case today for London. New York's job losses and bankruptcies in the securities industry right after 1987 pointed to the possibility of a major transformation in the role of Wall Street and other stock markets, most particularly in that large corporations can bypass stock markets to raise investment capital. We now know that the actual change proved to be far less drastic and that by the early 1990s Wall Street was once again booming, with a similar pattern evident after the far less severe 1997–98 financial crisis. These crises proved to be partly adjustment processes from which Wall Street emerged as a transformed market, but without losing an international base and continuing as a provider of the most specialized and complex services.

But then came the attacks on September 11, 2001.

New York City after September 2001

The multiple losses brought on by the September 11, 2001, attacks brought into question the benefits of the types of agglomeration economies at the heart of the global economic system.

The direct and indirect economic costs of the destruction of the World Trade Center (WTC) complex affected large and small firms, professional and blue-collar workers, high- and low-profit activities, rich and not-so-rich households. About 100,000 jobs were lost in Lower Manhattan, the area stretching south of 23rd Street to the southern tip of the island. This was 25% of all jobs in that area. Most of those who lost their jobs had modest incomes, under $25,000 yearly. This underlines a fact that is crucial to understanding a city like New York, even if we look at a small area. Wall Street was also the workplace for many low-wage workers. As for office space, 14 million square feet were destroyed and another 16 million damaged, accounting for more than 25% of all commercial office space in Lower Manhattan. The retail shopping area in the WTC—the third busiest in the entire United States—occupied 500,000 square feet of retail space; with it went the physical destruction of more than 700 small businesses. The towers' fall added to other losses in business volume, the departure of many firms for neighboring New Jersey and Connecticut (part of the tristate metro area), and a huge increase in the city's deficit. All these factors sharpened into a sense of profound unease about the economic future of the city—especially the Wall Street area.

And yet, not even the destructions of 9/11 and the emergence of global cities worldwide as leading targets for international terrorism (Sassen 2003) have actually reduced the levels of concentration. Already by the end of December 2001, the level of concentration in the global capital market had not only recovered but also grown. At the end of 2000, the leading nine stock markets in the world accounted for 76.4% of the global market; by the end of December 2001, this share stood at 87.5%. Perhaps even more remarkable: The New York Stock Exchange share went from 37% to 41%, although the absolute value stayed the same at about $11+ trillion. Most of the sharp decline in stock valuations in these markets that began in late March 2003 was not due to some aftereffect of September 11 but rather to a mix of (1) high-level scandals beginning with Enron, which produced major and widespread distrust among investors, and (2) what market analysts call *corrections* of excessively high market valuations in response to the fact that the Enron scandal had made certain accounting practices unacceptable and even illegal. The result was an enormous withdrawal of capital from the stock market. But by early 2004, the market was high again. The subsequent sharp declines in the fall of 2004 cannot be attributed to a September 11 effect, but rather to massive U.S. government deficits and sharp economic slowdowns.

I return to this post–September 11 phase in greater detail in Chapter 5 when I discuss spatial concentration and in Chapter 6, employment.

Conclusion: Cities as Postindustrial Production Sites

A central concern in this chapter is cities as production sites for the leading service industries of our time and hence the recovery of the infrastructure of activities, firms, and jobs necessary for running the advanced corporate economy. Specialized services are usually understood in terms of specialized outputs rather than the production process involved. A focus on the production process allows us (1) to capture some of the locational characteristics of these service industries and (2) to examine the proposition that there is a producer-services complex with locational and production characteristics that differ from those of the corporations it serves. It is this producer-services complex more than headquarters generally that benefits from, and even needs, a city location. We see this dynamic for agglomeration operating at different levels of the urban hierarchy, from the global to the regional.

At the global level, a key dynamic explaining the place of major cities in the world economy is that they concentrate the infrastructure and the servicing that produce a capability for global control. The latter is essential if geographic dispersal of economic activity—whether factories, offices, or financial markets—is to take place under continued concentration of ownership and profit appropriation. This capability for global control cannot simply be subsumed under the structural aspects of the globalization of economic activity. It needs to be produced. It is insufficient to posit, or take for granted, the power of large corporations, no matter how vast this power is.

By focusing on the production of this capability, I add a neglected dimension to the familiar issue of the power of large corporations. The emphasis shifts to the *practice* of global control: the work of producing and reproducing the organization and management of a global production system and a global marketplace for finance, both under conditions of economic concentration. Power is essential in the organization of the world economy, but so is production: in this case, the production of those inputs that constitute the capability for global control and the infrastructure of jobs involved in this production. This allows us to focus on cities and on the urban social order associated with these activities.

Notes

1. Mixed markets create measurement problems. These problems can be partly overcome by the fact that the consumer and business markets in these industries often involve very different sets of firms and different types of location patterns, and hence, they can be distinguished on this basis. Given the existence of mixed markets and the difficulty of distinguishing between markets in the organization of the pertinent data, it is helpful to group these services under the category of "mostly" producer services—that is, services produced mostly for firms rather than for individuals. It has become customary to refer to them, for convenience, as *producer services*.

2. Jobs were and remain far more concentrated in the central business district in New York City compared with other major cities in the United States. By the late 1980s, about 27% of all jobs in the consolidated statistical area were in Manhattan compared with 9% nationally (Drennan 1989). The 90% concentration ratio of finance was far above the norm.

3. The data on producer services are creating a certain amount of confusion in the United States. Faster growth at the national level and in medium-size cities is often interpreted as indicating a loss of share and declining position of leading centers such as New York or Chicago. Thus, one way of reading these data is as decentralization of producer services; that is, New York and Chicago are losing a share of all producer services in the United States—a zero-sum situation in which growth in a new location is construed ipso facto as a loss in an older location. Another way is to read it as growth everywhere. The evidence points to the second type of explanation: The growing service intensity in the economy nationwide is the main factor explaining growth in medium-size cities rather than the loss of producer-services firms in major cities and their relocation to other cities.

5

Issues and Case Studies in the New Urban Economy

S everal of the questions raised in Chapter 4 can be fruitfully addressed through a closer look at how individual cities developed global city functions. The organizing focus of this chapter is the growing concentration and specialization of financial and service functions that lies at the heart of the new urban economy at a time when we might expect the development of global telecommunications to be pushing these sectors toward geographic dispersal. These specific case studies provide insights into the dynamics of contemporary globalization processes as they materialize in specific places. They also present, in somewhat schematic form, a logic of inquiry into these issues that can be replicated in studies of other cities. Finally, I have chosen cities that are not among the absolute top tier and are less known as sites for global processes. These cases all function as natural experiments.

I begin with an examination of the formation of global city functions. I chose Miami to illustrate this process because it captures, at a fairly recent time and in a somewhat simple environment, the implantation of the growth dynamic described in Chapter 4. The question here is, Under what conditions do global city functions materialize? Miami brings an additional issue into the discussion: Can a city lacking a history as a world trade and banking center become a global city? The second case study is Toronto, a city that built up its financial district in the mid-1980s and hence could have opted for far more dispersal than old financial centers could. This helps disentangle something that is not clear in older centers where spatial concentration of the financial center might be a function of an old built environment inherited from an earlier economic era. The third city, Sydney, shows how these tendencies toward concentration operate in the case of a multipolar urban system and a vast, rich, continent-sized economy, as is Australia. Can we expect a similar multipolarity in the distribution of global city functions?

After looking at these cities as laboratory cases, we examine the general trend toward concentration in financial and top-level service functions against a broader historical and geographic perspective. Is this a new trend? Is it likely to remain unchanged? Finally, we examine the question of urban form: Have the new information technologies changed the spatial correlates of the center, the terrain where the international financial and business center and the producer-services complex materialize?

The Development of Global City Functions: The Case of Miami

Each of today's global cities has a specific history that has contributed to its current status. Many of the world's major cities enjoyed a long history as banking and trading centers or as capitals of commercial empires.[1] This fact raises two immediate questions: What aspects of today's global cities are continuations of past functions? How can global city functions emerge in cities that lack a long history as international banking and trading centers?

Miami is a case in point. On the one hand, it is a city with a short history, one mostly lacking any significant international functions. On the other hand, its large Cuban immigration led to the development in the 1960s and 1970s of an international trading complex oriented to Latin America and the Caribbean and small-scale investments into real estate by individuals and firms from Latin America. The relative simplicity of Miami's history and international-trading functions makes it relatively easy to disentangle two key processes: (1) the continuity of the Cuban-led trading complex and (2) the formation of a new business complex in the late 1980s that was not connected to the Cuban immigration but rather to the demands created by current processes of globalization.

The case of Miami thus helps us, first, to understand how a city that lacks a significant history as a world financial and business center can become a site for global city functions, and second, to disentangle the ways in which global city formation may or may not be related to an older internationalism.

The city already had a concentration of international trading operations in the 1970s, built and owned in good part by the prosperous resident Cuban elite (Portes and Stepick 1993). Since their arrival in the 1960s after the 1959 Castro revolution, the Cuban community has built an impressive international trading entrepôt, with a strong presence of firms and banks from Latin America and the Caribbean. Is the existence of the Cuban enclave, then, with its multiple trading operations for the Caribbean and Latin America, the base on which these new global city functions developed? Or is the latter a somewhat autonomous process that may benefit from the concentration of trading operations in Miami but that responds to a different logic? Does it represent a type of development that would have taken place anyway in the southern Atlantic region, although perhaps not in Miami without the Cuban enclave? In brief, what is the relationship between these two processes, one shaped by past events and the other by the current demands of economic globalization?

Some hypotheses in the research literature on global cities are of interest here, especially those that examine the spatial and organizational forms assumed by economic globalization today and the actual work of running transnational economic operations. Figures on the growth of Miami's foreign banks, foreign headquarters, prime office-space market, installation of major telecommunications facilities, high-income residential and commercial gentrification, and high-priced international tourism all point to developments that transcend both the Cuban enclave and the Caribbean import–export enterprises in its midst. They point to another dynamic, one at least partly rooted in the new forms of economic globalization, and suggest that the growth of Miami's new international corporate sector is part of this new dynamic rather than a mere expansion of the Cuban enclave's Latin American and Caribbean trading operations.

Overall international business transactions with Latin America rose sharply over a short period of time, from the end of the 1980s to the 1990s (see also Chapter 2). Total foreign direct investment in the Latin American economies grew from an average of US$6.1 billion in 1984–87 to $28.7 billion in 1994, nearly doubled to $56.1 billion in 1997, and reached more than US$95 billion in 1999; after this, it declined and stood at US$55 billion by 2004. Much of this capital was part of active entry by many foreign firms into several Latin American countries: They bought hotels, airlines, real estate of all sorts, factories, and so on. This in turn expanded the management and coordination work of these firms, which increasingly used Miami as a regional headquarters location. Privatization, deregulation of stock markets and other financial markets, and the new export-oriented development model in most of Latin America were major factors. These are all extremely complicated transactions that require vast specialized inputs—a far cry from the earlier type of trading that initiated the growth of Miami in the 1970s.

In the 1980s, a growing number of U.S., European, and Asian firms began to set up offices in Miami. Eastman Kodak moved its headquarters for Latin American operations from Rochester, New York, to Miami; Hewlett-Packard made a similar move from Mexico City to Miami; and GM relocated its headquarters for coordinating and managing Latin American operations from São Paulo, Brazil, to Miami. Firms and banks from Germany, France, Italy, South Korea, Hong Kong, and Japan, to name only a few, opened offices and brought in significant numbers of high-level personnel. Among these were major companies such as France's Aerospatiale, Italy's Rimoldi, and Japan's Mitsui, all of which opened operations in Miami. The city also received a significant inflow of secondary headquarters. Large U.S. firms reorganized and expanded their Miami offices to handle new trade with Latin America. For example, Texaco's Miami office increased its staff by 33% from the late 1980s to the early 1990s to handle new operations in Colombia and Venezuela. And so did Miami's AT&T headquarters, which at the time won 60% of a contract to upgrade Mexico's telecommunications infrastructure—no small job. The international shipping company DHL moved their headquarters near Miami, and Japan's Mitsubishi Power Systems chose the area for their American headquarters. By 2005, Southern Florida was home to 1,300 multinational corporations (Enterprise Florida 2005a).

There is a significant international banking presence—from Latin America, the Caribbean, Europe, and Asia. By 1992, Miami had 65 foreign bank offices, a small number compared with 464 in New York and 133 in Los Angeles at the time, but, close to Chicago's 80. It made Miami the fourth U.S. city in number of foreign bank offices. By 1998, Miami's number had grown to 77, and by 2005 it had about 100 international banking institutions (Enterprise Florida 2005b). This is not insignificant, considering that the 10 top cities (including Miami) accounted for over 90% of all foreign bank offices in the United States, with New York City accounting for almost half. Almost all Miami offices were bank agencies and representative offices, both of which are full banking offices. By the late 1990s, Miami had the fourth largest concentration of foreign bank offices in the United States, right behind New York, Los Angeles, and Chicago and ahead of San Francisco, Boston, and Atlanta.

Miami is also a key platform for the operations of Latin American firms in the United States and perhaps, eventually, even for operations with other Latin American countries. A specific role that Miami plays is as a bridge between cities and countries that are not particularly well articulated with the global economy. This is the case with many of Central America's banks.

Nijman (2000) reports on a study that is worth elaborating on. In 2000, the 22 most important banks headquartered in Central America maintained ties with a cumulative total of 319 "correspondent banks" outside the region; such correspondent banks provide services to clients of Central American banks when these banks cannot provide them, for example, because they do not have their own branch where the service needs to be provided. Of these 319 links, 168 were with Miami. New York was second with only 35 links. Miami is a major factor in the external financial connections of Central America.

Finally, Miami is becoming a major telecommunications center for the region. For example, AT&T laid the first undersea fiber-optic cable to South America, connecting southern Florida to Puerto Rico, the Dominican Republic, Jamaica, and Colombia. The company worked with Italy, Spain, and Mexico to build another fiber-optic link connecting those countries with the Caribbean and Florida. Finally, there is the significant concentration of telecommunication facilities associated with the large regional CIA head-quarters, which can benefit, often indirectly, commercial operations (Grosfoguel 1993), notably through established networks of highly specialized suppliers and a talent pool for servicing these often complex infrastructures.

These developments brought growth in financial and specialized services for business, which raised their share in the region's employment structure. Employment in services generally grew by 46.3% from 1970 to 1990 and was 90% of all employment in Dade County by 2003 (Miami-Dade County, Florida 2003). Although this growth is partly a function of population growth and general economic restructuring, there also has been a marked recomposition in the components of services. In the recent past, the driving growth sectors had been domestic tourism and retail; by the late 1980s, they were finance and producer services, as well as new types of tourism—mostly international and high priced—and new types of retail—mostly upscale and catering to the expanded national and foreign corporate sector and design world. One critical factor in the newly emergent Miami-area economy was the growth of producer-services industries. Employment in these sectors almost doubled from 1970 to 1989 in Dade County, particularly in the Miami metropolitan area, reaching 20% of all private sector employment (Perez-Stable and Uriarte 1993). Employment in banking and in credit agencies almost tripled. Business services more than doubled, as did specialized services, from engineering to accounting. The sharpest increase was the qua-drupling in legal services employment. (Although part of this increase may be a result of the growth of Miami's other major industries, drugs and guns, at least some of it is linked to the growth of international finance and service functions.) In the mid-1990s, employment in the leading sectors stabilized. By 2004, producer services were 42% of all private-sector employment;

major components were financial- and credit-services employment, at 19.4% of private-sector employment, and business services, at 17.8% (Florida Agency for Workforce Innovation 2005).

Industrial services are also a factor in these developments. Miami is a great transportation hub, with ports and airports that are among the busiest in the United States. The city and its neighboring ports move more containerized cargo to Latin America than any other U.S. port. In terms of turnover of foreign passengers and cargo, Miami International Airport is second only to New York City's Kennedy. In addition, the region now has a growing concentration of manufacturing firms aimed at the export market in the Caribbean and Latin America, as these areas become major buyers of U.S. goods. Miami's Free Trade Zone is one of the largest in the country.

All of this growth needs to be housed. By the end of the 1980s, Miami was in the top 15 U.S. metropolitan areas in terms of prime rental office-space supply. Although Miami's 44 million square feet were a fraction of top-listed New York City's 456.6 million square feet at the time, this was not insignificant. In addition, private investment in real estate, often for company housing by German, French, and Italian firms, grew sharply in the 1990s. By 1999, the Miami metropolitan area had 96.9 million square feet of office space compared with the New York metropolitan area's 688.4 million square feet (Lang 2000).

Why has this growth of a new international corporate sector taken place in Miami? One could argue that democratization and the opening of Latin American economies to foreign trade and investment should have made Miami less rather than more important. Yet Miami saw sharp growth in the concentration of top-level managerial and specialized service activities aimed at operations in Latin America. And, as described in Chapters 3 and 4, this is one type of evidence for cities that function as international business centers. This in turn raises a second question. Would these functions have been performed elsewhere had it not been for the Cuban enclave? The growth of the Cuban enclave supported the internationalization of the city by creating a pool of bilingual managers and entrepreneurs skilled in international business. This resource gave the city an edge in the competition for the Latin trade. But is it sufficient to explain the subsequent agglomeration of U.S., European, and Asian corporate headquarters and bank offices and the sharp expansion in financial services?

One angle into the question of the role of the Cuban enclave in these developments is offered by Nijman (2000), the leading researcher on Miami as a global city. He observes that while much attention has gone to the Cuban enclave, Miami actually has the most international immigrant population of all major U.S. cities, and that it is unique in the sense that no other major U.S. city has an absolute majority of recent immigrants. The absolute size of this population is much smaller than that of Los Angeles and any other major U.S. city, but the incidence is much higher: Miami has the highest proportion of foreign-born residents of any major city in the United States and the largest proportion of inhabitants who speak a language other than English. Finally, the socioeconomic status of a good share of its immigrant population is much higher than is typical in U.S. cities. A relatively large number of immigrants in Miami are wealthy, educated, and in possession of considerable entrepreneurial skills and experience; this holds not only for the first waves of Cuban migration but also for more recent migration from other Caribbean and Latin American nations, as well as other parts of the world, including high-level professionals and managers and leading design and fashion people from Europe and Asia. Unlike what is common in major U.S. cities, in Miami, many of the wealthiest people, entrepreneurs, politicians, and real estate owners are recent immigrants. "Miami's elite is a footloose cosmopolitan elite. . . . Los Angeles is the ultimate American place, made in America, with a mainstream American culture. . . . Miami, to most Americans, appears a 'foreign' place: hard to grasp and hard to say where it belongs. Perhaps that is because Miami is ahead of the curve, offering a glimpse of the urban future" (Nijman 2000:135).

Putting these immigration facts alongside the scale of developments described earlier suggests that although it is not quite a global city of the first rank, Miami has emerged as a site for global city functions. Because Miami's media image was so strongly associated with immigration and drugs, it took time for the media to recognize the formation of a new international corporate sector. Indeed it was not until the mid-1990s, when Miami had also become a destination for major and minor figures in the international fashion and design worlds, that it erupted on the global media stage. But the actual processes had started a decade earlier. Today, Miami concentrates multiple transnational-level functions that used to be located in a variety of other areas. We can think of the Miami metropolitan area as a platform for international business and the long-distance coordination of the Latin American and Caribbean transactions of firms from any part of the world.

The development of global city functions in Miami is centered on the recent sharp growth in the absolute levels of international investment in Latin America, the growing complexity of the transactions involved, and the trend for firms all over the world to operate globally—all three discussed in preceding chapters. The Cuban enclave represents a significant set of resources, from international servicing know-how to Spanish-speaking personnel. But the particular forms of economic globalization evident during the last decade have implanted a growth dynamic in Miami that is distinct from the enclave, although benefiting from it. At the same time, although the new international corporate sector has made Miami a site for the transnational operations of firms from all over the world, these operations are still largely confined to Latin America and the Caribbean. In that sense, Miami is a site for global city functions, although not a global city in the way that Paris or London is.

The Growing Density and Specialization of Functions in Financial Districts: Toronto

The leading financial districts in the world have all had rapid increases in the density of office buildings since the 1980s. There has also been a strong tendency toward growing specialization in the major activities housed in these buildings. It could be argued that one of the reasons for this continuing and growing concentration in a computer age is that these are mostly old districts that have inherited an infrastructure built in an earlier, pretelecommunications era and hence do not reflect a *necessary* built form for types of sectors. In other words, the new density evident today, as well as the increased specialization, would not be the result of agglomeration economies in the financial and corporate-services complex but, rather, would be an imposed physical form from the past.

The case of Toronto is interesting because so much of the city's current financial district was built in the mid- to late 1980s, a time when finance was beginning to boom, the use of new technologies had become fairly established, and spatial dispersal was a real option. Toronto entered the 1980s with a far smaller and less prominent financial district than cities such as New York, London, or Amsterdam (City of Toronto 1990; Todd 1993; 1995), thus conceivably rather free to redevelop its financial center according to the most desirable spatial pattern. Toronto had not yet gained ascendance over Montreal as a financial and business center (Levine 1990). Furthermore, massive construction of state-of-the-art office buildings for corporate users in the 1980s was shifting from the city to the wider metropolitan region, and included installation of all the most advanced communications facilities the 1980s offered. In terms of building and telecommunications technology, this might seem to be a case in which much of the office infrastructure of the financial sector could have been located outside the small confines of the downtown.

But that did not happen. According to Gunther Gad, a leading analyst of the spatial aspects of the office economy in Toronto, financial firms wanted a high-density office district. A survey aimed at these issues found that a

15-minute walk was seen as a "long walk" and was "resented" (Gad 1991: 206–207; see also Canadian Urban Institute 1993). The first trend that Toronto illustrates is that given the option of moving to a beautifully landscaped setting, surrounded by other major corporate headquarters, the financial sector insisted on a dense downtown location.

The second trend that Toronto illustrates sharply is the growing specialization of the downtown in financial and related specialized services. At one time, Toronto's downtown office district housed the headquarters of manufacturing and wholesaling firms, the printing plants of the two main newspapers, and a large number of insurance firms. Much space was also allocated to retail; at one time, there were street-level shops and eating places on most blocks, all of which were later put underground, further raising the actual and visual office density of the district. Until the 1950s, the present financial district was still the general office district of the metropolitan area, containing the headquarters of firms in all major industries. Beginning at that time and continuing into the subsequent two decades, firms in a broad range of industries—insurance, publishing, architecture, engineering—moved out. This is a pattern evident in other major cities, all of which saw the departure of the corporate headquarters of manufacturing firms, insurance companies, and other large offices. London lost many of its insurance headquarters; the downtowns of Frankfurt and Zurich became increasingly specialized financial districts; and in New York, a new midtown office district developed that accommodated growing industries such as advertising and legal services, leaving Wall Street to become an increasingly specialized financial district.

Between 1970 and 1989, office employment in Toronto's financial district doubled, and its share of all employment rose from 77.6% to 92.3%, with a corresponding fall in nonoffice jobs. But the composition of office jobs also changed from 1970 to 1989. Thus, the share of the insurance industry in all office activities fell from 14.6% to 9.8%, although it grew in absolute numbers; further, between 1996 and 1999, employment in Toronto's insurance industry fell by 11%, but professional jobs grew by 24% in 1996–98. By 1989, well over half of all office employment was in finance, insurance, and real estate (FIRE), and 28% was in producer services. Banks, trust companies, investment services (including securities dealers), and real estate developers grew strongly in the 1980s (Gad 1991). So did other producer services: legal services, accounting, management consulting, and computer services. But some, such as architectural and engineering consulting, did not. Since the 1990s, most of the new employment has been in business and technical services, including accounting, legal, management, computer, and engineering firms, followed by sectors with longer-term growth, especially finance and real estate services. "The FIRE sector grew at a rate of 38% between 1981 and 1996, exceeding that of Boston, Chicago, and San Francisco but it was outpaced by growth in Atlanta, Dallas, Seattle, Minneapolis, Philadelphia, and Seattle" (City of Toronto 2001); the financial services sector has consistently accounted for between 9% and 11% of Toronto's total employment in the 1990s and into 2000.

By the early 1990s, Toronto had the largest concentration of corporate offices in Canada. Fifty of Canada's largest financial institutions were headquartered in Toronto, with 39 of them in the financial district. They include the majority of Canada's banks, foreign banks, and trust companies. Canada's largest investment firms, several of the largest pension funds, and the various trade associations involved with finance and banking were also there by the early 1990s (Todd 1995). By 2004, Toronto was "home to 90 per cent of Canada's foreign banks, and its top accounting and mutual fund companies, and 80 per cent of Canada's largest R&D, law, advertising and high-tech firms" (City of Toronto 2005a). Many other financial institutions have Toronto head-office subsidiaries, and some insurance companies located elsewhere have investment departments in Toronto. "Toronto is today the 3rd largest financial centre in North America after New York and Chicago; 65 per cent of Canada's pension fund managers are headquartered in Toronto and it accounts for 50 per cent of the pension assets under management" (City of Toronto 2005b). By the early 1990s, Toronto's financial markets ranked fourth overall in North America (Todd 1995); by 2004, they ranked eighth in the world with a capitalization of US$1.1 trillion (see Exhibit 2.8).

A more detailed analysis shows yet other patterns. Until the 1970s, it was typical for a large bank in a major city of a developed country to consolidate all its operations in one building in a city's financial district. By the early 1980s, it had become common for such institutions to relocate back-office jobs and branch functions out of the main office in the financial district to other parts of a city's larger metropolitan region. The same pattern was evident in Toronto. Spatial dispersal of more routine operations also took place within other industries—again, a pattern fairly typical for all major business centers. These trends, together with the growth in the share of high-level professional and managerial jobs, led to an employment structure in Toronto's financial district that is highly bimodal, with 41% of all workers in top-level jobs by the end of the 1990s—up from 31.5% in 1980—and up to 52% by 2004.

Generally, top-level functions, and the most complex and innovative activities, are carried out in the financial districts of major cities. Routine operations can be moved outside these financial districts. The more risk-laden, speculative activities, such as securities trading, have increased their share of activity in financial districts. The financial district in Toronto is the place where large, complex loans can be put together; where complicated mergers and acquisitions can be executed; and where large firms requiring massive investment capital for risky activities, such as real estate development or mining, can secure what they need, often combining several lenders and multiple lending strategies.

This is the specialized production process that takes place in the financial districts of today's major cities. The nature of these activities—the large amounts of capital, the complexity, the risk, and the multiplicity of firms involved in each transaction—also contributes to the high density. There is a built-in advantage in being located in a financial district where all the crucial players are located; the risk, complexity, and speculative character of much of this activity raises the importance of face-to-face interaction. The financial district offers multiple possibilities for face-to-face contact: breakfast meetings, lunches, inter- and intrafirm meetings, cocktail parties, and, most recently, health clubs. These are all opportunities for regularly meeting with many of the crucial individuals, for developing trust (of a specific sort) with potential partners in joint offerings, and for making innovative proposals in terms of mergers and acquisitions or joint ventures. Further, as developed in Chapter 4, there is a work process that benefits from intersecting with multiple specialized forms of knowledge, including knowledge about conditions in other countries. Telecommunications cannot replace these networks (Garcia 2002). The complexity, imperfect knowledge, high risk, and speculative character of many endeavors, as well as acceleration in the circulation of information and in the execution of transactions, heighten the importance of both personal contact and spatial concentration.

The case of Toronto suggests that the high density and specialization evident in all major financial districts is a response to the needs generated by current trends in the organization of the financial and related industries. Toronto could have built its financial sector on a more dispersed model, as did the headquarters of the major national and foreign firms that spread over Toronto's metropolitan area along hypermodern communications facilities. But it didn't, suggesting, first, that the density of Toronto's downtown financial district is not the result of an inherited, old-fashioned built infrastructure, but a response to current economic requirements, and second, that the locational patterns and constraints of the financial sector in a global city are different from those of corporate headquarters.

The Concentration of Functions and Geographic Scale: Sydney

The analysis of Toronto revealed two forms of concentration: The first, the main focus of the previous section, was the disproportionate concentration of financial functions in one small district in the city when there was the option of locating in a larger metropolitan area with state-of-the-art infrastructure and building. The second is the disproportionate concentration of all national financial and headquarters functions of Canada in a single city, Toronto. Is it unusual to have such sharp concentration of top-level economic functions in one city when the country is the size of a continent and has a history of multiple growth poles oriented toward world markets?

Here, I examine in some detail this second tendency by focusing on Australia. Along with Canada and the United States, Australia has an urban system characterized by considerable multipolarity. This effect has been strengthened in Australia by the fact that it is an island-continent, which has promoted a strong outward orientation in each of its major cities. We might expect, accordingly, to find strong tendencies toward the emergence of several highly internationalized financial and business centers. Or is Australia's space economy also characterized by a disproportionate concentration of international business and financial functions in one city? If both Canada and Australia have gone from multipolar to a strengthened dominance of one city, we can posit a systemic trend in current economic dynamics (see Chapter 4). During the period from World War II to the 1970s, Australia became a very rich country with thriving agricultural and manufacturing exports, and low unemployment. In that period, Australia had several major urban areas and many growth poles. Melbourne, the old capital of the state of Victoria, had been and remained the traditional focus for commerce, banking, and headquarters and was generally the place of old wealth in Australia.

As did other developed economies, Australia experienced considerable restructuring beginning in the early 1970s: declines in manufacturing employment; growth in service employment; a shift to information-intensive industries; and a growing internationalization of production processes, services, and investment. In the mid-1980s, financial institutions were deregulated and integrated into global financial markets. There were massive increases in foreign direct investment, with a shift from agriculture, mining, and manufacturing to real estate and services and from European to Asian sources (Daly and Stimson 1992). Asian countries became and remain today the main source of foreign investment in all major industries, and generally there is a greater orientation of trading and investment toward the Pacific Rim. Producer services emerged as the major growth sector throughout all the metropolitan areas and (combined with wholesale and retail and community services) accounted for 48% of all employment nationwide in Australia by the end of the 1980s. The fastest-growing export sectors were producer services and tourism.

The shift in investment in the 1980s from manufacturing to finance, real estate, and services became particularly evident in metropolitan areas (Stimson 1993). Out of this conjunction, Sydney emerged as the major destination of investment in real estate and finance. In 1982–83, investment in manufacturing in Sydney was A$1.15 billion, compared with A$1.32 billion in finance, real estate, and business services. By 1984–85, these levels of investment had changed, respectively, to A$0.82 billion and A$1.49 billion. At lower levels, these trends were evident in other major urban areas (Stimson 1993:5). By 1986, however, the disproportionate concentration of finance and business services in Sydney increasingly outdistanced that of other major cities. A massive real estate boom from 1985 to 1988 made Sydney the dominant market in Australia, both in levels of investment and in prime office space.

Sydney became Australia's main international gateway city and its only "world city," according to Daly and Stimson (1992; see also Brotchie et al. 1995). By the late 1980s, Sydney had the largest concentration of international business and financial firms in Australia, surpassing Melbourne, once the main economic capital of the country (Exhibit 5.1). By 2005, more than half—77 (51.3%)—of the country's top 150 firms were headquartered in Sydney, compared with Melbourne's 34 (22.7%). Similar concentration exists in the banking sector. Sydney has also garnered a larger share of national employment in the major producer service sectors; it is home to 29.7% of the business-service sector, 33.3% of the financial and real estate sector, and 36.1% of the media and publishing sector (23.9%, 25.2%, and 19.9% in Melbourne, respectively). By 1990, Sydney's stock market ranked tenth in the world, a position it has overall kept ever since (see Exhibit 2.8). Approximately 67% of multinational corporations that establish an Asia-Pacific regional headquarters in Australia do so in Sydney, and when focusing solely on the finance and insurance sector, that number rises to 80% (Fitzgerald 2005). Australia has also become an attractive location for secondary headquarters of Asian firms, and Sydney, by far the country's most international city, became the preferred choice already in the 1980s (O'Connor 1990) and remains so today (Fitzgerald 2005).

The 1980s are the critical period for understanding the character of the change. Australia had long been dependent on foreign investment to develop its manufacturing, mining, and agricultural sectors, but the share, composition, origins, and size of foreign investment in the 1980s point to a qualitative transformation and, in that sense, to a distinct process of economic internationalization. From 1983–84 to 1988–89, foreign direct investment in Australia grew at an average of 34% a year, from A$81.9 billion to

Exhibit 5.1 Corporate Concentration in Sydney and Melbourne, 2004

	Firms[a]	Banking Locations[b]			Share of National Employment[c]		
	Top 150 Australian Corporations	Australian-Owned Banks	Foreign Subsidiary Banks	Branches of Foreign Banks	Business Services	Finance & Real Estate	Media & Publishing
Sydney	77	6	8	27	29.70%	33.30%	36.10%
Melbourne	34	3	1	0	23.90%	25.20%	19.90%

Sources:

a. Mayne (2005).

b. New South Wales Department of State and Regional Development (2005).

c. O'Connor (2003).

A\$222.9 billion. Foreign investment in manufacturing also grew at a high rate, at 29% per year. But it grew at 83% a year in finance, real estate, and business services. This investment increasingly came from Japan and Asia, with declining shares coming from the United States and the United Kingdom, the two major investors in the past. Japan's share rose by 280%, reaching almost 15% of all foreign direct investment by 1989. In the 1990s, Singapore, Hong Kong, Taiwan, Canada, and Germany also became, and remain, significant investors. In the second half of the 1980s, particularly following the deregulation of financial institutions, trading enterprises and banks were the major conduits through which capital entered the country. The real estate boom was directly linked to foreign investment, as was the real estate crisis of 1989–90, when foreign investors ceased pouring money into these markets. More than 28% of all foreign direct investment in 1985–86 went into real estate, rising to 46% by 1988–89. Japanese investors accounted for more than one-third of this investment. The subsequent financial and real estate crisis brought these shares down sharply, but from 1996 to 2004, the share of foreign investment in real estate rose once again, going from 21.5% to 28.2%; the composition of countries investing has become much more internationalized, with Singapore being the largest single investor in 2004 at only 12%. Foreign investment in the 1980s, the decade that marks the sharp shift toward Sydney, was disproportionately concentrated in New South Wales and Queensland, with each typically absorbing around one-third of total investment, rather than in the older regions such as Victoria, home to Melbourne. Almost half of all investments in New South Wales (home to Sydney) were in commercial real estate.

The geography of these investments is even more specific than the regional dimensions discussed earlier. The bulk of these investments were in the central business districts (CBDs) of major cities, with Sydney the leading recipient. Between 1975 and 1984, foreign investors had financed about 10% of total investment in commercial real estate; between 1980 and 1984, there were actually declines, reflecting the fall in global foreign investment in the early 1980s. But they picked up shortly after that, and by 1984, about 15% of CBD offices in Sydney were foreign owned, compared with about 12.5% in Melbourne (Adrian 1984). In the second half of the 1980s, there were sharp increases in investments in all CBDs of major cities but especially in Sydney, Melbourne, and Brisbane. Stimson (1993) notes that by 1990, the value of land held by Japanese investors in Sydney's CBD was estimated at A\$1.55 billion, all of which had been invested in the second half of the 1980s. At the height of the boom in 1988–89, the officially estimated value of land in Sydney's CBD was put at \$A17.4 billion, a tenth of which was owned by Japanese investors.

Melbourne's CBD was also the object of much foreign investment and acquisition, with record levels of construction in commercial real estate. In Brisbane, more than 40% of the total office floor space was built between 1983 and 1990. Since those boom years, levels of foreign investment have fallen equally sharply, leaving a depressed office market in CBDs, a situation evident in major business centers across the world at the time.

The 1990s and into the 2000s were years of great prosperity for Australia. But even so, Sydney captured a disproportionate share of that growth (O'Neill and McGuirk 2002; Connell 2000). Sydney now produces 30% of the country's GDP, is home to the regional headquarters of 500 global corporations operating in the Asia-Pacific area, and has further raised its concentration of financial and business services in Australia. The floor space in the city dedicated to property and business services has kept growing, as has that for financial services (Salmon 2006).

It would seem then that even at the geographic scale and economic magnitude of a country like Australia, the ascendance of finance and services along with the internationalization of investment contributed to the marked concentration of strategic functions and investment in one city. Several experts on the Australian economy have noted that its increasing internationalization and the formation of new linkages connecting regions, sectors, and cities to the global economy have been central elements in the economic restructuring of that country (Daly and Stimson 1992; O'Connor 1990; Rimmer 1988; Stimson 1993; O'Neill and McGuirk 2002; Connell 2000). Foreign investment patterns, international air passenger travel and tourism, and the location of activities and headquarters dependent on global networks all reflect this process of internationalization and concentration. But beneath these general trends lies the fact that Sydney has experienced much of this growth far more sharply than most other cities in Australia.

Globalization and Concentration: The Case of Leading Financial Centers

Perhaps with the exception of the United States, all the major economies in the developed world display a similar pattern of sharp concentration of financial activity and related producer services in one center: Paris in France, Milan in Italy, Zurich in Switzerland, Frankfurt in Germany, Toronto in Canada, Tokyo in Japan, Amsterdam in the Netherlands, and, as just shown, Sydney in Australia. The evidence also shows that the concentration of financial activity in such leading centers has actually increased over the last decade. Thus, Basel, formerly a very important financial center in

Switzerland, in the 1980s began to be overshadowed by Zurich (Keil and Ronneberger 1992); and Montreal, certainly the other major center in Canada, was overtaken by Toronto in the late 1980s (Levine 1990). Similarly, Osaka was once a far more powerful competitor with Tokyo in the financial markets in Japan than it had become by the late 1980s (Sassen [1991] 2001, chaps. 6, 7).

Is this tendency toward concentration within each country a new development for financial centers? A broader historical view points to some interesting patterns. Since their earliest beginnings, financial functions were characterized by high levels of concentration. They often operated in the context of empires, such as the British or Dutch empires, or quasi-empires, such as the disproportionate economic and military power of the United States in the world during the last 50 years. Although some of the first financial centers in Europe were medieval Italian cities such as Florence, a city whose currency, the florin, was one of the most stable in the continent, by the seventeenth century a single financial center became dominant. It was Amsterdam, which introduced central banking and the stock market, probably reflecting its vast international merchant and trading operations, and the city's role as an unrivaled international center for trading and exchange. One hundred years later, London had emerged as the major international financial center and the major market for European government debt. London remained the financial capital of the world, clearly as a function of the British Empire, until well into the twentieth century. By 1914, New York, which had won its competition with Philadelphia and Boston for the banking business in the United States, emerged as a challenger to London. London, however, was also the strategic cog in the international financial system, a role that New York was not quite ready to assume. But after World War II, the immense economic might of the United States and the destruction of Britain and other European countries left New York as the world's financial center. But the context had been changing, especially since World War I. Against the earlier pattern of empires, the formation of nation-states made possible a multiplicity of financial centers, typically the national capital in each country. Furthermore, the ascendance of mass manufacturing contributed to vast, typically regionally based fortunes and the formation of secondary financial centers in those regions: Chicago and Osaka are two examples. The Keynesian policies aimed at promoting a country's development of regional convergence became increasingly common across the world. By the 1960s, these various trends had contributed to a proliferation of financial centers inside countries (e.g., Italy had 11 financial centers, and Germany had 7), highly regulated banking systems, and strict national protections. The dominance of mass manufacturing over the preceding half century meant that finance and banking were to a large extent shaped by the needs of manufacturing economies and mass consumption. Although New York may have been the leading international financial center since the early twentieth century, it was so as part of a national U.S. government strategy seeking global dominance along patterns that differed from the contemporary phase (Sassen 2006, chap. 4).

The developments that took off in the 1980s represented a sharp departure from this pattern of fairly closed and protected national financial systems centered on mass production and mass consumption. The opening of national economies to foreign investors and the explosion in financial innovations that raised the speculative character of finance and began to replace highly regulated national commercial banking as a source of capital strengthened the tendencies toward concentration in a limited number of financial centers. Although this is reminiscent of older imperial patterns, the actual conditions and processes involved are different.

In the 1980s, there was massive growth in the absolute levels of financial activity worldwide. But this growth became more sharply concentrated in a limited number of countries and cities. International bank lending grew from US$1.89 trillion in 1980 to US$6.24 trillion in 1991—a threefold increase in a decade—and to US$9.03 trillion in 1998 (Exhibit 5.2). The same seven countries accounted for almost two-thirds of this lending in 1980, then saw their share rise to three-fourths in 1998 and fall back to 1980 levels by 2004, according to data from the Bank for International Settlements (2004), the leading institution worldwide in charge of overseeing banking activity. Much of this lending activity was executed in the leading financial center of each of these countries, or in specialized markets, such as Chicago, which dominates the world's trading in futures. By the late 1990s, five cities— New York, London, Tokyo, Paris, and Frankfurt—accounted for a disproportionate share of all financial activity. Strong patterns of concentration were also evident in stock market capitalization and in foreign-exchange markets (Exhibit 5.3).

Notice again that this unchanged level of concentration happened in the context of enormous absolute increases, deregulation, and globalization of the industry worldwide, which means that a growing number of countries have become integrated into the world markets. Furthermore, this unchanged level of concentration happened at a time when financial services are more mobile than ever before: Globalization, deregulation (an essential ingredient for globalization), and securitization have been the keys to this mobility—in the context of massive advances in telecommunications and electronic networks.[2] One result has been growing competition among centers for hypermobile financial activity. But there has been an overemphasis on competition in both general and specialized accounts of this subject. As

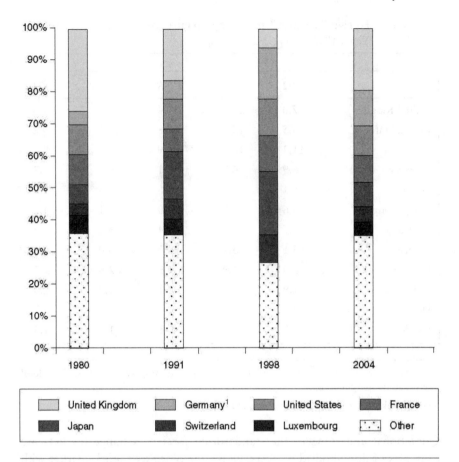

Exhibit 5.2   International Bank Lending by Country, Selected Years, 1980–2004 (percentage)

[1] 1980 figures based on West German reporting banks and institutions. 2004 data based on total external positions.

Source: Author's calculation based on data from the Bank for International Settlements, 62nd and 69th Annual Reports (Basel: B.I.S., 1992 and 1992), and BIS *Quarterly Review,* June 13, 2004

I argued in Chapter 3, there is also a functional division of labor among various major financial centers. In this sense, at work here is also a single global system with a division of function across multiple countries.

The hypermobility of financial capital puts added emphasis on the importance of technology. It is now possible to move money from one part of the world to another and make deals without ever leaving the computer terminal. Thanks to electronics, there are disembodied marketplaces—what we can think of as the cyberspace of international finance (Sassen 1998, chap. 9). NASDAQ (National Association of Securities Dealers Automated

Exhibit 5.3   Foreign Exchange Turnover by Country, Percentage Share, Selected Years 1992–2004 (US$ billions)

	1992	1995	1998	2001	2004
United Kingdom	27.0	29.5	32.4	31.2	31.3
United States	15.5	15.5	17.8	15.7	19.2
Japan	11.2	10.2	6.9	9.1	8.3
Singapore	6.9	6.7	7.1	6.3	5.2
Germany	5.1	4.8	4.8	5.4	4.9
Hong Kong	5.6	5.7	4.0	4.1	4.2
Australia	2.7	2.5	2.4	3.2	3.4
France	3.1	3.7	3.7	3.0	2.6
Canada	2.0	1.9	1.9	2.6	2.2
Netherlands	1.9	1.7	2.1	1.9	2.0
Denmark	2.5	2.0	1.4	1.4	1.7
Sweden	2.0	1.3	0.8	1.5	1.3

Note: Turnover of spot, outright forwards, and foreign exchange swaps (adjusted for local interdealer double counting).

Source: Bank for International Settlements (2005).

Quotations) and some of the standardized foreign-exchange markets are examples of disembodied markets, unlike the older-style stock market with its trading floor.

Yet the trend toward concentration still continues unabated—indeed, with renewed vigor. Further, the formation of a single European market and financial system raises the possibility, and even the need, for a European financial system made competitive by centralizing financial functions and capital in a limited number of cities, rather than maintaining the current structure in which each country has a financial center. Indeed, the consolidation of alliances, notably among Paris, Amsterdam, and Madrid (Euronext), is an emerging trend.

These tendencies toward concentration seem to be built into the nature of the financial system. Centers at the top are characterized by a multiplicity of financial institutions and markets and significant shares of world activity in various markets. They usually have a large number of banks and financial institutions that account for a significant share of international lending, foreign-exchange trading, and fund management. They also have large or significant markets in tradable securities—whether bonds, stocks, or their derivatives.

Among the large financial centers, some are dominated by international business, and others, by domestic business. Thus, London, with its enormous presence of foreign firms from all over the world and its strong Eurodollar and foreign-exchange markets, is extremely international, whereas New York and Tokyo, with their vast national economies, will inevitably have a very large number of domestic borrowers, lenders, and investors. Finally, the globalization of the industry has raised the level of complexity of transactions, and deregulation has promoted the invention of many new and increasingly speculative instruments. This change has contributed to the power of the leading centers, insofar as they are the only ones with the capability to produce authoritative innovations and to handle the levels of complexity in today's financial system.

In the next section, I examine these issues in greater detail with a particular focus on the networks that connect these centers and the impact of digitization on place.

Why Do We Need Financial Centers in the Global Digital Era?

The global financial system has reached levels of complexity that require the existence of a cross-border network of financial centers to service the operations of global capital. This network of financial centers differs sharply from earlier versions of the international financial system. In a world of largely closed national financial systems, each country duplicated most of the necessary functions for its economy; collaborations among different national financial markets were often no more than the execution of a given set of operations in each of the countries involved, as in clearing and settlement. With few exceptions, such as the offshore markets and some of the large banks, the international system consisted of a string of closed domestic systems and the limited, mostly routinized interactions among them.

The global integration of markets that took off in the 1980s led to the elimination of various redundant systems making collaboration a far more complex matter—it was no longer mere duplication of basic banking procedures in each country involved in a given transaction. Having something approaching one system embedded in all countries linked to the global financial system has had the perhaps ironic effect of raising the importance of leading financial centers; these centers have all the resources to execute the tasks, in part because they created many of the standards and rules that had to be adopted by all participating countries. Rather than each country with its own center for global operations, a leaner system is emerging, with fewer strategic centers and more hierarchy. In this context, London and New York, with their enormous concentrations of resources and talent, continue to be the powerhouses in the global network for the most strategic and complex operations for the system as a whole. They are the leading exporters of financial services and typically are part of any major international public offering, whether it is the privatization of British Telecom or France Telecom. This dominance, on the one hand, does not preclude the fact that one of the ways in which the global financial system grows is by incorporating more and more *national* economies, a process that happens through the development of a state-of-the-art financial center in each country—which often evolves into a second- or third-tier global city. On the other hand, in the case of the European Union, the formation of a single-currency Eurozone is spelling the end of an era in which each country had its full-fledged financial center. A steep hierarchy is very likely with Frankfurt and Paris at the top in the Eurozone and a crisscross of alliances centered in either of these major centers or among centers not included in those alliances.

The major financial centers of a growing number of countries worldwide are increasingly fulfilling gateway functions for the in-and-out circulation of national and foreign capital. Each of these centers is the nexus between that country's wealth and the global market and between foreign investors and that country's investment opportunities. The result is that the numbers of sources of, and destinations for, investment are growing. Gateway functions are their main mechanism for integration into the global financial market rather than, say, the production of innovations to package the capital flowing in and out; the production of innovations tends to remain concentrated in the leading centers, as these have not only the specialized talents but also the clout to persuade investors to buy innovative instruments. Further, the complex operations in most second- and third-tier financial centers tend to be executed by leading global investment, accounting, and legal services firms through affiliates, branches, or direct imports of those services.

These gateways for the global market are also gateways for the dynamics of financial crises: Capital can flow out as easily and quickly as it flows in. And what was once thought of as *national* capital can now as easily join the exodus. For example, during the Mexico crisis of December 1994, we now know that the first capitals to flee the Mexican markets were national, not foreign. In the financial crisis of 1997–98, much of the capital flight out of Brazil of an estimated US$1 billion a day by early September 1998 was not foreign.

Because the globally integrated financial system is not just about competition among countries, specialized collaborative efforts are increasing across borders. The financial system would not really gain from the downfall of Tokyo or Hong Kong, or for that matter, Buenos Aires. The ongoing growth of London, New York, Paris, or Frankfurt is in part a function of a global network of financial centers.

Finally, although electronic networks are growing in number and in scope, they are unlikely to eliminate the need for financial centers (Sassen 2006, chap. 7). Rather, they are intensifying the networks connecting such centers in strategic or functional alliances among exchanges in different cities. These alliances may well evolve into the equivalent of the cross-border mergers and acquisitions of firms. Electronic trading is also contributing to a radically new pattern whereby one market—for example, Frankfurt's Deutsche Eurex—can operate on screens in many other markets around the world, or one brokerage firm, notably Cantor Fitzgerald, could (since September 1998) have its prices of Treasury futures listed on screens used by traders all around the United States.

Electronic trading will not eliminate the need for financial centers because these combine multiple resources and talents necessary for executing complex operations and servicing global firms and markets. Frankfurt's electronic futures network is actually embedded in a network of financial centers. Broker Cantor Fitzgerald has an alliance with the Board of Trade of New York to handle its computerized sale of Treasury futures. Financial centers cannot be reduced to their exchanges. They are part of a far more complex architecture in the financial system, and they constitute far more complex structures within that architecture than the exchanges.

In the Digital Era: More Concentration than Dispersal

What really stands out in the evidence for the global financial industry is the extent to which there is a sharp concentration of the shares of many financial markets in a few financial centers. This trend toward consolidation in a few centers is also evident within countries. In the United States, for example, New York concentrates all the leading investment banks with only one other major international financial center, Chicago, in this enormous country. We already examined how Sydney and Toronto took over functions and market share from what were once the major commercial centers in their respective countries. So have São Paulo and Mumbai, which gained share and functions from, respectively, Rio de Janeiro in Brazil and New Delhi and Calcutta in India. These are all enormous countries, and one might have thought that they could sustain multiple major financial centers. In France, Paris today concentrates larger shares of most financial sectors than it did in the 1970s, and once-important stock markets such as Lyon have become "provincial," even though Lyon is today the hub of a thriving economic region. Milan privatized its exchange in September 1997 and electronically merged Italy's 10 regional markets. Frankfurt now concentrates a larger share of the financial market in Germany than it did in the early 1980s, as does Zurich in Switzerland. Further, these processes of growing concentration moved fast. For example, by 1997, Frankfurt's market capitalization was five times greater than all other regional markets in Germany combined, whereas in 1992, it was only twice as large. This story can be repeated for many countries. What stands out is that this pattern toward the consolidation of one leading financial center is a function of rapid growth in the sector, not necessarily of decay in the losing cities.

Note that there are both consolidation in fewer major centers across and within countries *and* a sharp growth in the numbers of centers that become part of the global network as countries deregulate their economies. São Paulo and Mumbai, for example, joined the global financial network after Brazil and India deregulated, at least partially, their financial systems in the early 1990s. This mode of incorporation into the global network is often at the cost of losing functions that they had when they were largely national centers; today, foreign financial, accounting, and legal services firms have entered their markets to handle the new cross-border operations. Incorporation of a country's financial center into the global network typically happens without a gain in the share of the global market that they can command even though their volume and value of operations will tend to grow sharply in absolute terms. In a globalized market, the owners or beneficiaries of the absolute growth in stock market value may well be foreign investors.

All of these trends bring up, once again, the question as to why this rapid growth in the network of financial centers, overall volumes, and electronic networks has resulted in, or failed to reduce, the high concentration of market shares in the leading financial centers of the world. Both globalization and electronic trading are about expansion and dispersal beyond what had been the confined realm of national economies and floor trading. Indeed, given globalization and electronic trading, one might well ask why financial centers matter at all.

Agglomeration in the Digital Era

The continuing weight of major centers is, in a way, countersensical, as is the existence of an expanding network of financial centers. The rapid development of electronic exchanges and the growing digitization of much financial activity suggest that location should not matter. In fact, geographic dispersal would seem to be a good option given the high cost of operating in major financial centers, and digitization would seem to eliminate most reasons for having a geographic base. Further, the geographic mobility of financial experts and financial services firms has continued to increase and has resulted in a variety of new industries catering to the needs of the transnational professional and managerial classes, thereby enabling even more mobility.

There has been geographic decentralization of certain types of financial activities, aimed at securing business in the growing number of countries becoming integrated into the global economy. Many of the leading investment banks now have operations in more countries than they did in the early 1980s. The same can be said for the leading accounting and legal services and other specialized corporate services, as well as some markets. For example, in the 1980s, all basic wholesale foreign-exchange operations were in London. Today, these are distributed among London and several other centers (even though the number of these centers is far smaller than the number of countries whose currency is being traded).

There are at least three reasons that explain the trend toward consolidation in a few centers rather than massive dispersal. I developed this analysis in *The Global City* (Sassen [1991] 2001), initially focusing on New York, London, and Tokyo in the 1980s, and since then on the larger network of financial centers. The reasons explaining the primacy of leading centers have become even clearer and sharper over the last few years, partly due to the rise in speculative finance and the fact that electronic markets have contributed to a new type of risk, one that might be called *market-risk*, whereby the so-called export of risk by a firm through the use of derivatives produces a boomerang effect for firms when electronic markets absorb the aggregate risk exported by all firms in such markets (Sassen 2006, chap. 7).

1. *Social Connectivity*. First, and as already discussed in Chapter 1 for firms, although the new telecommunications technologies do indeed facilitate geographic dispersal of financial activities without losing system integration, they have also had the effect of strengthening the importance of central coordination and control functions for financial firms and, even, markets. This is particularly so, given the trend toward making financial exchanges into private corporations and hence developing central management functions of sorts. While operating a widely dispersed network of branches and affiliates and operating in multiple markets has made central functions far more complicated for any firm, this is especially so in finance

given the speed of transactions possible in electronic markets. The exchanges are also increasingly subject to these trends. The execution of these central functions requires access to top talent and to innovative milieux—in technology, accounting, legal services, economic forecasting, and all sorts of other, many new, specialized corporate services. Financial centers have massive concentrations of state-of-the-art resources that allow them to maximize the benefits of telecommunications and, in the case of leading centers, to organize and govern the new conditions for operating globally. Even electronic markets such as NASDAQ and E*Trade rely on traders and banks located somewhere, with at least some in a major financial center.

One fact that has become increasingly evident is that to maximize the benefits of the new information technologies, you need not only the infrastructure but also a complex mix of other resources. Most of the value that these technologies can produce for advanced service firms lies in the externalities. And this means the material and human resources—state-of-the-art office buildings, top talent, and the social networking that maximize the benefits of connectivity. Any town can have fiber-optic cables. But do they have the rest?

A second fact emerging with greater clarity concerns the meaning of *information*. There are, one could say, two types of information. One is the datum: At what level did Wall Street close? Did Argentina complete the public sector sale of its water utility? Has Japan declared such-and-such bank insolvent? But there is a far more difficult type of information, akin to a mix of interpretation, evaluation, and judgment. It entails negotiating a series of data and a series of interpretations of other data in the hope of producing a higher-order datum. Access to the first kind of information is now global and immediate, thanks to the digital revolution. You can be a broker in the Colorado mountains and have access to this type of information. But the second type of information requires a complicated mixture of elements— the social infrastructure for global connectivity—and it is this that gives major financial centers a leading edge.

You can, in principle, reproduce the technical infrastructure anywhere. Singapore, for example, has technical connectivity matching Hong Kong's. But does it have Hong Kong's social connectivity? When the more complex forms of information needed to execute major international deals cannot be gotten from existing databases, no matter what a firm can pay, then that firm needs the social information loop with the associated interpretations and inferences that come with bouncing off information among talented, informed people. The importance of this input has given a whole new weight to credit-rating agencies, for example. Part of the rating has to do with interpreting and inferring the quality of a firm's or government's resources.

Credit-rating firms are in the business of producing *authoritative* interpretations and presenting them as information available to all. Firms, especially global firms in finance, often need more than what credit-ratings firms sell. They need to build this advanced type of interpretation into their daily work process, and this takes not only talent but also information-rich milieux. Financial centers generally, and leading ones especially, are such milieux.

Risk management, for example, which has become increasingly important with globalization as a result of the growing complexity and uncertainty that comes with operating in multiple countries and markets, requires enormous fine-tuning of central operations. We now know that many, if not most, major trading losses during the decade of the 1990s have involved human error or fraud. The quality of risk management depends more heavily on the top people in a firm than simply on technical conditions, such as electronic surveillance. Consolidating risk-management operations in one site, usually a central one for the firm, is now seen generally as more effective. This is the case of several major banks: Chase and Morgan Stanley Dean Witter in the United States, Deutsche Bank and Credit Suisse in Europe.

In brief, financial centers provide the social connectivity that allows a firm or market to maximize the benefits of its technological connectivity and to handle the added pressures that speed brings to financial firms.

2. Need for Enormous Resources. Global players in the financial industry need enormous resources, a trend that is leading, first, to rapid mergers and acquisitions of firms and, second, to strategic alliances between markets in different countries. Both of these are happening on a scale and in combinations few had foreseen a decade ago. Examples from the late 1990s, when these trends took off, are the mergers of Citibank with Travelers Group (which few had predicted just two years earlier), Salomon Brothers with Smith Barney, Bankers Trust with Alex Brown, and so on. This wave of mergers was so sharp that, subsequently, when powerful firms such as Deutsche Bank and Dresdner Bank each decided to purchase a U.S. security firm, they complained of a lack of suitable candidates. One common opinion among analysts emerging in the early 2000s is that midsize firms will find it difficult to survive in the global market given global megafirms such as Merrill Lynch, Morgan Stanley Dean Witter, and Goldman Sachs. Increasingly common are mergers among accounting firms, law firms, insurance brokers—in brief, firms that need to provide a global service. Analysts foresee a system dominated by a few global investment banks, about 25 large fund managers, and an increasingly consolidated set of specialized service firms. A similar trend is expected in the global telecommunications industry, which will have to consolidate to offer a state-of-the-art, globe-spanning service to its global clients, among which are the financial firms; indeed, the early 2000s saw the demise of several large telecommunications firms and their partial absorption by some of the remaining firms.

Another kind of merger is the consolidation of electronic networks that connect a very select number of markets. Europe's more than 30 stock exchanges have been seeking to shape various alliances. Euronext is Europe's largest stock exchange merger, an alliance among the Paris, Amsterdam, and Brussels bourses. Also, small exchanges are merging: In March 2001, the Tallinn Stock Exchange in Estonia and its Helsinki counterpart created an alliance. A novel pattern is hostile takeovers, not of firms, but of markets, such as the attempt by the owners of the Stockholm stock market to buy the London Stock Exchange (for a price of US$3.7 billion). There are some looser networks connecting markets that have been set up in the last few years. In 1999, NASDAQ, the second largest U.S. stock market after the New York Stock Exchange, set up NASDAQ Japan and in 2000 NASDAQ Canada. This gives investors in Japan and Canada direct access to the market in the United States. The Toronto Stock Exchange has joined an alliance with the New York Stock Exchange (NYSE) to create a separate global trading platform. The NYSE is a founding member of a global trading alliance, Global Equity Market (GEM), which includes 10 exchanges, among them Tokyo and Euronext. These developments are likely to strengthen intercity links in the worldwide network of about 40 cities through which the global financial industry operates and may well ensure the consolidation of a stratum of select financial centers at the top of the worldwide network.

Does the fact of fewer global players affect the spread of such operations? Not necessarily, but it will strengthen the hierarchy in the global network. For example, institutional money managers around the world controlled approximately $15 trillion by early 1999. The worldwide distribution of equities under institutional management shows considerable spread among a large number of cities that have become integrated in the global equity market with deregulation of their economies and the whole notion of emerging markets as an attractive investment destination over the last few years. Thomson Financial (1999), for example, has estimated that at the end of 1998 (the last year for which Thomson Financial produced this information), 25 cities accounted for 83% of the world's equities under institutional management. (At the time, these 25 cities also accounted for roughly 48% of the total market capitalization of the world, which stood at US$22 trillion at the end of 1998.) However, this global market is characterized by a disproportionate concentration in the top six or seven cities. London, New York, and Tokyo together accounted for a third of the world's total equities under institutional management at the end of 1998.

These developments make clear a second important trend that in many ways specifies the current global era. These various centers don't just compete with each other: There is collaboration and division of labor. In the international system of the postwar decades, each country's financial center, in principle, covered the universe of necessary functions to service its national companies and markets. The world of finance was, of course, much simpler than it is today. In the initial stages of deregulation in the 1980s, there was a strong tendency to see the relations between the major centers as one of straight competition, especially among the leading centers—New York, London, and Tokyo. But in my research at the time, I had already found a division of labor among these three centers, along with competition in certain areas. What we are seeing now is yet a third pattern: strategic alliances not only between firms across borders but also between markets. There is competition, strategic collaboration, and hierarchy.

In brief, the need for enormous resources to handle increasingly global operations and the growth of complex central functions discussed earlier produce tendencies toward concentration among the top centers and hierarchy in the expanding global network of financial centers.

3. Denationalization of the Corporate Elite. Finally, national attachments and identities are becoming weaker for these global players and their customers. Thus, the major U.S. and European investment banks have set up specialized offices in London to handle various aspects of their global business. Deregulation and privatization have further weakened the need for *national* financial centers. The nationality question simply plays differently in these sectors than it did as recently ago as the early 1980s. Global financial products are accessible in national markets, and national investors can operate in global markets. It is interesting to see that investment banks used to split up their analysts team by country to cover a national market; now they are more likely to do it by industrial sector.

In *Losing Control?* (Sassen 1996), I described this process as the incipient denationalizing of certain institutional arenas, a necessary condition for economic globalization as we know it today. The sophistication of the global economy lies in the fact that its organizational side (as opposed to the consumer side) needs to involve only strategic institutional areas—most national systems can be left basically unaltered. China is a good example. It adopted international accounting rules in 1993, an advantage for a country with an accounting system that differed sharply from the prevalent Anglo-American standards generally being used in international transactions. But China did not have to go through a fundamental reorganization to do this: It only used those standards when transacting with foreign firms. Japanese firms operating overseas adopted such standards long before Japan's government considered requiring them. In this regard, the organizational side of globalization is quite different from the global mass-consumer markets, in which success necessitates altering national tastes at a mass level.

This process of denationalization in the realm of the economy has an instrumental and practical connotation, unlike what might be the case in processes of identity formation or in the rising anti-immigrant politics evident in many of the European countries today, subjects examined in Chapter 6. For example, I argue that denationalization of key economic sectors in South Korea and Thailand was facilitated by the 1997–98 Asian financial crisis because it enabled foreign firms to buy up large numbers of firms and property in these countries where once their national elites had been in full control. In some ways, the Asian financial crisis has functioned as a mechanism to denationalize, at least partially, control over key sectors of economies that, while allowing the massive entry of foreign investment, never relinquished that control.

Major international business centers produce what can be thought of as a new subculture. In a witty insight, *The Economist,* in its coverage of the January 1997 World Economic Forum meeting held in Davos, titled one of its stories "From Chatham House Man to Davos Man," alluding to, respectively, the "national" and the "global" version of international relations. The resistance to mergers and acquisitions, especially hostile takeovers, in Europe in the 1980s and 1990s or to foreign ownership and control in East Asia points to national business cultures that are somewhat incompatible with the new global economic culture. I find that global cities and financial centers contribute to denationalizing the corporate elite. Whether this is good or bad is a separate issue; but it is, I believe, one of the conditions for setting in place the systems and subcultures necessary for a global economic system.

The Space Economy of Centrality

What are the spatial consequences of this new economic core of activities? What is the urban form that accommodates them?

Three distinct patterns are emerging in major cities and their regions in the developed countries and increasingly also in the rest of the world. First, beginning in the 1980s, there was an increase in the number of firms in the centers of major cities associated with growth in leading sectors and ancillary industries. This type of growth also took place in some of the most dynamic cities in developing countries, such as Seoul, Bangkok, Taipei,

Mumbai, São Paulo, Mexico City, and, toward the end of the decade, Buenos Aires. Second, along with this central city growth came the formation of dense nodes of commercial development and business activity in a broader urban region, a pattern less evident in developing countries, except in the export-oriented growth poles discussed earlier or in cities such as Johannesburg undergoing major social transformation. These nodes assumed different forms: suburban office complexes, edge cities, exopoles, and urban agglomerations in peripheral areas. *Edge cities* are significant concentrations of offices and business activities alongside residential areas in peripheral areas that are completely connected to central locations via state-of-the-art electronic means. Thus far, these forms are only rarely evident in developing countries, where vast urban sprawl with a seemingly endless metropolitanization of the region around cities has been the norm. In developed countries, the revitalized urban center and the new regional nodes together constitute the spatial base for cities at the top of transnational hierarchies. The third pattern is the growing intensity in the *localness*, or marginality, of areas and sectors that operate outside that world market-oriented subsystem, and this includes an increase in poverty and disadvantage. The general dynamic that emerges from these three patterns operates in cities with very diverse economic, political, social, and cultural arrangements. There is by now a vast scholarship on these various subjects and types of cities (see, among others, Benko and Dunford 1991; Cheshire and Hay 1989; Gans 1984; Hausserman and Siebel 1987; Henderson and Castells 1987; Cobos 1984; Scott 2001; Abrahamson 2004; Rutherford 2004; Krause and Petro 2003; Gugler 2004; Amen, Archer, and Bosman 2006).

A few questions spring to mind. One question is whether the type of spatial organization characterized by dense strategic nodes spread over the broader region might constitute a new form of organizing the territory of the center. This would contrast with the more conventional view that sees it as an instance of suburbanization or geographic dispersal. I argue that insofar as these various nodes are articulated through digital and other advanced communication systems, they represent the new geographic correlate of the most advanced type of center. The places that fall outside this new grid of digital highways are peripheralized. We might ask whether this is more so today than in earlier periods, when suburban and noncentral areas were integrated into the center because they were primarily geared *to* the center.

Another question is whether this new terrain of centrality is differentiated. Basically, is the old central city, which is still the largest and densest of all the nodes, the most strategic and powerful node? Does it have a sort of gravitational power over the region that makes the new grid of nodes and digital highways cohere as a complex spatial agglomeration? From a larger transnational perspective, these are vastly expanded central regions. This reconstitution of the center is different from the agglomerations still prevalent in most cities which fall outside the global city dynamic and the accumulation regime it entails. The reconstitution of the center at a larger metropolitan scale points to a reorganization of space/time dimensions in the urban economy (Sassen [1991] 2001, chap. 5).

Such a rescaling can enable the traditional perimeter of the city, a kind of periphery, to develop its full industrial and structural growth potential. For example, commercial and office space development lead to a reconcentration of economic activity into a variety of nodes in the urban periphery (Kotkin 2005). This geographic shift has much to do with the locational decisions of transnational and national firms that make the urban peripheries the growth centers of the most dynamic industries. It is not the same as largely residential suburbanization or metropolitanization.

There are differences in the pattern of global city formation in parts of the United States and in parts of Western Europe (e.g., Fainstein 1993; Hitz et al. 1995; Marcuse and Van Kempen 2000; Rutherford 2004; Abrahamson 2004; Graham and Marvin 1996; Kazepov 2005; Allen, Massey, and Pryke 1999). In the United States, major cities such as New York and Chicago have large centers that have been rebuilt many times, given the brutal neglect suffered by much urban infrastructure and the imposed obsolescence so characteristic of U.S. cities. This neglect and accelerated obsolescence produce vast spaces for rebuilding the center according to the requirements of whatever the prevalent regime of urban accumulation or pattern of spatial organization of the urban economy is at a given time.

In Europe, urban centers are far more protected, and they rarely contain significant stretches of abandoned space; the expansion of workplaces and the need for "intelligent" buildings necessarily will have to take place partly outside the old centers. One of the most extreme cases is the complex of La Defense, the massive, state-of-the-art office complex developed right outside Paris to avoid harming the built environment inside the city. This is an explicit instance of government policy and planning aimed at addressing the growing demand for central office space of prime quality. Yet another variant of this expansion of the center onto hitherto peripheral land can be seen in London's Docklands. This vast underutilized harbor area in London became the site of an expensive, state-of-the-art development project to accommodate the rapidly growing demand for office space, especially in the financial sector. The financial and real estate crisis of the early 1990s resulted in the collapse of the project. But by 1993, reorganization under a new consortium and a rapid demand by worldwide buyers brought full occupancy of the complex (Fainstein 2001). Similar projects for recentralizing peripheral areas were launched in several major cities in Europe, North America, and Japan during the late 1980s. What was seen in the 1980s as a derelict marginal area, Times Square in New York City, by the late 1990s had become a prime office, commercial, and entertainment area (Fainstein and Judd 1999). As with the Docklands and Times Square redevelopments, many of these did not succeed until the mid- or late 1990s, years after the crisis of 1990–91. What was once the suburban fringe and urban perimeter in many of today's global and other cities, has now been reconstituted as some variant of central city space.

Conclusion: Concentration and the Redefinition of the Center

The central concern in this chapter was to explain the counterintuitive tendency for the top-level functions of leading global and often digitized sectors to evince significant agglomeration economies. This concentration has occurred in the face of the globalization of economic activity and revolutionary changes in technology that have the power to neutralize distance.

In this chapter, I used specific cases as natural experiments to explore different aspects of this trend toward concentration. Miami represents the development of global city functions in a city lacking a long history as an international banking and business center, the typical trajectory for such global cities as New York or London. Miami shows in almost laboratory-like fashion how a new international corporate sector can become implanted in a site. It illuminates how globalization becomes embedded in place. Toronto is a city that decided to rebuild its financial district in the 1980s, when electronic markets were growing and many headquarters chose to leave the central city. Conceivably, these facts could have led to rebuilding the financial center in the metropolitan region alongside growing numbers of corporate headquarters. But it rebuilt in the downtown with high densities. The case of Toronto thus shows something about the advantages of agglomeration and that downtown financial centers are not simply a consequence of a built infrastructure from the past, as one might assume when examining older financial centers such as London or New York. Finally, the different locational preferences of corporate headquarters and the financial sector shows that certain industries and firms are more subject to agglomeration economies than others.

The case of Sydney explores the interaction of a vast, continental economic scale and pressures toward spatial concentration. Rather than strengthening the multipolarity of the Australian urban system, the developments of the 1980s—increased internationalization of the Australian economy; sharp increases in foreign investment; a strong shift toward finance, real estate, and producer services—all contributed to a greater concentration of major economic activities and actors in Sydney. This concentration included a declining share of such activities and actors in Melbourne, long the center of commercial activity and wealth in Australia.

Finally, I examined the case of the leading financial centers in the world today to see whether the concentration of financial activity and value has declined given globalization of markets and immense increases in the global volume of transactions. The levels of concentration remain unchanged in the face of massive transformations in the financial industry and in the technological infrastructure this industry depends on.

But what exactly is the space of the center in the contemporary economy, one characterized by growing use of electronic and telecommunication capabilities? The final section of the chapter examined the spatial correlates of the center and posited that today there is no longer a simple, straightforward relation between centrality and such geographic entities as the downtown or the central business district. In the past, and up until quite recently, in fact, the center was synonymous with the downtown or the CBD. Today, the spatial correlate of the center can assume several geographic forms. It can be the CBD, which remains as the most strategic center in most global cities, or it can extend into metropolitan areas in the form of a grid of nodes of intense business activity, as in Frankfurt and Zurich, for example.

Elsewhere (Sassen [1991] 2001), I argued that we are also seeing the formation of a transterritorial *center* constituted via intercity electronic networks and various types of economic transactions; I argued that the cross-border network of global cities can be seen as constituting such a transterritorial terrain of centrality *with regard to a specific complex of industries and activities*. At the limit, there exist terrains of centrality that are disembodied and lack any territorial correlate: These are electronic spaces of centrality.

One of the reasons for focusing on centrality and on its spatial correlates is to recover a particular kind of place—cities—in the operation of global processes. Such a recovery of place introduces questions concerning the social order associated with some of these transformations. This is the subject of Chapter 6.

Notes

1. For two extraordinary and different types of accounts, see Braudel (1984) and King (1990).

2. Securitization is the replacement of traditional bank finance by tradable debt; for example, a mortgage is bundled up along with thousands of others into a package that can be traded on specialized markets. This is one of the major innovations in the financial industry in the 1980s. Securitization made it possible to sell all kinds of (supposedly worthy) debt, thereby adding to the overall volume of transactions in the industry.

6

The New Inequalities
within Cities

W hat is the impact of the ascendance of finance and producer services on the broader social and economic structure of major cities? And what are the consequences of the new urban economy on the earnings distribution of a city's workforce? When manufacturing was the leading sector of the economy, it created the conditions for the expansion of a vast middle class because (1) it facilitated unionization; (2) it was based in good part on household consumption, and hence wage levels mattered in that they created an effective demand; and (3) the wage levels and social benefits typical of the leading sectors became a model for broader sectors of the economy.

In this chapter, I explore the place of workers lacking the high levels of education required by today's advanced economic sectors in these major cities. Have these workers become superfluous? I also examine the place in an advanced urban economy of firms and sectors that appear to be backward or to lack the advanced technological and human capital base of the new leading sectors. Have they also become superfluous? Or are significant shares of such workers, firms, and sectors actually articulated to the economic core, but under conditions of severe segmentation in the social, economic, racial, and organizational traits of firms and workers? Finally, I describe to what extent this segmentation is produced or strengthened by the existence of ethnic or racial segmentation in combination with racism and discrimination.

Remarkably enough, general tendencies are at work on the social level, just as they are on the economic level. Recent research shows sharp increases in socioeconomic and spatial inequalities within major cities of the developed world. This finding can be interpreted as merely a quantitative increase in the degree of inequality, one that is not associated with the emergence of new social forms or class realignments. But it can also be interpreted as social and economic restructuring and the emergence of new social forms: (1) the growth of an informal economy in large cities in highly developed countries, (2) high-income commercial and residential gentrification, and (3) the sharp rise in rich countries of a type of homelessness, for example, of families, that differs from older types, such as the proverbial hobo.

My concern in this chapter is to describe the general outlines of this transformation. The nature of the subject is such that a fully developed account would require introducing the specific conditions typical to each city, a task that falls outside the scope of this book (for a more detailed account, see Sassen [1991] 2001, chaps. 8, 9). For that reason, too, much of the empirical background shaping some of the specific statements made here comes from the case of the United States. Another reason for focusing particularly on the United States is that there are more detailed analyses available, and the trends under discussion are sharper.

The first half of the chapter discusses the transformation in the organization of the labor process, particularly as it materializes in large cities. The second half focuses on the earnings distribution in a service-dominated economy. This discussion includes somewhat more detailed accounts of the informal economy and of the restructuring of urban consumption, two key processes that are part of the changed earnings distribution.

Transformations in the Organization of the Labor Process

The consolidation of a new economic core of professional and servicing activities needs to be viewed alongside the general move to a service economy and the decline of manufacturing. New economic sectors are reshaping the job supply. So, however, are new ways of organizing work in both new and old sectors of the economy. The computer can now be used to do secretarial as well as manufacturing work. Components of the work process that even 10 years ago took place on the shop floor and were classified as production jobs today have been replaced by a combination of machine/service worker or worker/engineer. The machine in this case is typically computerized; for example, certain operations that required a highly skilled craftsperson can now be done through computer-aided design and calibration. Activities that were once consolidated in a single-service retail establishment have now been divided between a service delivery outlet and central headquarters. Finally, much work that was once standardized mass production is today increasingly characterized by customization, flexible specialization, networks of subcontractors, and informalization, even at times including sweatshops and industrial homework. In brief, the changes in the job supply evident in major cities are a function of new sectors as well as of the reorganization of work in both the new and the old sectors.

The historical forms assumed by economic growth in the post–World War II era that contributed to the vast expansion of a middle class—notably, fixed-capital intensity, standardized production, and suburbanization-led growth—deterred and reduced systemic tendencies toward inequality by constituting an economic regime centered on mass production and mass consumption. Further, so did the cultural forms accompanying these processes, particularly through their shaping the structures of everyday life: a large suburban middle class contributes to mass consumption and thus to standardization in production. These various trends led to greater levels of unionization and other forms of workers' empowerment helped by large scales of production and the centrality of mass production and mass consumption in national economic growth and profits. This form of economic growth, along with government programs, contributed to reduce poverty and expand the middle class in the United States (Exhibit 6.1) and in most highly developed economies.

It was also in that postwar period extending into the late 1960s and early 1970s that the incorporation of workers into formal labor-market relations reached its highest level in the most advanced economies. The formalization of the employment relation carries with it the implementation (albeit frequently precarious) of a set of regulations that have had the overall effect of protecting workers and securing the fruits of frequently violent labor struggles. But this formalization also entailed the exclusion of distinct segments of the workforce, such as women and minorities; this was particularly so in certain heavily unionized industries.

The economic and social transformations in the economy since the mid-1970s assume specific forms in urban labor markets. Changes in the functioning of urban labor markets since the mid-1970s have a number of possible origins. The most evident of these changes stem from the long-term shifts in the occupational and industrial balance of employment. Such shifts directly affect the mix of job characteristics, including earnings levels and employment stability, and the types of careers available to local workers. On the demand side, these developments include the new flexibility that employers

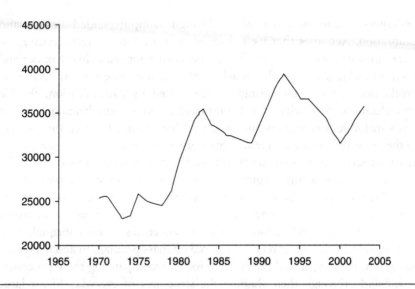

Exhibit 6.1   Poor People in the United States, 1970–2003 (in thousands)

Source: U.S. Bureau of the Census (2004a, Table B.1).

have tended to seek under the pressure of international competition, unstable product markets, and a weakening of political support for public sector programs. This new flexibility tends to mean more part-time and temporary jobs. On the supply side, a key factor has been the persistence of high unemployment in the 1970s and 1980s in many large cities, which notably altered the bargaining position of employers, and the insecurity or marginalization of the most disadvantaged groups in the labor market. Workers desperate for jobs in the 1980s became willing to take increasingly unattractive jobs. In combination, these major developments on both sides of the labor market, and especially strong in the urban core, seem likely to have induced, on the one hand, a growing destabilization of employment with increasing casualization and/or informalization of jobs and, on the other hand, an increasing polarization of employment opportunities with new types of social divisions.

Metropolitan labor markets tend to reflect a variety of background factors beyond particular restructuring effects. The most important include their sheer size and density, the particular industrial and occupational mix of their employment base, the overall state of tightness or slack in labor demand, and in many cities, the presence and characteristics of immigrant groups. Two traits of labor markets in major cities today, as in the past, are fluidity and openness; thus, the specific features of a given area can influence the types of activity prospering there and the labor-market experiences of residents. Labor markets in and around cities are *structured* through particular sets of jobs with distinctive combinations of rewards, security, and conditions of access (see Gordon and Sassen 1992).

The labor market characteristics of key industries in major cities have long evinced tendencies toward shorter-term employment relationships than in other types of settings. Whether it is fashion-oriented industries such as the garment trade, private consumer services, building contractors, or the current speculative financial services, a significant share of urban establishments operate in competitive and often highly unstable markets. The evidence shows much higher turnover rates in these activities than in large establishments and in monopolistic, bureaucratized organizations. Cities provide these more unstable activities easy access to workforces that can be adjusted up and down depending on demand for their products and services.

High rates of turnover also have implications on the supply side, adding to the attractions of the city for migrants, particularly for minorities who have difficulty gaining access to more closed sectors of employment and for young, single workers for whom job security may be a lower priority. The availability of these particular labor supplies must then have further implications for employers' strategies. The actual structure of urban labor markets has been more complex and changeable than agglomeration economies and the "natural selection" of activities and groups of workers can account for. The rapid growth in unemployment levels in many European cities captures the overall outcome of these various processes (Exhibit 6.2). The European case is particularly interesting because it has a stronger tradition of government protection of workers.

The potential importance of the presence or absence of a large immigrant labor force extends to a range of issues, including the level of wages in the lower part of the labor market and its implications for the cost of living and the competitiveness of local activities, as well as for patterns of segmentation and opportunities of advancement for indigenous workers. Furthermore, given the typical concentration of new migrants in central cities, immigration contributes to changes in spatial patterns in labor supply. The marked decentralization of the white population into the outer rings of metropolitan regions, again, especially in the United States where it has often taken the form of white flight to the suburbs, was counterbalanced by mostly third-world immigration into urban centers from the mid-1970s on. Beginning in the 1980s, there was a positive influx of young, highly educated whites into central cities, and most recently, there has been significant growth in suburban immigrant settlement, especially in the United States. Today, major U.S.

Exhibit 6.2   Unemployment in Select European Cities, 1980, 1990, and 2001
(percentage)

City	Unemployment		
	1980	*1990*	*2001*
Amsterdam	8.2	19.5 (1988)	4.3
Barcelona	15.5 (1981)	14.6 (1988)	10.4
Birmingham	15	10.3	9.5
Brussels	6	16.7 (1989)	18.3
Copenhagen	7.8	11.3 (1988)	4.5
Dortmund	5.7	11.9	13.5
Dublin	9.9	18.4 (1987)	6.7
Glasgow	8	15	10.8
Hamburg	3.2	11.2	7.6
Liverpool	16	20	11.1
Lyons	6.1	8.3	11.5
Madrid	12	12.5	12.4
Marseilles	12.2	18.1	20.3
Montpellier	6.8	10.3	18
Paris	7	8.4	11.7
Rennes	8.1	10.1	9
Rotterdam	8.8	17.1 (1988)	5.9
Seville	18.7	25.2	22.8
Valencia	9.9	17.5	14.2

Sources: (1980–1990 data) Based on European Institute of Urban Affairs (1992:83–87). (2001 data) EUROSTAT (2005). *The Urban Audit.* Data accessible online at http://www.urbanaudit .org.

cities tend to have higher shares of immigrants and highly educated high-income professionals than was the case in the 1960s and 1970s.

Trends toward concentration of immigrants and ethnic populations in the center are also evident in other major cities in the developed world, from the well-known case of London to the little-known one of Tokyo. Thus, in 1991, greater London had 1.35 million residents, or 20% of the population, classified as ethnic minorities. Ethnic minorities were 25.7% of the population of inner London and about 17% in outer London. Some of London's inner boroughs have extremely high concentrations: Brent, about 45%; Newham, more than 42%; and Tower Hamlets, more than 35%. The 2001 census (Office for National Statistics 2002) showed increases in most of these figures. We see here a very high degree of spatial segregation and heavy concentration in central urban areas. In Tokyo, 250,000 foreign residents were officially registered in 1991. This figure is an understatement because it excludes the growing illegal immigration (see Morita 1993; Sassen 1998, chap. 4). But also in Tokyo, there is a pattern of spatial concentration in the center of the city. Thus, 85% of these registered foreigners were living in central Tokyo, with a disproportionate number, especially those of Asian origin, concentrated in a few small areas in the center of the city. Although the registered foreign population represents a mere 2.3% of the total population of central Tokyo, its share rises to 5% in the center of the city. In some inner-city areas known to have many of the unregistered, mostly undocumented new immigrants, foreigners account for a much larger proportion of residents. In Shinjuku ward, the new site of the city's government and a major commercial center, there are sections where foreigners account for 15% to 20% of all residents. About two-thirds of these foreigners are Korean and Chinese, but there are also rapidly growing numbers of foreigners from other Asian countries.

The expansion of low-wage jobs as a function of growth trends implies a reorganization of the capital–labor relation. To see this effect clearly, we must distinguish the *characteristics* of jobs from their sectoral location. That is, highly dynamic, technologically advanced growth sectors may well contain low-wage, dead-end jobs. Furthermore, the distinction between sectoral characteristics and sectoral growth patterns is crucial: Backward sectors such as downgraded manufacturing or low-wage service occupations can be part of major growth trends in a highly developed economy. It is often assumed that backward sectors express decline trends. Similarly, there is a tendency to assume that advanced industries, such as finance, have mostly good, white-collar jobs, when in fact they also have a significant share of low-paying jobs, from cleaners to stock clerks.

It is easy to think of finance and specialized services as a matter of expertise rather than of production. High-level business services, from accounting to decision-making expertise, are not usually analyzed in terms of their production processes. Insufficient attention has gone to the actual array of jobs, from high paying to low paying, involved in the production of these services. The production process itself, moreover, includes a variety of workers and firms not usually thought of as part of the information economy—notably, secretaries, maintenance workers, and truckers. These jobs are also key components of the service economy. No matter how high a place a city occupies in the new transnational hierarchies, it will have a significant share of low-wage jobs, often viewed as irrelevant in an advanced information economy, when they are actually an integral component.

There have been transformations in the forms of organizing manufacturing, with a growing presence of small-batch production, high product differentiation, and rapid changes in output. These elements have promoted subcontracting and the use of flexible ways of organizing production, both of which can be found in advanced or in backward industries. Such ways of organizing production assume distinct forms in the labor market, in the components of labor demand, and in the conditions under which labor is employed. Indications of these changes are the decline of unions in manufacturing, the loss of various contractual protections, and the increase of involuntary part-time and temporary work and other forms of contingent labor. An extreme indication of this downgrading is the growth of sweatshops and industrial homework. The expansion of a downgraded manufacturing sector partly involves the same industries that used to have largely organized plants and reasonably well-paid jobs, but it replaces these with different forms of production and organization of the work process, such as piecework and industrial homework. But it also involves new kinds of activity associated with the new major growth trends. The possibility for manufacturers to develop alternatives to the organized factory becomes particularly significant in growth sectors. The consolidation of a downgraded manufacturing sector—whether through social or technical transformation—can be seen as a politico-economic response to the growing average wages and militancy in the 1960s and early 1970s in a growing number of countries.

New types of labor market segmentation began to emerge in the 1980s. Two characteristics stand out. One is a shift of some labor market functions and costs to households and communities. The second one is the weaker role of the firm in structuring the employment relation; more is now left to the market. The first is particularly evident in the immigrant community. But it is part possibly of a more generalized pattern that deserves further research (see Sassen 1995). There is a large body of evidence showing that once one or a few immigrant workers are hired in a given workplace, they will bring in other members from their communities as job openings arise. There is also evidence showing great willingness on the part of immigrant workers to help those they bring in with some training on the job, teaching the language, and just generally socializing them into the job and workplace. This amounts to a displacement of traditional labor market functions such as recruitment, screening, and training from the labor market and the firm to the community or household. This displacement of labor market functions to the community or household raises the responsibility and the costs for workers of participating in the labor force, even if these costs are often not monetized.[1] These are all subjects that require new research given the transitions we are living through.

As for the weaker role of the firm in organizing the employment relation, it takes on many different forms. One is the declining weight of internal labor markets in structuring employment. This corresponds both to the shrinking weight of vertically integrated firms and the restructuring of labor demand in many firms toward bipolarity—a demand for highly specialized and educated workers alongside a demand for basically unskilled workers whether for clerical work, services, industrial services, or production jobs. The shrinking demand for intermediate levels of skill and training has in turn reduced the need and advantages for firms of having internal labor markets with long promotion lines that function as training-on-the-job mechanisms. The decentralization of the large, vertically integrated manufacturing firms, including the offshoring of parts of the production process, has contributed to the decline in the share of unionized shops, the deterioration of wages, and the expansion of sweatshops and industrial homework. This process includes the downgrading of jobs within existing industries and the job-supply patterns of some of the new industries, notably electronics assembly. The recomposition in household consumption patterns particularly evident in large cities contributes to a different organization of work from that prevalent in large, standardized establishments. This difference in the organization of work is evident in both the retail and the production phases. High-income gentrification generates a demand for goods and services that are frequently not mass-produced or sold through mass outlets. Customized production, small runs, specialty items, and fine food dishes are generally produced through labor-intensive methods and sold through small, full-service outlets. Subcontracting part of this production to low-cost operations, as well as sweatshops or households, is common. The overall outcome for the job supply and the range of firms involved in this production and delivery is rather different from that characterizing the large department stores and supermarkets where standardized products and services are prevalent, and hence acquisition from large, standardized factories located outside the city or the region are the norm. Proximity to stores is of far greater importance with customized producers. Further, unlike customized production and delivery, mass production and mass distribution outlets facilitate unionizing.

The observed changes in the occupational and earnings distribution are outcomes not only of industrial shifts but also of changes in the organization of firms and of labor markets. There has been a strengthening of differences within major sectors, notably within services. One set of service industries tends toward growing capital–labor ratios, growing productivity, and intensive use of the most advanced technologies; and the other, toward continued labor intensity and low wages. Median earnings and median educational levels are also increasingly divergent for each of these subsectors. These characteristics in each set of industries contribute to a type of cumulative causation within each set: The first group of industries experiences pressures toward even higher capital–labor ratios and productivity levels, given high wages; while in the second group of industries, low wages are a deterrent toward greater use of capital-intensive technologies, and low productivity leads to even more demand for very-low-wage workers. These conditions in turn contribute to reproduce the difference in profit-making capacities embedded in each of these subsectors.

Finally, what I call urban manufacturing (see Mitchell and Sassen 1996) remains a crucial economic sector in all of these economies, even when more traditional forms of manufacturing may have ceased to be so in some of these cities. Manufacturing in a city like New York ranges from apparel production for the fashion industry to woodwork and metal making for architects, furniture designers, and other design industries. Such leading cultural industries as theater and opera demand significant inputs from manufacturing for costumes and stage sets. I define urban manufacturing as a kind of manufacturing that (1) inverts the traditional relationship of manufacturing and services, in that this is manufacturing that services service industries, and (2) needs an urban location because (a) that is where its demand is located, (b) its production process is deeply networked in terms of suppliers and subcontractors, and (c) it typically requires rather fast turnover times and much detailed consulting and checking with the customer. At the level of policy, urban manufacturing is typically not receiving the kind of support and recognition it needs in order to survive in today's urban economies dominated by high-profit-making firms. Yet, a strong urban manufacturing sector is necessary for many of today's key service industries.

Finally, two rather contrasting components of advanced service-based urban economies that characterize all global cities are the so-called cultural sector and a new type of informal economy. Beginning in the 1980s and taking off in the late 1990s the so-called cultural industries saw raped growth (Clark 2003; Lloyd 2005; Florida 2004, 2006). Although these have long played a critical role in major cities around the world, what happened during the last decade is a sort of industrializing of culture and an expansion of the designation of the economics involved. The development of conference and entertainment complexes is one case in point. Festivals of all kinds are another growth sector. Even street performers are now seen as value-adding and licensed in a growing number of cities. The notion of creative cities is the latest addition: It encompasses not only this mix of cultural and entertainment industries but also the fact that the growing specialized service industries employ increasingly talented creative people who in turn want culturally developed cities to live and work in. There is today a vast literature on these issues, among which the volume by Zukin (2005) stands out (but see also Florida 2006). The best work in this field, combining the notion of "creative industries" with a critical political economy, is Lloyd's book on neo-bohemias (2005). Two features of this cultural turning of cities are the emergence of cities as tourism destinations (Fainstein and Judd 1999) and as informal spaces for cultural work (Lloyd 2005). As more and more people live in suburbs and in small towns, large complex cities become a form of exotic landscape. A growing number of tourists want to go to a city not simply for its museums or antiquities but also to experience what might be called *urban exotica*—the punk scene, the mix of people from all over the world, the latest brand-name architecture, and street performers, to name just a few. The current vigor of informal cultural work in cities—parades, street performance, and the theatricalization of politics—is a whole subject unto itself. What matters for the purposes of this book is that these transformations in the world of the political also contribute to the experience of a renaissance in cities.

The Informal Economy

A good part of the downgraded manufacturing sector is an instance of the informalization of a growing range of economic activities in today's large cities. Although such informal sectors are thought to emerge only in global South cities, rapid growth of informal work is happening in most major cities in highly developed countries, from New York and Los Angeles to Paris and Amsterdam (Portes, Castells, and Benton 1989; Renooy 1984; Sassen 1998, chap. 8; WIACT 1993; Komlosy et al. 1997). Although this is a controversial subject because there are no definitive data, several detailed field studies in major cities of developed countries are providing important insights into the scale and dynamics of the informal economy. See the studies by Lazzarato (1997), Peraldi and Perrin (1996), Komlosy et al. (1997), Tabak and Chrichlow (2000), Martin (1997), Russell and Rath 2002, to name but a few that have detailed field studies on the informal economy in advanced economies.

Two spheres need to be distinguished for the circulation of goods and services produced in the informal economy. One sphere circulates internally and mostly meets the demands of its members, such as small immigrant-owned shops in the immigrant community; the other circulates through the "formal" sector of the economy. In this second sphere, informalization represents a direct profit-maximizing strategy, one that can operate through subcontracting, the use of sweatshops and homework, or direct acquisition of goods or services. All these options also raise the flexibility for contractors.

Informalization tends to downgrade manufacturing work and, perhaps increasingly, also to downgrade mass-consumer services, whether public or private. But it also contributes to lowering the costs of high-priced goods and services for non-mass-consumer markets.

The combination of several trends particularly evident in major cities provides inducements to informalization: (1) the increased demand for high-priced, customized services and products by the expanding high-income population; (2) the increased demand for extremely low-cost services and products by the expanding low-income population; (3) the demand for customized services and goods or limited runs from firms that are either final or intermediate buyers, a trend that also leads to the growth of subcontracting; (4) the increasing inequality in the bidding power of different types of firms in a context of acute pressures on land because of the rapid growth and strong agglomeration patterns of the leading industries; and (5) the continuing demand by various firms and sectors of the population—including demand from leading industries and high-income workers—for goods and services typically produced in firms with low profit rates that find it increasingly difficult to survive aboveground, given rising rents and production costs and multiple regulations.

The transformation of final and intermediate consumption and the growing inequality in the bidding power of firms and households create inducements for informalization in a broad range of activities and spheres of the economy. The existence of an informal economy in turn emerges as a mechanism for reducing costs, even in the case of firms and households that do not need it for survival, and for providing flexibility in instances where this is essential or advantageous (Sassen 1998, chap. 8).

The Earnings Distribution in a Service-Dominated Economy

What is the impact that these various shifts have had on the earnings distribution and income structure in a service-dominated economy? A growing body of studies on the occupational and earnings distribution in service industries finds that services produce a larger share of low-wage jobs than does manufacturing, although the latter may increasingly be approaching parity with services; moreover, several major service industries also produce a larger share of jobs in the highest-paid occupations (Economic Policy Institute 2005b; Munger 2002; Goldsmith and Blakely 1992; Harrison and Bluestone 1988; Nelson and Lorence 1985; Sheets, Nord, and Phelps 1987; Silver 1984; Stanback and Noyelle 1982).

Much scholarly attention has been focused on the importance of manufacturing in reducing income inequality in the 1950s and 1960s (Blumberg 1981; Stanback et al. 1981). Central reasons typically identified for this effect are the greater productivity and higher levels of unionization found in manufacturing. Clearly, however, these studies tend to cover a period largely characterized by such conditions. Since the 1970s, the organization of jobs in manufacturing has undergone pronounced transformation. In what was at the time a major breakthrough and the most detailed analysis of occupational and industry data, Harrison and Bluestone (1988) found that earnings in manufacturing in the 1980s were lower than in the preceding two decades in many industries and occupations. This type of analysis has not been replicated with more updated data sets. Glickman and Glasmeier (1989) found that a majority of manufacturing jobs in the Sunbelt during the high-growth years of the 1970s and 1980s were low wage, and Fernandez-Kelly and Sassen (1992) found growth of sweatshops and homework and declining wages in several industry branches in New York and Los Angeles in the late 1980s.

A considerable number of studies with a strong theoretical bent (Hill 1989; Lipietz 1988; Massey 1984; Sassen 1988; Scott and Storper 1986) argue that the declining centrality of mass production in national growth and the shift to services as the leading economic sector contributed to the demise of a broader set of arrangements. In the post–World War II period, the economy functioned according to a dynamic that transmitted the benefits accruing to the core manufacturing industries onto more peripheral sectors of the economy. The benefits of price and market stability and increases in productivity could be transferred to a secondary set of firms, including suppliers and subcontractors, but also to less directly related industries, for example through the consumption of high-wage factory workers. Although there was still a vast array of firms and workers that did not benefit from this shadow effect, their number was probably at a minimum in the postwar period. By the early 1980s, the wage-setting power of leading manufacturing industries had fallen sharply (see generally Exhibits 6.4 and 6.5).

Scholarship on the impact of services on the income structure of cities is only now beginning to emerge for most countries. Several detailed analyses of the social impact of service growth in major metropolitan areas in the United States for the period of the shift of concern here are worth discussing (Fainstein et al. 1992; Nelson and Lorence 1985; Ross and Trachte 1983; Sheets et al. 1987; Stanback and Noyelle 1982). Sheets et al. (1987) found that from 1970 to 1980 several service industries had a significant effect on the growth of underemployment, which they define as employment paying below poverty-level wages in the 199 largest metropolitan areas. The strongest effect was associated with the growth of producer services and retail trade. The highest relative contribution resulted from what the authors call "corporate services" (FIRE [finance, insurance, and real estate], business services, legal services, membership organizations, and professional services), such that a 1% increase in employment in these services was found to result in a 0.37% increase in full-time, year-round, low-wage jobs. Furthermore, a 1% increase in distributive services resulted in a 0.32% increase in full-time, year-round, low-wage jobs. In contrast, a 1% increase in personal services was found to result in a 0.13% increase in such full-time jobs and a higher share of part-time, low-wage jobs. The retail industry had the highest effect on the creation of part-time, year-round, low-wage jobs, such that a 1% increase in retail employment was found to result in a 0.88% increase in such jobs.

But what about the impact of services on the expansion of high-income jobs? Nelson and Lorence (1985) examined this question using census data on the 125 largest urban areas. To establish why male earnings are more unequal in metropolises with high levels of service-sector employment, they measured the ratio of median earnings over the 5th percentile to identify the difference in earnings between the least affluent and the median metropolitan male earners; and they measured the ratio at the 95th percentile to establish the gap between median and affluent earners. Overall, they found that inequality in the 125 areas appeared to be the result of greater earnings disparity between the highest and the median earners than between the median and the lowest earners (Nelson and Lorence 1985:115). Furthermore, they found that the strongest effect came from the producer services and that the next strongest was far weaker (social services in 1970 and personal services in 1980). What had been only dimly perceived and discarded by many as measurement quirks became a full-blown reality in the 1990s. By 2003, these trends were still continuing. The growth in the share of income going to the top fifth of families in the United States grew, while other sectors of the population lost share (see Exhibit 6.3); average hourly wages of workers with top levels of education grew while those of workers with lower levels fell (see Exhibits 6.4 and 6.5); and household income grew increasingly unequal (see Exhibit 6.6).

These trends also hold to variable extents for other major cities. For example, the occupational composition of residents in central Tokyo has undergone considerable change. There has been a marked tendency for growing numbers of upper-level professional workers and low-level workers to live in central cities: Sonobe (1993) found that the share of the former grew from 20% of all workers in 1975 to more than 23% in 1985, and (although difficult to measure) the numbers of low-wage legal and undocumented

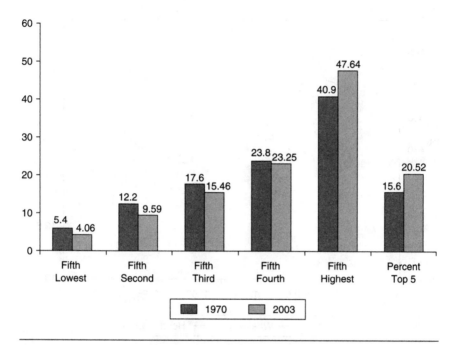

Exhibit 6.3   Share of Aggregate Income Received by Each Fifth and Top 5% of Families in the United States, 1970 and 2003 (percentage)

Source: Based on the U.S. Bureau of the Census (2004a).

immigrants also grew, up to that time, and certainly have grown sharply since then. The share of middle-level workers, however, fell: For example, the share of skilled workers fell from 16% in 1975 to 12% in 1985. Similar patterns hold for other areas of the city (Sonobe 1993). The total size of the resident workforce stayed the same, at about 4.3 million in 1975 and in 1985. The sharp growth of high-income professional and managerial jobs in the second half of the 1980s and again in the late 1990s further reinforced this trend.

Gottschalk and Smeeding (1997) have reviewed the research on earnings trends taking off in the 1980s across developed countries and find four facts: (1) Almost all industrial economies experienced some increase in wage inequality among prime aged men in the 1980s, with Germany and Italy the exceptions; (2) there are large differences across countries, with the United States and the United Kingdom showing the sharpest inequality in earnings and Europe's Nordic countries the least; (3) the increasing demand for more skilled workers, coupled with the differences across countries in the growth in the supply of skilled workers, explains a large part of differences in trends

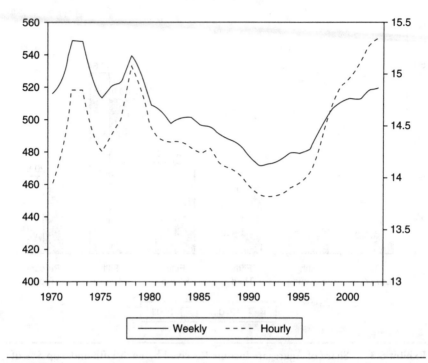

Exhibit 6.4   Real Average Weekly and Hourly Earnings of Production and
Nonsupervisory Workers in the United States, 1970–2003
(2003 US$)

Notes: Values are adjusted for inflation using the CPI-U-RS deflator.

Production and nonsupervisory workers account for more than 80% of wage and salary
employment.

Source: Economic Policy Institute (2005b, Table 2.4). Reprinted with permission from the
Economic Policy Institute, www.epinet.org.
(Analysis of U.S. Bureau of the Census Current Population Survey data described in Appendix
B of the publication)

and returns to education and experience, but it does not explain the whole
difference; and (4) institutional constraints on wages also seem to matter.
The fact that there was not a relative increase in unemployment among the
least skilled in countries with centralized wage-setting institutions suggests
that these institutions helped to limit the rise of inequality. In the 1990s, the
United States and the United Kingdom stand out among all developed
countries as showing the most pronounced increase in inequality (OECD
1996:63).

A second group showed substantial increases but not as sharp as those
in the United States: Canada, Australia, and Israel. Small changes over the

Exhibit 6.5   Average Real Hourly Wages of All Workers by Education in the
United States, 1973–2003 (2003 US$)

Year	Less than High School	High School	Some College	College	Advanced Degree
1973	$11.83	$13.56	$14.60	$19.77	$23.90
1974	11.56	13.17	14.15	19.10	24.29
1975	11.24	13.10	14.12	18.96	24.26
1976	11.45	13.23	14.23	18.90	23.59
1977	11.51	13.10	13.92	18.67	23.53
1978	11.62	13.44	14.42	19.09	24.00
1979	12.07	13.55	14.48	18.99	23.19
1980	11.71	13.11	14.20	18.70	22.74
1981	11.45	12.96	14.05	18.76	22.61
1982	11.21	12.97	14.05	19.01	23.24
1983	11.01	12.83	13.96	19.14	23.72
1984	10.91	12.78	14.05	19.40	24.23
1985	10.83	12.85	14.22	19.73	24.76
1986	10.90	13.00	14.52	20.35	25.64
1987	10.73	13.01	14.54	20.74	26.09
1988	10.73	13.06	14.48	20.80	26.37
1989	10.38	12.65	14.20	19.91	25.68
1990	10.17	12.48	14.25	20.12	25.82
1991	10.04	12.51	14.20	19.90	26.22
1992	9.95	12.43	14.05	20.24	25.74
1993	9.84	12.43	14.06	20.25	26.04
1994	9.66	12.58	14.02	20.56	27.32
1995	9.39	12.42	13.89	20.61	27.19
1996	9.37	12.37	13.91	20.40	27.16
1997	9.40	12.60	14.21	21.03	27.41
1998	9.76	12.85	14.49	21.91	27.80
1999	9.75	13.04	14.70	22.46	28.93
2000	9.76	13.13	14.93	22.93	29.00
2001	9.87	13.31	15.17	23.42	29.21
2002	10.04	13.51	15.25	23.46	29.94
2003	10.12	13.57	15.23	23.44	29.58

Note: Values are adjusted for inflation using the CPI-U-X1 deflator.

Source: Economic Policy Institute (2005b, Table 2.17). Reprinted with permission from the Economic Policy Institute, www.epinet.org.

(Analysis of U.S. Bureau of the Census Current Population Survey data described in Appendix B of the publication)

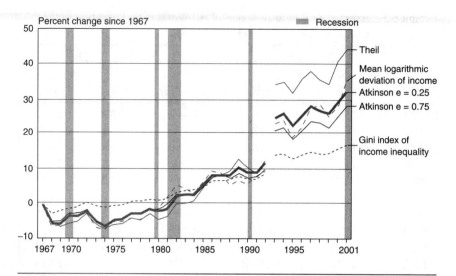

Exhibit 6.6   Index of Change for Various Measures of Household Income
Inequality, 1967–2001

Note: Because of changes in data collection methodology, 1992 and earlier estimates of
income inequality are not comparable with those for 1993 and beyond. (See *Current
Population Reports,* Series P60-204, "The Changing Shape of the Nation's Income
Distribution: 1947–1998" for more details.)

Source: U.S. Bureau of the Census (2004b, Fig. 3).

period were evident in Japan, France, the Netherlands, Sweden, and Finland,
though inequality began rising more sharply toward the end of the 1980s.
Many of the Nordic countries started from a very low level of inequality,
thus making its increase far less evident than in the United States. Thus what
we are seeing are diverse outcomes but all going in the same general direc-
tion of growing earnings inequality. While the absolute decline at the bottom of the earnings distribution holds almost exclusively for the United
States, even where no absolute declines are evident there were relative
declines in some countries, notably Japan and the United Kingdom (OECD
1993, Table 5.2). A recent study of 25 developed and developing nations
showed all but one country rising in equality from the late 1980s to the late
1990s. Furthermore, in 15 of the 25, inequality rose by more than 7%
through those years, with two of those 15 rising by more than 15% (New
Zealand and the Czech Republic). This same study reveals that while average incomes were generally rising across these nations, since 1973 the
incomes of the top 5th percentile have risen by nearly 50%, while the bottom 5th's have declined by approximately 4% (Smeeding 2002).

In many OECD (Organization for Economic Cooperation and Development) countries large shares of workers are covered by collective bargaining and the centralization of wage setting. This explains part of the difference in the degree of increases in inequality. The lower income segments are especially likely not to be allowed to fall through some basic safety net level, unlike what is the case in the United States. This means that in the United States the bottom 10% actually wind up with lower living standards than the bottom 10% in the other 14 developed countries, even though the latter have a lower median than that of the United States. Even countries whose median is only about 70% of the U.S. median have a better standard of living in the bottom percentile than the United States.

The growth in earnings inequality evident at the national level in the United States is fully evident in the New York area. From 1979 to 1996, earnings inequality in the New York–New Jersey region grew by more than 50%, notwithstanding the strong growth of the second half of the 1990s (Brauer, Khan, and Miranda 1998), a figure we arrive at by using the top and bottom percentiles for year-round, full-time workers, both men and women. Full-time, year-round male workers ages 25 to 64 in the 90th percentile saw a 26% increase in real earnings from 1979 to 1996 (from $63,700 to $80,000), while earnings of those at the 10th percentile fell by 21% (from $19,000 to $15,000). The trend was similar for women with a gain from $39,300 to $54,000 at the top and a loss from $13,200 to $12,300 at the bottom. These gains at the 90th percentile were sharper than the 10% gain for the country. Between 1989 and 1996, total declines in earnings for full-time male workers at the 10th percentile were nearly double the nation's, while those at the top rose much faster than the nation's. The higher degree of inequality in the New York City (NYC) area is due largely to the financial-services industry. It pushed earnings in the top percentile higher. From 1989 to 1996, earnings at the 90th percentile grew by 8%, compared with 0.6% in the country as a whole. In that same period, earnings at the 10th percentile fell by 27% in the NYC region, compared with 7.8% for the country as a whole. Recent data show 34% of NYC families having annual incomes under $12,000, compared with the national average of only 16%. Manhattan also has the highest income disparity of all 3,200 counties in the United States (see Brauer et al. 1998; Orr and Rosen 2000; Nepomnyaschy and Garfinkel 2002; Beveridge 2003).

In the United States, much of the decline in the relative economic well-being of the least skilled has taken the form of collapsing real wages. Gottschalk and Smeeding (1997) describe who lost and who gained from 1973 to 1994: 78% of male workers in 1994 earned less than their counterparts in 1973. The growth in inequality in this period was driven in large part by this decline in real earnings of workers with the least education. The real weekly earnings of college graduates increased by 5%, while that of high school grads declined by 20%. Robert Topel (1997:57) offers another angle: Indexed to 1969, real wages at the 90th percentile (high-wage workers) rose slightly, but fell substantially at the 50th percentile, and collapsed at the bottom of the distribution—the bottom 10th percentile. "As a measure of inequality, then, the 90–10 wage differential among American men expanded by a startling 49 percent in 26 years, with over two-thirds of this gap attributable to a decline in real wages among those in the 10th percentile." Several studies estimate that the decline in the real minimum wage accounts for 30% of the increase in earning inequality (Fortin and Lemieux 1997). According to Gordon (1996:206), the most important factor has to do with management's decisions and practices. Estimates of the impact of unions put their decline at 20% of the increase in male earnings inequality, but for little in that of women (Freeman 1994; Fortin and Lemieux 1997). Economic growth since the mid-1990s has helped raise real wages for all quintiles back above their 1970s levels (e.g., Exhibit 6.4), but this recovery has not been a balanced one; from 1992 to 2003, the incomes of those in the 90th percentile rose 40.8%, compared with the 10th percentile's 12.6%. "These more aggregate statistics have also been suggestive of increasing inequality, as a larger-than-usual share of national income took the form of non-labor income (e.g., investment income and profits) that tend to accrue to those at the upper end of the wealth scale" (Economic Policy Institute 2005a).

The Restructuring of Urban Consumption

The rapid growth of industries with a strong concentration of high- and low-income jobs has assumed distinct forms in the consumption structure, which in turn has a feedback effect on the organization of work and the types of jobs being created. In the United States, the expansion of the high-income work-force in conjunction with the emergence of new cultural forms has led to a process of high-income gentrification that rests, in the last analysis, on the availability of a vast supply of low-wage workers. High-income gentrification is labor-intensive, in contrast to the typical middle-class suburb that represents a capital-intensive process: tract housing, road and highway construction, dependence on private automobiles or commuter trains, marked reliance on appliances and household equipment of all sorts, and large shopping malls. Directly and indirectly, high-income gentrification replaces much of this capital intensity with workers. Similarly, high-income residents in the city depend to a much larger extent on hired maintenance staff than does the middle-class suburban home, with its concentrated input of family labor and machinery.

City	0	2	4	6	8
Oslo					
Milan					
Copenhagen					
Stockholm					
Rome					
Sydney					
London					
Helsinki					
Prague					
Amsterdam					
Lugano					
Dublin					
Miami					
Geneva					
Basel					
Chicago					
Toronto					
Warsaw					
Auckland					
Zurich					
New York					
Los Angeles					
Lagos					
Ljubljana					
Barcelona					
Lisbon					
Frankfurt					
Vienna					
Brussels					
Hong Kong					
Tokyo					
Sofia					
Montreal					
Berlin					
Athens					
Tallinn					
Moscow					
Mexico City					
Madrid					
Taipei					
Bratislava					
Luxembourg					
Tel Aviv					
Singapore					
Budapest					
Riga					
Mumbai					
Vilnius					
Paris					
Kiev					
Manila					
Istanbul					
Kuala Lumpur					
Dubai					
Lima					
São Paulo					
Jakarta					
Buenos Aires					
Nairobi					
Seoul					
Bangkok					
Santiago de Chile					
Johannesburg					
Shanghai					
Manama					
Bucharest					
Caracas					
Karachi					
Rio de Janeiro					
Bogotá					

Ratio of net pay between:

▓ Highly and low-qualified occupations

■ Highly and medium-qualified occupations

Methodology

In order to study country-specific and city-specific pay differentials, the 13 occupations in the study were divided into three income categories. The lowest of these includes occupations that require no qualifications above and beyond statutory schooling, examples being factory workers and building laborers. The middle category includes occupations that require a higher level of training or an apprenticeship, such as car mechanics and skilled staff, while the top category is reserved for graduates and/or people with many years' experience like department heads and product managers.

Note

In the low-ranked cities, a product manager or head of department's gross earnings are seven to nine times as much as a construction or factory worker's. In high-ranked cities, higher paid staff gross earnings are at most double or triple those of low-wage workers.

Exhibit 6.7   Income Disparities by City, 2003

Source: Union Bank of Switzerland (2003:31).

Although far less dramatic than in large cities in the United States, the elements of these patterns are also evident in major Western European cities, Latin American cities, and, increasingly, Asian cities (e.g., Roulleau-Berger 1999; Schiffer Ramos 2002; Parnreiter 2002). The growth of the high-income population in the resident and commuting workforce has contributed to changes in the organization of the production and delivery of consumer goods and services. Behind the delicatessens and specialty boutiques that have replaced many self-service supermarkets and department stores lies a very different organization of work from that prevalent in large, standardized establishments. This difference in the organization of work is evident in both the retail and the production phases (Gershuny and Miles 1983; Sassen 1998, chaps. 7, 8). High-income gentrification generates a demand for goods and services that are frequently not mass produced or sold through mass outlets. Customized production, small runs, specialty items, and fine food dishes are generally produced through labor-intensive methods and sold through small, full-service outlets. Subcontracting part of this production to low-cost operations and to sweatshops or households is common. The overall outcome for the job supply and the range of firms involved in this production and delivery differ from that characterizing the large department stores and supermarkets—through Wal-Mart has launched a new phase combining mass production, large standardized factories located outside of the region, and no unionization of workers. Proximity to stores is of far greater importance with customized producers, while historically mass-production and mass-distribution outlets have facilitated unionizing (see Sayer and Walker 1992; Munger 2002).

The pronounced expansion of the high-income workers stratum in major cities and their high levels of spending contribute to this outcome. All major cities have long had a core of wealthy residents or commuters. By itself, however, this core of wealthy people could not have created the large-scale residential and commercial gentrification in the city. As a stratum, the new high-income workers are to be distinguished from this core of wealthy residents. Their disposable income is generally not enough to make them into major investors. It is, however, sufficient for a significant expansion in the demand for highly priced goods and services—that is, to create a sufficiently large demand so as to ensure economic viability for the producers and providers of such goods and services. Furthermore, the level of disposable income is also a function of lifestyle and demographic patterns, such as postponing having children and larger numbers of two-earner households.

The expansion in the low-income population has also contributed to the proliferation of small operations and the move away from large-scale standardized factories and large chain stores for low-price goods. In good part, the consumption needs of the low-income population are met by manufacturing and retail establishments that are small, rely on family labor, and often fall below minimum safety and health standards. Cheap, locally produced sweatshop garments, for example, can compete with low-cost Asian imports. A growing number of products and services ranging from low-cost furniture made in basements to "gypsy cabs" and family day care is available to meet the demand for the growing low-income population (see Komlosy et al. 1997; Russell and Rath 2002; Sassen 1998, chap. 8).

There are many instances of how the increased inequality in earnings reshapes the consumption structure and how this reshaping in turn has feedback effects on the organization of work. Some examples are the creation of a special taxi line for Wall Street that services only the financial district and an increase of gypsy cabs in low-income neighborhoods not serviced by regular cabs; the increase in highly customized woodwork in gentrified areas and low-cost informal rehabilitation in poor neighborhoods; the increase of homeworkers and sweatshops making either very expensive designer items for boutiques or very cheap products.

Conclusion: A Widening Gap

Developments in cities cannot be understood in isolation from fundamental changes in the larger organization of advanced economies. The combination of economic, political, and technical forces that has contributed to the decline of mass production as the central driving element in the economy brought about a decline in a broader institutional framework that shaped the employment relation. The group of service industries that were one of the driving economic forces beginning in the 1980s, and continue as such today, is characterized by greater earnings and occupational dispersion, weak unions, and a growing share of casualized low-wage jobs along with a growing share of high-income jobs. The associated institutional framework shaping the employment relation diverges from that of the growth period of mass manufacturing: Today, there are more part-time and temporary jobs and generally fewer protections and fringe benefits for growing portions of the workforce. These changes in the employment relation have contributed to reshaping the sphere of social reproduction and consumption, which in turn has a feedback effect on economic organization and earnings. Whereas in the earlier period this feedback effect contributed to expanding and reproducing the middle class, currently it reproduces growing earnings disparity, labor market casualization, and consumption restructuring along high- and low-end markets. A good fifth of the residents in major cities are part of a new high-income professional stratum that contributes to high-income consumption and customized production and services.

The greater intensity of these diverse trends in major cities than in medium-size towns results from at least three conditions. First is the concentration of major growth sectors with either sharp earnings dispersion or disproportionate concentration of either low- or high-paying jobs in major cities. Second is the proliferation of small, low-cost service operations made possible by the massive concentration of people in such cities, in addition to a large daily inflow of nonresident workers and tourists. The ratio between the number of these service operations and the resident population is probably significantly higher in a very large city than in an average-size city. Further, the large concentration of people in major cities tends to create intense inducements to open up such operations, as well as intense competition and very marginal returns. Under such conditions, the cost of labor is crucial, and hence the likelihood of a high concentration of low-wage jobs increases. Third, for these same reasons together with other components of demand, the relative size of the downgraded manufacturing sector and the informal economy tends to be larger in big cities such as New York or Los Angeles than in average-size cities.

The overall result is a tendency toward increased economic polarization. Looking at polarization in the use of land, the organization of labor markets, the housing market, and the consumption structure, I do not necessarily mean that the middle class is disappearing. I am rather referring to a dynamic whereby growth contributes to inequality rather than to expansion of the middle class, as was the case in the middle of the century and into the 1970s in the United States and even into the 1980s in several of the developed countries. In many of these cities, the middle class represents a significant share of the population and hence represents an important channel through which income and lifestyle coalesce into a social form. But as the growth dynamics of new or newly reorganized economic sectors become more and more prevalent, the core of the middle class will continue to thin out, as the sectors that ensure its reproduction are a smaller part of developed economies.

The middle class in the United States is a very broad category. It contains prosperous segments of various recent immigrant populations as well as established ethnic communities in large cities. Beginning in the 1980s, certain segments of the middle class gained income and earnings, thus becoming wealthier, while others became poorer. In the 1990s, these trends also became evident in major cities of the global South—whether São Paulo, Mumbai, or Shanghai. In brief, the middle class has become segmented in a way that has a sharper upward and downward slant than has been the case in other periods. The argument put forth here is that while the middle strata still constitute the majority, the conditions that contributed to their expansion and politico-economic power—the centrality of mass production and mass consumption in economic growth and profit realization—have been displaced by new sources of growth. This is not simply a quantitative transformation; here are the elements for a new economic regime.

The growth of service employment in cities, including advanced services, and the evidence of the associated growth of inequality raise questions about how fundamental a change this shift entails. Several of these questions concern the nature of service-based urban economies. The observed changes in the occupational and earnings distribution are outcomes not only of industrial shifts but also of changes in the organization of firms and of labor markets in both old and new sectors. There is considerable articulation of firms, sectors, and workers that may appear to have little connection to an urban economy dominated by finance and specialized services but in fact fulfill a series of functions that are an integral part of advanced service based urban economies. They do so, however, under conditions of sharp social, earnings, and often racial or ethnic segmentation.

Note

1. There is an interesting parallel here with the earlier analysis in Gershuny and Miles (1983) showing that one of the components of the service economy is the shift of tasks traditionally performed by the firm onto the household: for example, furniture and even appliances sold unassembled to be put together by the buyer.

7

Global Cities and
Global Survival Circuits

A lthough this whole book is an effort to recover the meaning of place
and of multiple diverse social groups in constituting globalization, it is
important to emphasize that this is not part of today's dominant account
about the global economy in media and policy circles, nor of much academic
research. Key concepts in that dominant account—global information economy, instant communication, electronic markets—all suggest that place no
longer matters and that the only type of worker that matters is the highly
educated professional. This account privileges the capability for global transmission over the material structures and work processes necessary for such
transmission. In this type of account, immigrant workers belong to older,
backward histories, not to the present; it cannot even incorporate the global
migration of maids and nannies, so clearly connected to the new high-
income professionals in global cities. From the dominant perspective, this
migration of maids and nannies has little to do with global cities: These are
just women deciding to take a go at it. Their migrations and the jobs they do
once they get there supposedly, then, tell us little about economic globalization. Further, many of these migrations existed long before the current phase
of economic globalization.

This chapter examines the possible links between particular features of
globalization and particular components of international migration that are
especially evident in global cities. It will examine whether the conditions and

dynamics brought on by globalization are altering or reinscribing often old histories of migration, as well as generating new ones. There are two distinct issues here: One is whether globalization has enabled older processes that used to be national or regional to become global, and the other is whether it has produced new conditions and dynamics. Given the enormous variety of migrations and the places where they wind up, the chapter will focus on one specific issue as a way of understanding the intersection of migration and globalization in cities: the global migration and trafficking of maids, nannies, nurses, and sex workers that has risen sharply since the 1990s and has vastly expanded its geography.

One way of formulating this sharply has been provided by Ehrenreich and Hochschild (2003): the current migration and trafficking of women for jobs that used to be part of the first-world woman's domestic role.

Women in the Global Economy

Analytically, we can anchor the current global migration of women for largely female-typed activities in two specific sets of dynamic configurations. One of these is the global city, and the other, a set of survival circuits emerging as a response to growing immiseration of governments and whole economies in the global South. Global cities are key sites for not only the specialized servicing, financing, and management of global economic processes but also the incorporation of large numbers of immigrants in activities that service the strategic sectors. This incorporation happens directly through the demand for mostly low-paid clerical and blue-collar service workers, such as janitors and repair workers. And it happens indirectly through the consumption practices of high-income professionals, which in turn generates a demand for maids and nannies as well as low-wage workers in expensive restaurants and shops. Low-wage workers get incorporated into the leading sectors. But it is a mode of incorporation that renders these workers invisible, therewith breaking the nexus between being workers in leading industries and the opportunity to become—as had been historically the case in industrialized economies—an empowered sector of the organized working class. In this sense, "women and immigrants" emerge as the systemic equivalent of the off-shore proletariat being produced via outsourcing.

The global migration of maids and nannies particularly brings out the demands placed on the top-level professional and managerial workforce in global cities: The usual modes of handling household tasks and lifestyle issues do not apply in this case. This is a type of household that could be described as the *professional household without a wife*, regardless of the fact that it may have a couple composed of man and woman, or man and man, or woman and woman, so long as they are both in demanding jobs. As a consequence, this is creating the return of the so-called serving classes in all the global cities around the world, made up largely of immigrant and migrant women (Sassen [1991] 2001, chap. 9; Hondagneu-Sotelo 2003; Parrenas 2001). Put this way, the new transnational corporate culture turns out to be partly anchored in a worl of work to which it seems unconnected. The immigrant cultures within which many of the other jobs of the global information economy take place. (See also Aguiar and Herod 2005 on janitors in the corporate sector.)

As for the second site, in the 1990s and onward, there has been a proliferation of new or renewed survival circuits built on the backs of women— as trafficked workers for low-wage jobs and the sex industry and as migrant workers—sending remittances back home. A key aspect here is that through their work and remittances, women enhance the government revenue of deeply indebted countries and offer new profit-making possibilities to quasi-entrepreneurs who have seen other opportunities vanish as a consequence of global firms and markets entering their countries or to longtime criminals who can now operate their illegal trades globally. These survival circuits are often complex, involving multiple locations and sets of actors, constituting increasingly global chains of traders and workers.

Both in the global city and in these survival circuits, women emerge as crucial actors for new and expanding types of economies. It is through these supposedly rather valueless economic actors that key components of these new economies have been built. Globalization plays a specific role here in a double sense, first, contributing to the formation of links between sending and receiving countries and, second, enabling local and regional practices to become global in scale. On the one hand, the particular dynamics that come together in the global city produce a strong demand for these types of workers, while the dynamics that mobilize women into these survival circuits produce an expanding supply of workers who can be pushed, or are sold, into those types of jobs. On the other hand, the technical infrastructure and transnationalism that underlie some of the key globalized industries are also making it possible for other types of actors to deploy their activities at global scales, whether money laundering or trafficking.[1]

Localizing the Global

Throughout this book I have argued that economic globalization entails multiple localizations, many of which do not generally get coded as having anything to do with the global economy. The global city is one of the key places for many of these localizations. Cities are a nexus where many of the new organizational tendencies of economies and societies come together in specific localized configurations. They are also the sites for a disproportionate concentration of all immigrants in the global North.

One of the localizations of the dynamics of globalization is the process of economic restructuring in global cities, which has generated a large growth in the demand for low-wage workers and jobs that offer few advancement possibilities (chapter 6). This, amid an explosion in the wealth and power concentrated in these cities—in conditions where there is also a visible expansion in high-income jobs and high-priced urban space. *Women and immigrants* emerge as the labor supply that facilitates the imposition of low wages and few benefits, even when there is high demand and these jobs are in high-growth sectors. Access to women and immigrants breaks the historic nexus that would have led to empowering workers under these conditions, and, further, it legitimates this break culturally. The demographic transition evident in such cities, where a majority of resident workers are today women—often women of color, both native and immigrant—can be understood as mediating between the new kinds of economic organization (as discussed in preceding chapters) and the chipping away of hard-earned higher wages and benefits among global North workers.

Another localization that is rarely associated with globalization is the growing informalization of an expanding range of activities briefly discussed in Chapter 6. *Informalization* reintroduces the community and the household as important economic spaces in global cities. I see informalization in this setting as the low-cost (and often feminized) equivalent of deregulation at the top of the system. As with deregulation (e.g., as in financial deregulation), informalization introduces flexibility, reduces the so-called burdens of regulation, and lowers costs, in this case especially of labor. Informalization in the cities of the global North—whether New York, London, Paris, or Berlin—can be seen as a downgrading of a variety of activities for which there is an effective and often growing demand located inside these cities. Immigrant women are important actors in the new informal economies of these cities. They absorb the costs of informalizing these activities.

Yet another important localization of the dynamics of globalization is that of the new professional women stratum. Elsewhere I have examined the impact of the growth of top-level professional women in high-income gentrification in these cities—both residential and commercial—as well as in the reurbanization of middle class family life (see Sassen [1991] 2001, chap. 9). The vast expansion in the demand for high-level professionals has brought with it a sharp increase in the employment of women in corporate professional jobs.[2] The complex and strategic character of these jobs requires long work hours and intense engagement with their jobs and work lives. This places heavy demands on their time. Urban residence is far more desirable than the suburbs, especially for single professionals or two-professional career households. As a result, high-income residential areas in global cities have expanded, creating a reurbanization of family life, insofar as these professionals want it all, including dogs and children, even if they may not have the time for either. Given demanding and time-absorbing jobs, the usual modes of handling household tasks and lifestyle are inadequate. This is the type of household that I describe as the *professional household without a "wife,"* alluded to earlier. Growing shares of household tasks are relocated to the market; they are bought directly as goods and services or indirectly through hired labor. Here is a dynamic akin to a double movement: A shift to the labor market of functions that used to be part of household work, but also a shift of what used to be labor-market functions in standardized workplaces to the household and, in the case of much informalization, to the immigrant community.[3] This reconfiguration of economic spaces associated with globalization in cities has had different impacts on women and men, on male-typed and female-typed work cultures, on male- and female-centered forms of power and empowerment.

These transformations contain possibilities, even if limited, for women's autonomy and empowerment. For example, we might ask whether the growth of informalization in advanced urban economies reconfigures some types of economic relations between men and women. With informalization, the neighborhood and the household—including both the immigrant and the high-level professional household—reemerge as sites for economic activity. This condition has its own dynamic possibilities for women. Economic downgrading through informalization creates so-called opportunities for low-income women and thus reconfigures some of the work and household hierarchies that women find themselves in. This becomes particularly clear in the case of immigrant women who come from countries with rather traditional male-centered cultures.

There is a large literature showing that immigrant women's regular wage work and improved access to other public realms has an impact on their gender relations, as it allows them to gain greater personal autonomy and independence. However, immigrant men function in a more confined sociopolitical space. Women gain more control over budgeting and other domestic decisions and greater leverage in requesting help from men in domestic chores. Also, their access to public services and other public resources gives them a chance to become incorporated in the mainstream society—and they are often the ones in the household who mediate in this process. It is likely that some women benefit more than others from these circumstances; more research is needed to establish the impact of class, education, and income on such gendered outcomes. Besides the relatively greater empowerment of women in the household associated with waged employment, there is a second important outcome: their greater participation in the public sphere and their possible emergence as public actors.

There are two arenas where immigrant women are active: institutions for public and private assistance and the immigrant/ethnic community. The incorporation of women in the migration process strengthens the settlement likelihood and contributes to greater immigrant participation in their communities and vis-à-vis the state. Immigrant women come to assume more active public and social roles, which further reinforces their status in the household and the settlement process (Hondagneu-Sotelo 1994; Mahler 1995). Women are more active in community building and community activism, and they are positioned differently from men regarding the broader economy and the state. They are the ones that are likely to have to handle the legal vulnerability of their families in the process of seeking public and social services. This greater participation by women suggests the possibility that they may emerge as more forceful and visible actors and make their role in the labor market more visible as well.

Here is, to some extent, a joining of two different dynamics in the condition of immigrant women in global cities described earlier. On the one hand, they are constituted as an invisible and disempowered class of workers in the service of the strategic sectors constituting the global economy. This invisibility keeps them from emerging as whatever would be the contemporary equivalent of the strong proletariat of earlier forms of economic organization, when workers' positions in leading sectors had the effect of empowering them. On the other hand, the access to wages and salaries (even if low), and the growing feminization of the job supply and business opportunities brought about with informalization, do alter the gender hierarchies in which they find themselves.

The Other Workers in the Advanced Corporate Economy

In the day-to-day work of the leading sectors in global cities, a large share of the jobs involved are low paid and manual, many held by immigrant women. Even the most advanced professionals will require clerical, cleaning, and repair workers for their state-of-the-art offices, and they will require truckers to bring not only the software but also the light bulbs. Although these types of workers and jobs are never represented as part of the global economy, they are in fact part of the infrastructure of jobs involved in running and implementing the global economic system, including such an advanced form of it as international finance.

As already discussed in this book, high-level corporate services, from accounting to decision-making expertise, are not usually analyzed in terms of their work process. Such services are usually seen as a type of output, that is, high-level technical knowledge. Thus, insufficient attention has gone to the actual array of jobs, from high paying to low paying, involved in the production of these services. A focus on the work process brings to the fore the labor question. Information outputs need to be produced, and the buildings that hold the workers need to be built and cleaned. The rapid growth of the financial industry and highly specialized services generates not only high-level technical and administrative jobs but also low-wage unskilled jobs. In my research on New York and other cities, I found that between 30% and 50% of the workers in the leading sectors are actually low-wage workers (Sassen [1991] 2001, chaps. 8, 9).

Further, the similarly state-of-the-art lifestyles of the professionals in these sectors have created a whole new demand for a range of household workers, particularly maids and nannies. As discussed earlier, the presence of a highly dynamic sector with a polarized income distribution has its own impact on the creation of low-wage jobs through the sphere of consumption (or, more generally, social reproduction). The rapid growth of industries with strong concentrations of high- and low-income jobs has assumed distinct forms in the consumption structure, which in turn has a feedback effect on the organization of work and the types of jobs being created. The expansion of the high-income workforce in conjunction with the emergence of new lifestyles has led to a process of high-income gentrification that rests, in the last analysis, on the availability of a vast supply of low-wage workers. High-price restaurants, luxury housing, luxury hotels, gourmet shops, boutiques, French hand laundries, and special cleaning services are all more labor-intensive than their lower price equivalents. This has reintroduced—to an extent not seen in a very long time—the whole notion of the serving classes in contemporary high-income households.[4] The immigrant woman serving the white middle-class professional woman has replaced the traditional image of the black female servant serving the white master. These trends give cities an increasingly sharp tendency toward social polarization.

The consumption needs of the growing low-income population in large cities are also increasingly met through labor-intensive rather than standardized and unionized forms of producing goods and services: manufacturing and retail establishments that are small, rely on family labor, and often fall below minimum safety and health standards. Cheap, locally produced sweatshop garments and bedding, for example, can compete with low-cost Asian imports. A growing range of products and services, from low-cost furniture made in basements to "gypsy cabs" and family day care, are available to meet the demand for the growing low-income population. There are numerous instances of how the increased inequality in earnings reshapes the consumption structure, and how this in turn has feedback effects on the organization of work, both in the formal and in the informal economy.

This disparity between the high- and low-income classes has resulted in the formation of global labor markets at the top and at the bottom of the economic system. At the bottom, much of the staffing occurs through the efforts of individuals, largely immigrants, though an expanding network of organizations is getting involved (as well as illegal traffickers, as I discuss in the second half of this chapter). For example, Kelly Services, a Fortune 500 services company in global staffing, which operates offices in 25 countries, now has added a homecare division, which provides a full range of help. It is particularly geared to people who need assistance with daily living activities but also for those who lack the time to take care of the needs of household members who in the past would have been taken care of by the mother/wife figure in the household.[5] More directly pertinent to the professional households under discussion here are a growing range of global staffing organizations whose advertised services cover various aspects of day care, including dropping off and picking up, as well as in-house tasks, from child minding to cleaning and cooking.[6] One international agency for nannies and au pairs (EF Au Pair Corporate Program) advertises directly to corporations, urging them to make the service part of their employment offers to potential employees to help them address household and child care needs. Increasingly, the emergent pattern is that the transnational professional class can access these services in the expanding network of global cities among which they are likely to circulate. (See Sassen [1991] 2001, chap. 7.) At the top of the system several major Fortune 500 global staffing companies provide firms with experts and talent for high-level professional and technical jobs. In 2001, the largest of these was the Swiss multinational Adecco, with offices in 58 countries; in 2000, it provided firms worldwide with 3 million workers. Manpower, with offices in 59 different countries, provided 2 million workers. Kelly Services, mentioned earlier, provided 750,000 employees in 2000.

Note that it is at the top and bottom of the occupational distribution that internationalization is happening; midlevel occupations, although increasingly handled through temporary employment agencies, have not internationalized their supply. The types of occupations involved at both the top and bottom are, in very different yet parallel ways, sensitive. Firms need reliable and, ideally, somewhat talented professionals, and they need them specialized but standardized, so they can use them globally. And professionals want the same in the workers they employ in their homes. The move of staffing organizations into the provision of domestic services signals both the emergence of a global labor market and efforts to standardize the service delivered by maids, nannies, and homecare nurses.

In brief, the top end of the corporate economy—the high-paid professionals and the corporate towers that project engineering expertise, precision, "techne"—is far easier to recognize as necessary for an advanced economic system than are truckers and other industrial service workers, or maids and nannies, even though all of them are necessary ingredients. Firms, sectors, and workers that may appear as though they have little connection to an urban economy dominated by finance and specialized services, can in fact be an integral part of that economy. They do so, however, under conditions of sharp social, earnings, and often gender and racial or ethnic segmentation. They become part of an increasingly dynamic and multifaceted lower circuit of global capital that partially parallels the upper circuit of professionals—the lawyers, accountants, and telecommunications experts that service global capital.

Producing a Global Supply of the New Caretakers: The Feminization of Survival

The immigrant women described in the first half of this chapter enter the migration process in many different ways (Pessar and Mahler 2003). For some, it is family reunion; others come on their own. Many features of these migration processes have little to do with globalization. Here, I am concerned with one specific set of processes that I see as deeply linked to certain features of economic globalization today. These are migrations largely organized by third parties, typically governments or illegal traffickers. These women wind up in work situations that involve a far broader range of worlds than the ones described earlier, though they also include those jobs. What they share, analytically so to speak, with the women described here, is that they also are taking over tasks previously associated with the domain of the housewife.

The last decade has seen a growing presence of women in a variety of cross-border circuits. These circuits are enormously diverse but share one feature: They are profit- or revenue-making circuits developed on the backs of the truly disadvantaged. They include the illegal trafficking in people for the sex industry and for various types of formal and informal labor markets. And they include cross-border migrations, both documented and not, which have become an important source of hard currency for governments in home countries. The formation and strengthening of these circuits is in good part a consequence of broader structural conditions. Among the key actors emerging out of these broader conditions to give shape to these particular circuits are the women themselves in search of work, but also, and increasingly so, illegal traffickers and contractors as well as governments of home countries.

I conceptualize these circuits as countergeographies of globalization. They are deeply imbricated with some of the major dynamics constitutive of globalization: the formation of global markets, the intensifying of transnational and translocal networks, and the development of communication technologies that easily escape conventional surveillance practices. The strengthening and, in some of these cases, the formation of new global circuits is embedded or made possible by the existence of a global economic system and its associated development of various institutional supports for cross-border money flows and markets.[7] These countergeographies are dynamic and changing in their locational features. They are partially in the shadow economy, yet also use some of the institutional infrastructure of the regular, even corporate economy.

Crucial to the formation of a global supply of caretakers in demand in global cities are the systemic links between the growth of these alternative circuits for survival, for profit-making, and for hard-currency earning, on the one hand, and major conditions in developing countries that are associated with economic globalization, on the other. Among these conditions are a growth in unemployment, the closure of a large number of typically small and medium-size enterprises oriented to national rather than export markets, and large, often increasing government debt. Although these economies are frequently grouped under the label *developing*, they are in some cases struggling or stagnant and even shrinking. (For the sake of briefness, I will use *developing* as shorthand for this variety of situations.) Many of these developments have produced additional responsibilities for women toward their households, as men have lost earnings opportunities and governments have cut back on social services that supported women and their family responsibilities.[8]

One way of articulating this in substantive terms is to posit that (1) the shrinking opportunities for male employment in many of these countries, (2) the shrinking opportunities for more traditional forms of profit making in these same countries as they increasingly accept foreign firms in a widening range of economic sectors and are pressured to develop export industries, and (3) the fall in revenues for the governments in many of these countries, partially linked to these conditions and to the burden of debt servicing, have (4) all contributed to raising the importance of alternative ways of making a living, making a profit, and securing government revenue.[9]

The variety of global circuits that are incorporating growing numbers of women have strengthened at a time when major dynamics linked to economic globalization have had significant impacts on developing economies, including the so-called middle-income countries of the global South. These countries have had to implement a bundle of new policies and accommodate new conditions associated with globalization: structural adjustment programs, the opening of these economies to foreign firms, the elimination of multiple state subsidies, and, it would seem almost inevitably, financial crises and the prevailing types of programmatic solutions put forth by the International Monetary Fund (IMF). It is now clear that in most of the countries involved, whether Mexico or Ukraine, Ghana or Thailand, these conditions have created enormous costs for certain sectors of the economy and of the population. Further, after 20 years of these programs, it is clear that in several of these countries these conditions have not fundamentally reduced government debt.

These conditions also play a substantial role in the lives of a growing number of women from developing or struggling economies, even when the articulations are often not self-evident or visible—a fact that has marked much of the difficulty of understanding the role of women in development generally. These are, in many ways, old conditions. What is different today is their rapid internationalization and considerable institutionalization.

One effort analytically here—paralleling the analysis on the significance of women and immigrants in the global city—is to uncover the systemic connections between, on the one hand, what are considered poor, low-earning, and low-value-added individuals, often represented as a burden rather than a resource, and on the other hand, what are emerging as significant sources for profit making, especially in the shadow economy, and for government revenue enhancement. Prostitution and labor migration are growing in importance as ways of making a living; illegal trafficking in women and children for the sex industry and in laborers are growing in importance as ways of making a profit; and the remittances sent by emigrants, as well as the organized export of workers, are increasingly important sources of revenues for some of these governments. Women make up by far the majority in prostitution and trafficking for the sex industry, and they are becoming a majority group in migration for labor. The employment and/or use of foreign-born women cover an increasingly broad range of economic sectors, some illegal and illicit (e.g., prostitution), and some in highly regulated industries (e.g., nursing). (See generally Chant and Craske 2002.)

These circuits can be thought of as indicating the, albeit partial, feminization of survival, because it is increasingly on the backs of women that these forms of making a living, making a profit, and securing government revenue are realized. Thus, in using the notion of feminization of survival, I mean not only that households and indeed whole communities are increasingly dependent on women for their survival, but also that governments are dependent on women's earnings in these various circuits, and so are types of enterprises whose ways of profit making exist at the margins of the licit economy. Finally, by using the term *circuits*, I want to underline the fact that there is a degree of institutionalization in these dynamics—they are not simply aggregates of individual actions.

Alternative Survival Circuits

It is in this context that alternative circuits of survival emerge and can be seen as articulated with more general conditions of economic decline and deeply indebted governments in the less developed world, which have been forced to make major cuts in general expenditures on health, education and development. This is a context marked by a systemic condition characterized by high unemployment, poverty, bankruptcies of large numbers of firms, and shrinking resources in the state to meet social needs. Here, I want to focus briefly on some of the issues in the trafficking of women for sex industries and for work, the growing weight of this trafficking as a profit-making option and the growing weight of emigrants' remittances in the account balance of many of the sending states.

Trafficking involves the forced recruitment and/or transportation of people within and across states for work or services through a variety of forms, all involving coercion. Trafficking is a violation of several distinct types of rights: human, civil, political. Trafficking in people appears to be mainly related to the sex market, labor markets, and illegal migration. Much legislative work has been done to address trafficking: international treaties and charters, United Nations resolutions, and various bodies and commissions.[10] Nongovernmental organizations (NGOs) are also playing an increasingly important role.[11]

As tourism has grown sharply over the last decade and become a major development strategy for cities, regions, and whole countries, the entertainment sector has seen a parallel growth and recognition as a key development strategy (Fainstein and Judd 1999; Wonders and Michalowski 2001). In many places, the sex trade is part of the entertainment industry and has grown alongside the latter. At some point, the sex trade itself has become a development strategy in areas with high unemployment and poverty and governments desperate for revenue and foreign exchange reserves. When local manufacturing and agriculture can no longer function as sources of employment, profits, and government revenue, what was once a marginal source of earnings, profits, and revenues now becomes a far more important one. The increased importance of these sectors in development generates growing tie-ins. For example, when the IMF and the World Bank see tourism as a solution to some of the growth challenges in many poor countries and provide loans for its development or expansion, they may well be contributing to develop a broader institutional setting for the expansion of the entertainment industry and indirectly of the sex trade. This tie-in with development strategies signals that there may be a sharp expansion in the trafficking in women.

The entry of organized crime in the sex trades, the formation of cross-border ethnic networks, and the growing transnationalization in so many aspects of tourism suggest that further development of a global sex industry is likely. This could mean greater attempts to enter into more and more markets and a general expansion of the industry. It is a worrisome possibility, especially in the context of growing numbers of women with few if any employment options. And such growing numbers are to be expected given high unemployment and poverty, the shrinking of a world of work opportunities that were embedded in the more traditional sectors of these economies, and the growing debt burden of governments rendering them incapable of providing social services and support to the poor.

Women in the sex industry become—in certain kinds of economies—a crucial link supporting the expansion of the entertainment industry and therefore of tourism as a development strategy, which in turn becomes a source of government revenue. These tie-ins are structural, not a function of conspiracies. Their weight in an economy will be raised by the absence or limitations of other sources for securing a livelihood, profits, and revenues for, respectively, workers, enterprises, and governments.

Conclusion

The global migration and trafficking of women is anchored in particular features of the current globalization of economies in both the North and the South. To understand how globalization actually relates to the globalized extraction of services that used to be part of the first-world woman's domestic role requires that we look at globalization in ways that are different from the mainstream view. Rather than confining the description of globalization to the hypermobility of capital and to the ascendance of information economies, this book has sought to recover the fact that specific types of places and work processes are also part of economic globalization. This chapter focused on two such concrete conditions. One is the globalizing of often older survival and profit-making activities that contribute today to producing a global supply of low-wage women workers. The other, the growing demand for migrant nannies, maids, nurses, and sex workers in the global North, amounts to a sharp reorganization of labor demand. These dynamics are particularly visible in global cities, also strategic sites for global corporate capital.

The growing immiseration of governments and whole economies in the global South has promoted and enabled the proliferation of survival and profit-making activities that involve the migration and trafficking of women. To some extent, these are older processes that used to be national or regional and can today operate at global levels. The same infrastructure that facilitates cross-border flows of capital, information, and trade is also making possible a whole range of cross-border flows not intended by the framers and designers of the current globalization of economies. Growing numbers of traffickers and smugglers are making money off the backs of women, and many governments are increasingly dependent on their remittances. A key aspect here is that through their work and remittances, women enhance the government revenue of deeply indebted countries and offer new profit-making possibilities to so-called entrepreneurs who have seen other opportunities vanish as a consequence of global firms and markets entering their countries or to longtime criminals who can now operate their illegal trades globally. These survival circuits are often complex, involving multiple locations and sets of actors constituting increasingly global chains of traders and workers.

But globalization has also produced new conditions and dynamics. Strategic among these both for global corporate capital and some of the new labor demand dynamics that involve women from the global South are global cities. These are places that concentrate some of the key functions and resources for the management and coordination of global economic processes. The growth of these activities has in turn produced a sharp growth in the demand for highly paid professionals. Both the firms and the lifestyles of their professionals generate a demand for low-paid service workers. In this way, global cities are also sites for the incorporation of large numbers of low-paid women and immigrants into strategic economic sectors. This incorporation happens directly through the demand for mostly low-paid clerical and blue-collar service workers, such as janitors and repair workers. And it happens indirectly through the consumption practices of high-income professionals, which in turn generates a demand for maids and nannies as well as low-wage workers in expensive restaurants and shops. Low-wage workers get incorporated into the leading sectors, but they do so under conditions that render them invisible, therewith undermining what had historically functioned as a source of workers' empowerment—being employed in growth sectors.

Both in the global city and in these survival circuits women emerge as crucial actors for new and expanding types of economies. It is through these supposedly rather valueless economic actors that key components of these new economies have been built. Globalization plays specific roles here. First, it contributes to the formation of links between sending and receiving countries. The technical infrastructure and transnationalism that underlie some of the key globalized industries are also making it possible for other types of actors to deploy their activities at global scales, whether money laundering or trafficking. Second, it enables local and regional practices to become global in scale. Third, it promotes dynamics that come together in global cities (and in tourism enclaves) to produce a strong demand for these types of workers; on the other hand, globalization also promotes dynamics that mobilize women into these survival circuits, thereby producing an expanding supply of workers who can be pushed, or are sold, into those types of jobs.

Notes

1. In my larger research project, I also focus on a range of what we could call liberating activities and practices that are enabled by globalization, for example, specific aspects of the human rights and environmental movements as well as particular activities of the antiglobalization network. One way of thinking about this is to posit that globalization enables the production of both exploitative and emancipatory countergeographies.

2. Indeed, women represent a specific type of resource in many of these settings since they are seen—whether rightly or not—as better cultural brokers, a significant issue for firms with global operations. Further, women are also seen as crucial in the interface with consumers in the financial services industry in that they are seen as inspiring more trust, and thereby making it easier for individual investors to put their money in what are often known to be highly speculative endeavors (Fisher 2004).

3. I have developed this at length in Sassen 1995.

4. Some of these issues are well illustrated in the emergent research literature on domestic service (see, among others, Ehrenreich and Hochschild 2003; Parrenas 2001; Ribas-Mateos 2005) and in the rapid growth of international organizations catering to various household tasks discussed here.

5. Homecare services include assistance with bathing and dressing, food preparation, walking and getting in and out of bed, medication reminders, transportation,

housekeeping, conversation, and companionship. Although less directly related to the needs of high-income professional households, many of these tasks used to be in the care of the typical housewife of the global North.

6. Very prominent in this market are the International Nanny and Au Pair Agency, headquartered in Britain, Nannies Incorporated, based in London and Paris, and the International Au Pair Association (IAPA), based in Canada.

7. I have argued this for the case of international labor migrations (e.g., Sassen 1998, chaps. 2–4; 1999; see also, e.g., Castro 1999; Bonilla et al. 1998).

8. There is, also, an older literature on women and the debt, focused on the implementation of the first generation of structural adjustment programs in several developing countries linked to the growing debt of governments in the 1980s; this literature has documented the disproportionate burden these programs put on women. It is a large literature in many languages; it also includes a vast number of limited-circulation items produced by various activist and support organizations. For overviews, see, for example, Ward (1991); Ward and Pyle (1995); Bose and Acosta-Belen (1995); Beneria and Feldman (1992); Bradshaw et al. (1993); Tinker (1990); Moser (1989). And now there is a new literature on the second generation of such programs, one more directly linked to the implementation of the global economy in the 1990s (Buchman 1996; Chang and Abramovitz 2000; Chant and Craske 2002). In the context of crisis, trafficking becomes a significant source of revenue. In 2005 global remittances sent by immigrants to their home countries reached over US$ 230 billion (World Bank 2006). The illegal trafficking of migrants generates estimated revenues of US$ 9.5 billion annually for organized crime associations and is ranked as their third most profitable operation after narcotics and arms dealing (U.S. Department of State 2004).

9. Among the components under (1) and (2) are the closure of a large number of firms in often fairly traditional sectors oriented to the local or national market, and the promotion of export-oriented cash crops that have increasingly replaced survival agriculture and food production for local or national markets.

10. See, for example, Chuang (1998). Trafficking has become sufficiently recognized as an issue that it was also addressed in the G8 meeting in Birmingham in May 1998 (International Organization for Migration 1998). The heads of the eight major industrialized countries stressed the importance of cooperation against international organized crime and trafficking in persons. The U.S. president issued a set of directives to his administration to strengthen and increase efforts against trafficking in women and girls. This in turn generated the legislation initiative by Senator Paul Wellstone; Bill S. 600 was introduced in the U.S. Senate in 1999.

11. The Coalition Against Trafficking in Women has centers and representatives in Australia, Bangladesh, Europe, Latin America, North America, Africa, and Asia Pacific. The Women's Rights Advocacy Program has established the Initiative Against Trafficking in Persons to combat the global trade in persons. Other organizations are referred to throughout this book.

8

A New Geography of
Centers and Margins

Summary and Implications

Three important developments that took off in the 1980s laid the foundation for the analysis of cities in the world economy presented in this book. They are captured in the four broad propositions organizing the preceding chapters.

1. *The territorial dispersal of corporate economic activities, of which globalization is one form, contributes to the growth of centralized functions and operations.* This entails a new logic for agglomeration and is a key condition for the renewed centrality of cities in advanced economies. Information technologies, often thought of as neutralizing geography, actually contribute to spatial concentration of central headquarters functions. These technologies are capabilities that enable the simultaneous geographic dispersal and integration of many activities. The particular conditions under which the utilities of such capabilities can be maximized have promoted centralization of the most advanced users and providers of information services in the most advanced urban economies. Parallel developments exist in cities that function as regional nodes—that is, at smaller geographic scales and lower levels of complexity than global cities.

2. *Centralized control and management over a geographically dispersed array of economic operations does not come about inevitably as part of a world system.* It requires the production of a vast range of highly specialized services, telecommunications infrastructures, and industrial services. Major cities are centers for the servicing and financing of international trade,

investment, the international art market, and many other activities that have complex requirements. Headquarters increasingly outsource some of their critical operations to this speclialized service sector. This makes global cities strategic production sites for today's leading economic sectors. Cities that serve as regional centers exhibit similar developments but with lower levels of agglomeration and complexity. The built environments of cities partly represent the spatial effects of the growing service intensity in the organization of all industries.

3. *Economic globalization has contributed to a new geography of centrality and marginality.* This new geography assumes many forms and operates in many terrains, from the distribution of telecommunications facilities to the structure of the economy and of employment. Global cities become the sites of immense concentrations of economic power, while cities that were once major manufacturing centers suffer inordinate declines. Parallel inequalities develop inside cities. Professionals see their incomes rise to unusually high levels, while low- or medium-skilled workers see theirs sink. Financial services produce superprofits, while industrial services barely survive.

4. *Emergent transnational urban systems also enable a proliferation of sociopolitical networks.* The making of an infrastructure for the global operations of firms and markets is increasingly also used for purposes other than narrow corporate economic ones. Immigrants, diasporic groups, environmental and human-rights activists, global justice campaigns, and groups fighting the trafficking of people, among many others, are contributing to strengthen these emergent transnational urban systems. What distinguishes both the economic and sociopolitical networks examined in this book is that they constitute globalities centered in cities rather than running through the bureaucracies of national states or supranational agencies. Sociopolitical networks illuminate the ways in which powerlessness can become a complex condition in the concrete space of cities where multiple groups and projects intersect. The recurrence of such projects across cities contributes to an emergent horizontal multisited globality among growing numbers and types of disadvantaged groups.

Let us look more closely now at the two last and most encompassing propositions. They point to the emergence of two strategic geographies. One, inside global cities, brings the most powerful sectors of global capital together with some of the most disadvantaged workers from a large number of countries. The other, an increasingly developed intercity geography, produces transnational spaces that are beginning to be used by actors other than the firms and professionals who partly developed them.

The Locus of the Peripheral

The sharpening distance between the extremes evident in all major cities of developed countries raises questions about the notion of *rich* countries and cities. It suggests that the geography of centrality and marginality, which in the past was seen in terms of the duality of highly developed and less developed countries, is now also evident within developed countries and especially within their major cities.

One line of theorization posits that the intensified inequalities described in this book represent a transformation in the geography of center and periphery. They signal that peripheralization processes are occurring inside areas that were once conceived of as *core* areas—whether at the global, regional, or urban level—and that alongside the sharpening of peripheralization processes, centrality has also become sharper at all three levels.

The condition of being peripheral is installed in variable geographic terrains and institutional contexts depending on the prevailing economic dynamic. We see new forms of peripheralization at the center of major cities in developed countries not far from some of the most expensive commercial land in the world: the inner city next to the central city or the downtown. These juxtapositions are evident not only in the United States and large European cities but also now in Tokyo (Sassen [1991] 2001, chap. 9), in Mumbai (Weinstein 2006), Shanghai (Gu and Tang 2002), and just about all other cities becoming incorporated into the global economy (Gugler 2004). Peripheralization operates at the center also in organizational terms (e.g., garment sweatshops and the growing range of informal operations), a trend that began in the 1970s in U.S. cities (Sassen-Koob 1982) and also in major European cities, such as Paris (Lazzarato 1997), Amsterdam (Russell and Rath 2002), and urban regions such as Northern Italy (Bagnasco 1977). We have long known about segmented labor markets, but today's downgrading of manufacturing sectors that are actually part of advanced urban economies and sharp devaluing of nonprofessional workers in leading industries go beyond segmentation and in fact represent an instance of peripheralization at the core.

Furthermore, the new forms of growth evident at the urban perimeter also mean crisis: violence in the immigrant ghetto of the *banlieues* (the French term for inner-ring *suburbs*), exurbanites clamoring for growth controls to protect their environment, and new forms of urban governance (Body-Gendrot 1999; Rae 2003; Keil 1999). The regional mode of regulation in many of these cities is based on the old city-suburb model and may hence become increasingly inadequate to deal with intraperipheral conflicts—conflicts between different types of constituencies at the urban perimeter or urban region (Frug 2001). Frankfurt, for example, is a city that cannot function without its region's towns; yet this particular *urban region* would not have emerged without the specific forms of growth in Frankfurt's center. Keil and Ronneberger (1995) noted the ideological motivation in the late 1980s in the call by politicians to officially *recognize* the region so as to strengthen Frankfurt's position in the global interurban competition (Brenner 2004). This call also provides a rationale for coherence and the idea of common interests among the many objectively disparate interests in the region: It displaces the conflicts between unequally advantaged sectors onto a project of regional competition with other regions. Regionalism then emerges as the concept for bridging the global orientation of leading sectors with the various local agendas of various constituencies in the region (Brenner 2004; Scott 2001).

In contrast, the city discourse rather than the ideology of regionalism dominates in cities such as Chicago or São Paulo (see Schiffer Ramos 2002) even when their regions are massive economic complexes. The challenge is how to bridge the inner city, or the squatters at the urban perimeter, with the center. In multiracial cities, multiculturalism has emerged as one form of this bridging. A *regional* discourse is perhaps beginning to emerge, but it has until now been totally submerged under the suburbanization banner, a concept that suggests both escape from and dependence on the city. The notion of conflict within the urban periphery between diverse interests and constituencies (Schiffer 2002) has not really been much of a factor in the United States. The delicate point at the level of the region has rather been the articulation between the residential suburbs and the city (Madigan 2004).

Contested Space

Large cities have emerged as strategic territories for these developments. *First, cities are the sites for concrete operations of the global economy.* For our purposes, we can distinguish two forms of such concrete operations: (1) In terms of economic globalization and place, cities are strategic places that concentrate command functions, global markets, and production sites for the advanced corporate service industries. (2) In terms of day-to-day work in the leading economic complex, a large share of the jobs involved are low paid and manual, and many are held by women and (im)migrants. Although these types of workers and jobs are never represented as part of the global economy, they are in fact as much a part of globalization as international finance is. We see at work here a dynamic of valorization that has sharply increased the distance between the devalorized and the valorized—indeed overvalorized—sectors of the economy. These joint presences have made cities a contested terrain.

The structure of economic activity has brought about changes in the organization of work that are reflected in a pronounced shift in the job supply, with strong polarization occurring in the income distribution and occupational distribution of workers. Major growth industries show a greater incidence of jobs at the high- and low-paying ends of the scale than do the older industries now in decline. Almost half the jobs in the producer services are lower-income jobs, and the other half are in the two highest earnings classes. In contrast, large shares of manufacturing workers were in middle-earning jobs during the postwar period of high growth in these industries in the United States and most of Western Europe.

One particular concern here is to understand how new forms of inequality actually are constituted into new social forms, such as gentrified neighborhoods, informal economies, or downgraded manufacturing sectors. To what extent these developments are connected to the consolidation of an economic complex oriented to the global market is difficult to say. Precise empirical documentation of the linkages or impacts is impossible; the effort here was focused, then, on a more general attempt to understand the consequences of both the ascendance of such an international economic complex and the general move to a service economy.

Second, the city concentrates diversity. Its spaces are inscribed with the dominant corporate culture and also with a multiplicity of other cultures and identities, notably through immigration. The slippage is evident: The dominant culture can encompass only part of the city. And although corporate power inscribes noncorporate cultures and identities with *otherness*, thereby devaluing them, they are present everywhere. The immigrant communities and informal economy described in Chapters 6 and 7 are only two instances. Diverse cultures and ethnicities are especially strong in major cities in the United States and Western Europe, regions that also have the largest concentrations of corporate power.

We see here an interesting correspondence between great concentrations of corporate power and large concentrations of Others. It invites us to see that globalization is constituted not only in terms of capital and the new international corporate culture (international finance, telecommunications, information flows) but also in terms of people and noncorporate cultures. There is a whole infrastructure of low-wage, nonprofessional jobs and activities that constitutes a crucial part of the so-called corporate economy.

A focus on the *work* behind command functions, *production* in the finance and services complex, and market*places* has the effect of incorporating the material facilities underlying globalization and the whole range of jobs and workers typically not seen as belonging to the corporate sector of the economy: secretaries and cleaners, the truckers who deliver the software, the variety of technicians and repair workers, and all the people with jobs related to the maintenance, painting, and renovation of the buildings where the corporate economy is housed.

This expanded focus helps us recognize that a multiplicity of economies is involved in constituting the so-called global information economy. It recognizes types of activities, workers, and firms that have never been installed in the "center" of the economy or that have been evicted from that center in the various restructuring phases that began in the 1980s and have therefore been devalued in a system with a narrow conception of what is the center of the economy. But this expended focus also allows us to recognize segments of the workforce that are in the center but have been evicted from the *account about* that center. Economic globalization, then, can be seen as a process that involves multiple economies and work cultures.

In this book, I showed that cities are of great importance to the dominant economic sectors. Large cities in the highly developed world are the places where globalization processes assume concrete, localized forms. These localized forms are, in good part, what globalization is about. We can then think of cities also as one key place where the contradictions of the internationalization of capital either come to rest or to conflict. If we consider, further, that large cities concentrate a growing share of disadvantaged populations—immigrants in both Europe and the United States, African Americans and Latinos in the United States—then we can see that cities have become a strategic terrain for a whole series of conflicts and contradictions.

On the one hand, they concentrate a disproportionate share of corporate power and are one of the key sites for the overvalorization of the corporate economy; on the other, they concentrate a disproportionate share of the disadvantaged and are one of the key sites for their devalorization. This joint presence happens in a context in which (1) the globalization of the economy has grown sharply and cities have become increasingly strategic for global capital and the latter increasingly makes claims on these cities, and (2) marginalized people have come into representation and also are making claims on the city as well. This joint presence is further brought into focus by the sharpening of the distance between the two. The center, both as space and as social form, now concentrates immense power, a power that rests on the capability for global control and the capability to produce superprofits. And marginality, notwithstanding weak economic and political power, has become an increasingly strong presence through the new politics of culture and identity.

If cities were irrelevant to the globalization of economic activity, the key economic and political actors could simply abandon them and not be bothered by any of this. Indeed, this is precisely what some politicians argue—that cities have become hopeless reservoirs for all kinds of social despair. The dominant economic narrative argues that place no longer matters, firms can be located anywhere, thanks to telematics, and major industries now are information based and hence not placebound. This line of argument devalues cities at a time when they are major sites for the new cultural politics. It also allows the corporate economy to extract major concessions from city governments under the notion that firms can simply leave and relocate elsewhere, which is not quite the case for a whole complex of firms, as much of this book showed.

In seeking to show that (1) cities are strategic to economic globalization because they are command points, global marketplaces, and production sites for the information economy, and (2) many of the devalued sectors of the urban economy actually fulfill crucial functions for the center, in this book, I recover the importance of cities specifically in a globalized economic system and the importance of those overlooked sectors that rest largely on the labor of women, immigrants, and, in large U.S. cities, African Americans and Latinos. In fact, the intermediary sectors of the economy (such as routine office work, headquarters that are not geared to the world markets, the variety of services demanded by the largely suburbanized middle class) and of the urban population (the middle class) can and have left cities. The two sectors that have stayed, the center and the *other*, find in the city the strategic terrain for their operations.

Appendix

The tables in this appendix provide more detailed information about some of the issues discussed in the book. Exhibit A.1 shows the considerable variation in income levels among cities in different regions of the world, and within those cities, it shows the differences among three types of workers: industrial workers, primary school teachers, and engineers. I selected these three types of workers from a longer list in the original data set, which can be found in the original source of the table. Average household payments on rent show less differentiation across regions than earnings. The sharpest relative differences, though not necessarily in absolute value, in rent occur between cities within regions that lie outside the most developed core of countries—between Johannesburg and Lagos in Africa, between Tallinn and Istanbul in Central and Eastern Europe, or between Karachi and Hong Kong in Asia. Not unexpectedly, the pattern of acute international differentiation in these regions is evident in incomes for different types of work as well. The highest rents and the highest earnings for these workers are found in a group of cities in the highly developed world: Geneva, Milan, and London.

Exhibit A.2 presents information on the same cities of Exhibit A.1, adding prices and hours worked. In addition, the information in Exhibit A.2 is standardized on the levels that obtain in one particular city used as a benchmark. This city is Zurich, used most likely because the report where these data are presented was produced by the Union Bank of Switzerland of Zurich. Exhibit A.2 helps to understand the differences among all the cities on the list and among the regions. It makes clear that Zurich has higher wages and salaries than just about every city on the list, and that its price index is also the highest, except for a group of cities in highly developed countries—Oslo, New York, and Tokyo, as well as the still quasi-city-state that is Hong Kong. A larger group of cities in the same development rank are close to Zurich in their price indices: Geneva, Copenhagen, Stockholm, Dublin, and London.

The last two exhibits show basic descriptive information on the largest urban agglomerations, the share of total population of a country residing in the particular city listed, and the share of the total urban population of a country residing in the city listed. The largest urban agglomerations today are overwhelmingly in Asia and Latin America (see Exhibit A.3). Tokyo, New York, Los Angeles, Osaka-Kobe, and Moscow are the only very large cities that are not in the developing world. The shares of national populations residing in country's largest urban agglomeration vary considerably, ranging from 34% in Buenos Aires and Santiago and 29% in Lima, to a low of around 1% in Mumbai, Delhi, Calcutta, Shanghai, and Beijing. Similar marked variations are evident in the percentage of the total urban population of a country accounted for by the major cities in those countries, ranging from 42% for Tokyo, and 39% each for Santiago and Lima, to 5.8% for Mumbai and about 2% each in Beijing and Shanghai.

Exhibit A.4 shows the list of countries that have three or more urban agglomerations with more than 1 million inhabitants. In this case, the numbers are consistently higher than in Exhibit A.3, and several of the highly developed countries appear on the list. It is a far more mixed picture and points to a range of dynamics. Thus the relatively high number (13) of cities with more than a million inhabitants in Germany is linked to its administrative territorial organization into "Landers," each with considerable political autonomy, making for a rather balanced space economy. The 39 such cities in the United States account for a share of the total U.S. population similar to Germany's 42%, pointing to a fairly balanced urban system, and also one organized with a measure of administrative autonomy among the 56 states. However, the 93 such cities in China and 37 in India are in good part a function of enormous population sizes rather than balanced space economies. Thus India's 37 cities with more than 1 million inhabitants account for a mere 11% of the total population.

Exhibit A.1   Household Rent per Month and Gross Yearly Income by
Occupation, 2003 (US$)

| City | Normal Household Rent per Month[a] | Gross Yearly Income | | |
		Industrial Workers[b]	Primary School Teachers[c]	Engineers[d]
Africa				
Lagos	100	2,700	1,700	3,200
Nairobi	320	2,900	1,900	3,900
Johannesburg	480	15,900	7,500	50,400
Central and Eastern Europe				
Bratislava	350	5,600	4,100	9,100
Bucharest	150	3,500	1,800	12,800
Budapest	440	9,400	6,200	15,100
Istanbul	890	15,100	10,400	18,600
Kiev	310	5,300	600	3,700
Ljubljana	170	12,000	17,800	14,100
Moscow	590	3,800	1,800	3,400
Prague	310	6,800	5,700	10,200
Sofia	150	3,300	2,100	4,300
Tallinn	100	6,400	5,100	9,200
Vilnius	340	5,900	3,700	10,100
Riga	140	10,100	2,400	7,700
Warsaw	440	6,900	5,300	11,300
Western Europe				
Amsterdam	890	40,600	34,300	36,300
Athens	620	20,700	19,500	26,800
Barcelona	590	17,700	25,500	32,400
Basel	930	52,600	78,500	76,900
Berlin	630	32,600	45,000	50,600
Brussels	590	37,800	30,600	39,900
Copenhagen	940	47,700	42,500	63,500
Dublin	1,320	35,700	41,700	46,900
Frankfurt	920	34,300	41,900	54,800
Geneva	1,630	49,600	76,400	62,200
Helsinki	560	32,300	30,500	48,500
Lisbon	810	10,300	16,000	18,700
London	1,930	28,800	33,700	40,800
Lugano	950	51,400	59,500	69,900
Luxembourg	700	30,700	58,000	71,800
Madrid	740	16,800	27,600	41,300

(Continued)

Exhibit A.1   (Continued)

City	Normal Household Rent per Month[a]	Gross Yearly Income		
		Industrial Workers[b]	Primary School Teachers[c]	Engineers[d]
Milan	1,660	16,100	20,600	33,200
Oslo	1,000	54,200	35,700	46,000
Paris	1,270	19,300	24,900	42,900
Rome	1,210	15,700	17,300	25,800
Stockholm	750	40,000	32,300	47,700
Vienna	1,020	29,100	28,900	40,600
Zurich	1,380	59,600	75,300	81,300
Latin America				
Bogotá	200	4,100	4,100	14,400
Buenos Aires	150	5,100	2,400	10,500
Caracas	290	10,700	3,500	14,900
Lima	300	6,800	4,100	16,800
Rio de Janeiro	230	6,900	2,400	14,600
Santiago de Chile	430	8,300	5,900	15,500
São Paulo	200	6,500	2,700	13,400
Middle East				
Dubai	1,350	13,300	22,800	42,500
Manama	800	22,500	13,300	51,000
Tel Aviv	790	13,300	13,400	43,300
North America				
Chicago	1,430	43,800	47,200	57,100
Los Angeles	1,060	43,400	46,700	74,500
New York	1,790	47,000	54,200	75,000
Mexico City	770	3,600	8,300	9,000
Miami	700	40,900	34,000	54,000
Montreal	410	28,700	30,700	48,500
Toronto	850	29,800	26,500	66,200
Southeast Asia and Pacific Rim				
Auckland	780	30,200	22,000	39,800
Bangkok	120	4,200	4,200	9,800
Hong Kong	1,750	17,300	47,100	39,200
Jakarta	1,110	3,300	2,300	6,700
Karachi	90	1,300	2,000	4,700
Kuala Lampur	460	11,100	10,200	15,900
Manila	650	4,200	4,000	5,500

| | Normal Household Rent per Month[a] | Gross Yearly Income | | |
City		Industrial Workers[b]	Primary School Teachers[c]	Engineers[d]
Mumbai	200	1,900	1,400	6,000
Seoul	710	34,600	27,200	32,900
Shanghai	480	4,600	4,300	12,100
Singapore	790	1,700	23,000	26,700
Sydney	1,010	18,400	24,300	32,400
Taipei	1,410	22,200	22,300	25,800
Tokyo	1,010	50,000	45,800	71,500

Notes:

a. Average monthly rents on the open housing market at the time of this survey; apartments built after 1980 that represent the average gross monthly rent paid by the majority of local households (typical size and comfort).

b. Skilled workers with vocational training and about 10 years' experience with a large company in the metal working industry; about 35 years old, married, two children.

c. Primary school teachers who have taught in the public school system for about 10 years; about 35, married, 2 children.

d. Employed by an industrial firm in the electrical engineering sector, university or technical college graduate with at least 5 years' work experience; about 35 years old, married, 2 children.

Source: Based on Union Bank of Switzerland (2003). (c) UBS 1998-2003. All rights reserved.

Exhibit A.2   Price and Wage Indices and Working Hours per Annum, 2003
(numbers)

City	Prices (excl. rent) (Zurich = 100)[a]	Gross Wages and Salary (Zurich = 100)[b]	Working Hours per Year[c]
Africa			
Lagos	59.4	5.0	1,723
Nairobi	53.6	4.2	2,165
Johannesburg	44.9	19.1	1,910
Central and Eastern Europe			
Bratislava	38.3	9.7	1,881
Bucharest	33.2	7.2	1,992
Budapest	55.9	16.6	2,012
Istanbul	54.9	17.9	2,154
Kiev	32.5	5.0	1,958
Ljubljana	55.0	21.2	1,830
Moscow	53.6	11.1	1,784
Prague	40.5	11.8	1,946
Sofia	35.4	5.3	1,824
Tallinn	50.0	12.4	1,826
Vilnius	48.8	11.2	1,833
Riga	43.4	12.6	1,862
Warsaw	50.7	13.0	1,901
Western Europe			
Amsterdam	77.3	64.7	1,741
Athens	73.8	34.6	1,744
Barcelona	63.0	38.0	1,743
Basel	97.5	97.7	1,868
Berlin	75.4	63.9	1,666
Brussels	79.2	67.9	1,722
Copenhagen	98.9	98.9	1,658
Dublin	82.8	63.5	1,779
Frankfurt	78.5	70.0	1,682
Geneva	95.6	91.1	1,895
Helsinki	86.1	58.2	1,714
Lisbon	65.1	23.6	1,804
London	97.6	65.6	1,787
Lugano	93.9	84.3	1,921
Luxembourg	78.2	69.4	1,768
Madrid	68.4	35.3	1,782
Milan	74.4	44.5	1,718
Oslo	117.8	94.9	1,703
Paris	89.3	53.4	1,561
Rome	73.4	37.1	1,810
Stockholm	91.1	64.7	1,775
Vienna	84.2	55.8	1,696
Zurich	100.0	100.0	1,872

City	Prices (excl. rent) (Zurich = 100)[a]	Gross Wages and Salary (Zurich = 100)[b]	Working Hours per Year[c]
Latin America			
Bogotá	38.0	8.3	1,987
Buenos Aires	30.6	7.9	2,044
Caracas	47.6	9.2	1,989
Lima	45.4	9.9	2,152
Rio de Janeiro	38.2	8.4	1,802
Santiago de Chile	41.5	12.7	2,195
São Paulo	41.7	10.4	1,936
Middle East			
Dubai	65.1	26.4	2,233
Manama	66.1	22.8	2,034
Tel Aviv	70.2	32.8	1,977
North America			
Chicago	97.2	82.5	1,858
Los Angeles	84.3	72.2	2,022
New York	104.5	84.7	1,843
Mexico City	61.1	9.2	2,281
Miami	74.6	62.4	1,856
Montreal	65.6	50.1	1,829
Toronto	66.6	52.6	1,909
Southeast Asia and Pacific Rim			
Auckland	62.1	34.5	2,022
Bangkok	45.8	6.9	2,184
Hong Kong	108.1	31.1	2,398
Jakarta	50.4	6.5	2,175
Karachi	32.7	3.5	2,302
Kuala Lampur	42.9	14.5	2,152
Manila	36.8	5.4	2,301
Mumbai	28.7	3.1	2,347
Seoul	76.5	30.6	2,270
Shanghai	69.7	12.8	1,958
Singapore	72.1	26.8	2,056
Sydney	66.1	40.2	1,757
Taipei	73.1	32.3	2,327
Tokyo	106.7	68.3	1,864

Notes:

a. Prices are based on the cost of a basket of 114 goods and services weighted in favor of European consumer habits.

b. Hourly wages calculated on data from 13 occupations that are represented universally around the world. Wage index is weighted by the share of each occupation in overall employment, overall income, gender, net of taxes, and social security contributions.

c. Working hours are based on 12 occupations excluding primary school teachers.

Source: Based on Union Bank of Switzerland (2003). (c) UBS 1998-2003. All rights reserved.

Exhibit A.3 Largest Urban Agglomerations, 2003 (millions and percentages)

Urban Agglomeration	Country	2003 Population (millions)	Percentage of Total Population	Percentage of Urban Population
Urban Agglomerations with 10 Million or More				
Tokyo	Japan	35.0	27.4	41.9
Mexico City	Mexico	18.7	18.0	23.9
New York	United States of America	18.3	6.2	7.7
São Paulo	Brazil	17.9	10.0	12.0
Mumbai (Bombay)	India	17.4	1.6	5.8
Delhi	India	14.1	1.3	4.7
Calcutta	India	13.8	1.3	4.6
Buenos Aires	Argentina	13.0	34.0	37.7
Shanghai	China	12.8	1.0	2.5
Jakarta	Indonesia	12.3	5.6	12.3
Los Angeles	United States of America	12.0	4.1	5.1
Dhaka	Bangladesh	11.6	7.9	32.5
Osaka-Kobe	Japan	11.2	8.8	13.5
Rio de Janeiro	Brazil	11.2	6.3	7.6
Karachi	Pakistan	11.1	7.2	21.2
Beijing	China	10.8	0.8	2.2
Cairo	Egypt	10.8	15.1	35.8
Moscow	Russian Federation	10.5	7.3	10.0
Metro Manila	Philippines	10.4	12.9	21.2
Lagos	Nigeria	10.1	8.1	17.4
Urban Agglomerations between 5 and 10 Million				
Paris	France	9.8	16.3	21.3
Seoul	Republic of Korea	9.7	20.4	25.4

Urban Agglomeration	Country	2003 Population (millions)	Percentage of Total Population	Percentage of Urban Population
Istanbul	Turkey	9.4	13.1	19.8
Tianjin	China	9.3	0.7	1.8
Chicago	United States of America	8.6	2.9	3.6
Lima	Peru	7.9	29.1	39.4
London	United Kingdom	7.6	12.9	14.4
Santa Fé de Bogotá	Colombia	7.3	16.5	21.6
Tehran	Iran (Islamic Republic of)	7.2	10.4	15.6
Hong Kong[a]	China, Hong Kong SAR	7.0	100.0	100.0
Chennai (Madras)	India	6.7	0.6	2.2
Rhein-Ruhr North	Germany	6.6	8.0	9.0
Bangkok	Thailand	6.5	10.3	32.4
Bangalore	India	6.1	0.6	2.0
Lahore	Pakistan	6.0	3.9	11.4
Hyderabad	India	5.9	0.6	1.9
Wuhan	China	5.7	0.4	1.1
Baghdad	Iraq	5.6	22.3	33.2
Santiago	Chile	5.5	34.7	39.8
Saint Petersburg	Russian Federation	5.3	3.7	5.0
Kinshasa	Dem. Rep. of the Congo	5.3	10.0	31.6
Philadelphia	United States of America	5.3	1.8	2.2
Miami	United States of America	5.2	1.8	2.2
Riyadh	Saudi Arabia	5.1	21.2	24.1
Madrid	Spain	5.1	12.4	16.2
Belo Horizonte	Brazil	5.0	2.8	3.4

Note:

a. As of July 1, 1997, Hong Kong became a Special Administrative Region (SAR) of China.

Source: Author's calculations based on United Nations Department of Economic and Social Affairs, Population Division (2004).

Exhibit A.4   Countries with Three or More Urban Agglomerations
(> 1 million), 2003

Country	Total Number of Urban Agglomerations (UA)	Total Percentage Residing in UA
Argentina	4	44.0
Australia	5	61.5
Bangladesh	3	11.5
Brasil	16	36.6
Canada	5	39.7
China*	93	14.6
Colombia	5	35.4
France	4	22.6
Germany	13	41.6
India	37	11.0
Indonesia	6	10.6
Iran (Islamic Rep. of)	6	20.9
Iraq	3	31.5
Italy	4	18.9
Japan	6	43.7
Mexico	9	33.5
Nigeria	4	13.1
Pakistan	8	17.2
Republic of Korea	8	49.0
Russian Federation	12	19.2
Saudi Arabia	3	41.9
South Africa	5	28.0
Turkey	5	24.8
Ukraine	5	14.8
United Kingdom	5	24.5
United States	39	42.2
Venezuela	4	33.3
Viet Nam	3	13.1

*Does not include Hong Kong (SAR).

Source: Author's calculations based on United Nations Department of Economic and Social Affairs, Population Division (2004).

References and Suggested Reading

Abrahamson, Mark. 2004. *Global Cities*. New York and Oxford: Oxford University Press.

Abreu, A., M. Cocco, C. Despradel, E. G. Michael, and A. Peguero. 1989. *Las Zonas Francas Industriales: El Exito de una Politica Economica*. Santo Domingo: Centro de Orientacion Economica.

Abu-Lughod, Janet Lippman. 1980. *Rabat: Urban Apartheid in Morocco*. Princeton, NJ: Princeton University Press.

———. 1994. *From Urban Village to "East Village": The Battle for New York's Lower East Side*. Cambridge, MA: Blackwell.

———. 1999. *New York, Chicago, Los Angeles: America's Global Cities*. Minneapolis, MN: University of Minnesota Press.

Acemoglu, Daron. 2002. "Technical Change, Inequality, and the Labor Market." *Journal of Economic Literature* 40(1):7–72.

Acosta-Belen, Edna and Carlos E. Santiago. 2006. *Puerto Ricans in the United States: A Contemporary Portrait*. Boulder, CO: Lynne Reinner Publishers.

Adrian, C. 1984. *Urban Impacts of Foreign and Local Investment in Australia*. Publication 119. Canberra: Australian Institute of Urban Studies.

Aguiar, Luis L.M. and Andrew Herod, eds. 2005. *Cleaning Up the Global Economy*. Malden, MA: Blackwell.

Alderson, Arthur S. and Jason Beckfield. "Power and Position in the World City System." *American Journal of Sociology* 109(4):811–51.

Allen, John. 1999. "Cities of Power and Influence: Settled Formations." Pp. 181–228 in *Unsettling Cities*, edited by John Allen, Doreen Massey, and Michael Pryke. New York: Routledge.

———. 2003. *Lost Geographies of Power*. Malden, MA: Blackwell Publishers.

———, Doreen Massey, and Michael Pryke, eds. 1999. *Unsettling Cities*. London, UK: Routledge.

Allison, Eric. 1996. "Historic Preservation in a Development-Dominated City: The Passage of New York City's Landmark Preservation Legislation." *Journal of Urban History* 22(3):350–76.

Amen, Mark M., Kevin Archer, and M. Martin Bosman, eds. 2006. *Relocating Global Cities: From the Center to the Margins.* New York: Rowman & Littlefield.

Amin, Ash, ed. 1997. *Post-Fordism.* Oxford, UK: Blackwell.

———. 2002. *Placing the Social Economy.* London: Routledge.

——— and Kevin Robins. 1990. "The Re-emergence of Regional Economies? The Mythical Geography of Flexible Accumulation." *Environment and Planning D: Society and Space* 8(1):7–34.

AMPO. 1988. "Japan's Human Imports: As Capital Flows Out, Foreign Labor Flows In." Special issue of *Japan-Asia Quarterly Review* 19(1, Special issue).

Anderson, E. 1990. *Streetwise, Chicago.* Chicago, IL: University of Chicago Press.

Appadurai, Arjun. 1996. *Modernity at Large.* Minneapolis, MN: University of Minnesota Press.

Arroyo, Monica, Milton Santos, Maria Adelia A. De Souze, and Francisco Capuano Scarlato, eds. 1993. *Fim de Seculo e Globalizacao.* São Paulo, Brazil: Hucitec.

Ascher, François. 1995. *Metapolis ou l'Avenir des Villes.* Paris, France: Editions Odile Jacob.

Asian Women's Association. 1988. *Women from Across the Seas: Migrant Workers in Japan.* Tokyo, Japan: Asian Women's Association.

Australian Government Foreign Investment Review Board. 1996. *Annual Report 1995–96.* Canberra, Australia: Australian Government Publishing Service.

———. 2004. *Annual Report 2003–04.* Canberra, Australia: CanPrint Communications.

Avgerou, Chrisanthi. 2002. *Information Systems and Global Diversity.* Oxford: Oxford University Press.

Axel, Brian K. 2002. "The Diasporic Imaginary." *Public Culture* 14(2):411–428.

Bagnasco, Arnaldo. 1977. *Tre Italie: La Problematica Territoriale Dello Sviluppo Italiano.* Bologna, Italy: Il Mulino.

Bailey, Thomas. 1990. "Jobs of the Future and the Education They Will Require: Evidence from Occupational Forecasts." *Educational Researcher* 20(2):11–20.

Balbo, Laura and Luigi Manconi. 1990. *I Razzismi Possibili.* Milano, Italy: Feltrinelli.

Bank for International Settlements. 1992. *62nd Annual Report.* Basel, Switzerland: BIS.

———. 1998. *Central Bank Survey.* Basel, Switzerland: BIS.

———. 1999. *69th Annual Report.* Basel, Switzerland: BIS.

———. 2002. *Central Bank Survey.* Basel, Switzerland: BIS.

———. 2004. *Quarterly Review—June 13, 2004.* Basel, Switzerland: BIS.

———. 2005. *Triennial Central Bank Survey.* Basel, Switzerland: BIS.

———. 2005. *Quarterly Review—December, 2005.* Basel, Switzerland: BIS.

Barr, J. B. and Budd, L. 2000. "Financial Services and the Urban System: An Exploration." *Urban Studies,* 37(3):593–610.

Bartlett, Anne (2006). "Political Subjectivity in the Global City." Ph.D. Dissertation, Department of Sociology, University of Chicago.

Bavishi, V. and Wyman, H. E. 1983. *Who Audits the World: Trends in the Worldwide Accounting Profession.* Storrs, CT: University of Connecticut, Center for Transnational Accounting and Financial Research.

Beck, Ulrich. 2000. *The Risk Society and Beyond: Critical Issues for Social Theory.* Thousand Oaks, CA: Sage

Beneria, Lourdes. 1989. "Subcontracting and Employment Dynamics in Mexico City." Pp. 173–188 in *The Informal Economy: Studies in Advanced and Less Developed Countries,* edited by A. Portes, M. Castells, and L. Benton. Baltimore, MD: Johns Hopkins University Press.

────── and Marta Roldan. 1987. *Crossroads of Class and Gender: Homework, Subcontracting, and Household Dynamics in Mexico City.* Chicago, IL: University of Chicago.

────── and Shelley Feldman, eds. 1992. *Unequal Burden: Economic Crises, Persistent Poverty, and Women's Work.* Boulder, CO: Westview.

Benko, Georges and Mick Dunford, eds. 1991. *Industrial Change and Regional Development: The Transformation of New Industrial Spaces.* London and New York: Belhaven/Pinter.

Berger, Suzanne and Michael J. Piore. 1980. *Dualism and Discontinuity in Industrial Societies.* New York and London, UK: Cambridge University Press.

Berque, Augustin. 1987. *La Qualité de la Ville: Urbanite Française, Urbanite Nippone.* Tokyo, Japan: Maison Franco-Japonaise.

Bestor, Theodore. 1989. *Neighborhood Tokyo.* Stanford, CA: Stanford University Press.

Beveridge, Andrew A. 2003. "The Affluent of Manhattan." *Gotham Gazette* June 2003.

Bhachu, Parminder. 1985. *Twice Immigrants.* London, UK: Tavistock.

Bhagwati, J. 1988. *Protectionism.* Boston, MA: MIT Press.

Bini, Paolo Calza. 1976. *Economia Periferica e Classi Sociali.* Napoli, Italy: Liguori.

Blaschke, J. and A. Germershausen. 1989. "Migration und Ethnische Beziehungen." *Nord-Sud Aktuell* 3–4(Special issue).

Blumberg, P. 1981. *Inequality in an Age of Decline.* New York: Oxford University Press.

Bodnar, Judit. 2000. *Fin de Millénaire Budapest: Metamorphoses of Urban Life.* Minneapolis, MN: University of Minnesota Press.

Body-Gendrot, S. 1993. *Ville et violence.* Paris, France: Presses Universitaires de France.

──────. 1999. *The Social Control of Cities.* London, UK: Blackwell.

──────, Emmanuel Ma Mung, and Catherine Hodier, eds. 1992. "Entrepreneurs entre Deux Mondes: Les Creations d'Entreprises par les Etrangers: France, Europe, Amerique du Nord." *Revue Européenne des Migrations Internationales* 8(1, Special issue):5–8.

Boissevain, Jeremy. 1992. "Les Entreprises Ethniques aux Pays-Bas." *Revue Européenne des Migrations Internationales* 8(1, Special issue):97–106.

Bolin, Richard L., ed. 1998. *The Global Network of Free Zones in the 21st Century.* Flagstaff, AZ: The Flagstaff Institute.

Bonacich, Edna. 2000. *Behind the Label: Inequality in the Los Angeles Garment Industry.* Berkeley, CA: University of California Press.

Bonacich, Edna, Lucie Cheng, Nora Chinchilla, Norma Hamilton, and Paul Ong, eds. 1994. *Global Production: The Apparel Industry in the Pacific Rim*. Philadelphia, PA: Temple University Press.

Bonamy, Joel and Nicole May, eds. 1994. *Services et Mutations Urbaines*. Paris, France: Anthropos.

Bonilla, Frank, Edwin Melendez, Rebecca Morales, and Maria de los Angeles Torres, eds. 1998. *Borderless Borders*. Philadelphia, PA: Temple University Press.

Boris, Eileen. 1994. *Home to Work*. Cambridge, UK: Cambridge University Press.

Bose, Christine E. 2001. *Women in 1900: Gateway to the Political Economy of the 20th Century*. Philadelphia, PA: Temple University Press.

—— and E. Acosta-Belen, eds. 1995. *Women in the Latin American Development Process*. Philadelphia, PA: Temple University Press.

Bourgois, P. 1996. *In Search of Respect: Selling Crack in El Barrio*. Structural Analysis in the Social Sciences Series. New York: Cambridge University Press.

Boyer, Christine. 1983. *Dreaming the Rational City*. Cambridge, MA: MIT Press.

Boyer, Robert, ed. 1986. *La Flexibilité du Travail en Europe*. Paris, France: La Découverte.

Bradshaw, Y., R. Noonan, L. Gash, and C. Buchmann. 1993. "Borrowing against the future: Children and third world indebtedness." *Social Forces* 71(3):629–56.

Braudel, Fernand. 1984. *The Perspective of the World*. Vol. III. London, UK: Collins.

Brauer, David, Beethika Khan and Elizabeth Miranda. 1998. "Earnings Inequality, New York–New Jersey Region." New York: Federal Reserve Bank of New York (July).

Brettell, Caroline, and James F. Hollifield, eds. 2000. *Migration Theory: Talking Across the Disciplines*. New York: Routledge.

Brenner, Neil. 1998. "Global Cities, Glocal States: Global City Formation and State Territorial Restructuring in Contemporary Europe." *Review of International Political Economy* 5(1):1–37.

——. 2004. *New State Spaces: Urban Governance and The Rescaling of Statehood*. Oxford, UK: Oxford University Press.

—— and Nik Theodore, eds. 2002. *Spaces of Neoliberalism: Urban Restructuring in Western Europe and North America*. Malden, MA: Blackwell Publishers.

—— and Roger Keil. 2006. *The Global Cities Reader*. London: Routledge.

Brosnan, P. and F. Wilkinson. 1987. *Cheap Labour: Britain's False Economy*. London, UK: Low Pay Unit.

Brotchie, J., M. Barry, E. Blakely, P. Hall, and P. Newton, eds. 1995. *Cities in Competition: Productive and Sustainable Cities for the 21st Century*. Melbourne, Australia: Longman Australia.

Brown, C. 1984. *Black and White Britain*. London, UK: Heinemann.

Brusco, Sebastiano. 1986. "Small Firms and Industrial Districts: The Experience of Italy." Pp. 182–202 in *New Firms and Regional Development*, edited by David Keeble and Francis Weever. London, UK: Croom Helm.

Bryson, J. R. and P. W. Daniels, eds. 2005. *The Service Industries Handbook*. Cheltenham, UK: Edward Elgar.

Buchler, Simone. 2002. "Women in the informal economy of São Paulo." Paper prepared for the National Academy of Sciences, forthcoming in *Background Papers. Panel on Cities.* Washington, DC: National Academy of Sciences.

Buck, Nick, Matthew Drennan, and Kenneth Newton. 1992. "Dynamics of the Metropolitan Economy." Pp. 68–104 in *Divided Cities: New York & London in the Contemporary World,* edited by Susan Fainstein, Ian Gordon, and Michael Harloe. Oxford, UK: Blackwell.

Buntin, Jennifer. (In Process). "Transnational Suburbs? The Impact of Immigration Communities on the Urban Edge." Ph.D. Dissertation, Department of Sociology, University of Chicago.

Burgel, Guy. 1993. *La Ville Aujourd'hui.* Paris, France: Hachette, Collection Pluriel.

Cadena, Sylvia. 2004. "Networking for Women or Women's Networking." A report for the Social Science Research Council's Committee on Information Technology and International Cooperation. Accessible at: [http://www.ssrc .org/programs/itic/publications/civsocandgov/cadena.pdf].

Canadian Urban Institute. 1993. *Disentangling Local Government Responsibilities: International Comparisons.* Urban Focus Series 93–1. Toronto, Canada: Canadian Urban Institute.

Canevari, Annapaola. 1991. "Immigrati Prima Accoglienza: E Dopo?" *Dis T Rassegna di Studi e Ricerche del Dipartimento di Scienze del Territorio del Politecnico di Milano* 9(September):53–60.

Cardew, R. V., J. V. Langdale, and D. C. Rich, eds. 1982. *Why Cities Change: Urban Development and Economic Change in Sydney.* Sydney, Australia: Allen and Unwin.

Carleial, L. and M. R. Nabuco. 1989. *Transformacoes na DiviSao Inter-regional no Brasil.* São Paulo, Brazil: Anpec/Caen/Cedeplar.

Castells, M. 1983. *The City and the Grassroots: A Cross-Cultural Theory of Urban Social Movements.* Berkeley, CA: University of California Press.

———. 1989. *The Informational City.* London, UK: Blackwell.

———. 1998. *The Information Age: Economy, Society, and Culture. Vol. 3: End of Millennium.* Malden/Oxford, UK: Blackwell.

——— and Yuko Aoyama. 1994. "Paths Toward the Informational Society: Employment Structure in G-7 Countries, 1920–1990." *International Labour Review* 133(1):5–33.

——— and P. Hall. 1994. *Technopoles of the World: The Making of Twenty-First-Century Industrial Complexes.* London, UK: Routledge.

Castles, S. and M. Miller. 2003. *The Age of Migration: International Population Movements in the Modern World. (3rd Ed.)* London, UK: Macmillan.

Castro, Max, ed. 1999. *Free Markets, Open Societies, Closed Borders.* Coral Gables, FL: University of Miami, North-South Center Press.

CEMAT (European Conference of Ministers Responsible for Regional Planning). 1988. *Draft European Regional Planning Strategy.* Vols. 1 and 2. Luxembourg: CEMAT.

Chant, Sylvia H., and Nikki Craske. 2002. *Gender in Latin America.* New Brunswick, NJ: Rutgers University Press.

Chaney, E. and M. Garcia Castro. 1993. *Muchacha Cachifa Criada Empleada Empregadinha Sirvienta Y . . . Mas Nada.* Caracas, Venezuela: Nueva Sociedad.

Chang, Grace. 1998. "Undocumented Latinas: The New 'Employable Mothers'." Pp. 311–319 in *Race, Class, and Gender,* 3d ed., edited by M. Andersen and Patricia Hill Collins. Belmont, CA: Wadsworth.

——— and Mimi Abramovitz. 2000. *Disposable Domestics: Immigrant Women Workers in the Global Economy.* Boston, MA: South End Press.

Chase-Dunn, C. 1984. "Urbanization in the World System: New Directions for Research." Pp. 111–120 in *Cities in Transformation,* edited by M. P. Smith. Beverly Hills, CA: Sage.

Chen, Xiangming. 2005. *As Borders Bend: Transnational Spaces on the Pacific Rim.* New York: Rowman & Littlefield.

Cheshire, P. C. and D. G. Hay. 1989. *Urban Problems in Western Europe.* London, UK: Unwin Hyman.

Chinchilla, Norma and Nora Hamilton. 2001. *Seeking Community in the Global City: Salvadorans and Guatemalans in Los Angeles.* Philadelphia, PA: Temple University Press.

Chuang, Janie. 1998. "Redirecting the Debate over Trafficking in Women: Definitions, Paradigms, and Contexts." *Harvard Human Rights Journal* 10(Winter): 65–108.

Ciccolella, Pablo. 1998. "Territorio de Consumo: Redefinición del Espacio en Buenos Aires en el Fin de Siglo." Pp. 201–30 in *Ciudades y Regiones al Avance de la Globalización,* edited by S. Sorenstein and R. Bustos Cara. UNS (Universidad Nacional del Sur), Bahia Blanca, Argentina.

———. 2002. "Buenos Aires: Sociospatial Impacts of the Development of Global City Functions." Pp. 309–326 in *Global Networks, Linked Cities,* edited by Saskia Sassen. New York and London: Routledge.

City of Toronto. 2005a. Business and Economic Development facts. Toronto, Canada. Retrieved December 7, 2005 (http://www.city.toronto.on.ca/toronto_facts/business_econdev.htm).

———.2005b. Toronto's Economic Profile. Toronto, Canada. Retrieved December 7, 2005 (http://www.city.toronto.on.ca/economic_profile/index.htm).

———. 2001. *Toronto's Financial Services Cluster: A Review.* Toronto, Canada: City of Toronto, Economic Development. Retrieved December 7, 2005 (http://www.city.toronto.on.ca/business_publications/finance_review.pdf).

———. 1990. *Cityplan '91: Central Area Trends Report.* Toronto, Canada: City of Toronto, Planning and Development Department.

Clark, Terry Nichols (ed). 2003. *The City as an Entertainment Machine.* St. Louis, MO: Elsevier.

——— and Vincent Hoffman-Martinot, eds. 1998. *The New Political Culture.* Oxford, UK: Westview.

Clavel, P. 1986. *The Progressive City.* New Brunswick, NJ: Rutgers University Press.

Cobos, Emilio Pradilla. 1984. *Contribución a la Critica de la "Teoria Urbana": Del "Espacio" a la "Crisis Urbana."* Mexico, D.F.: Universidad Autonoma Metropolitana Xochimilco.

Cohen, R. 1987. *The New Helots: Migrants in the International Division of Labour.* London, UK: Avebury.

Cohen, Stephen S. and John Zysman. 1987. *Manufacturing Matters: The Myth of the Post-industrial Economy.* New York: Basic Books.

Colomina, Beatriz, ed. 1992. *Sexuality & Space.* Princeton Papers on Architecture. Princeton, NJ: Princeton Architectural Press.

Colon, Alice, Marya Munoz, Neftali Garcia, and Idsa Alegria. 1988. "Trayectoria de la Participación Laboral de las Mujeres en Puerto Rico de los Años 1950 a 1985." In *Crisis, Sociedad y Mujer: Estudio Comparativo entre Paises de America 1950–1985).* Havana: Federación de Mujeres Cubanas.

Connell, J. 2000. *Sydney: The Emergence of a World City.* Melbourne, Australia: Oxford University Press.

Consalvo, Mia and Susanna Paasonen, eds. 2002. *Women and Everyday Uses of the Internet: Agency and Identity.* New York: Peter Lang.

Copjec, Joan and Michael Sorkin, eds. 1999. *Giving Ground.* London, UK: Verso.

Corbridge, S. and J. Agnew. 1991. "The U.S. Trade and Budget Deficit in Global Perspective: An Essay in Geopolitical Economy." *Environment and Planning D: Society and Space* 9:71–90.

Corbridge, Stuart, Ron Martin, and Nigel Thrift, eds. 1994. *Money, Power, and Space.* Oxford, UK: Blackwell.

Cordero-Guzman, Hector R., Robert C. Smith, and Ramon Grosfoguel, eds. 2001. *Migration, Transnationalization, and Race in a Changing New York.* Philadelphia, PA: Temple University Press.

Cornelius, Wayne A., Philip L. Martin, and James F. Hollifield, eds. 1994. *Controlling Immigration: A Global Perspective.* Stanford, CA: Stanford University Press.

———, Takeyuki Tsuda, Philip L. Martin, and James F. Hollifield, eds. 2004. *Controlling Immigration: A Global Perspective* (2nd Ed.). Stanford, CA: Stanford University Press.

Crichlow, Michaeline A. 2004. *Negotiating Caribbean Freedom: Peasants and The State in Development.* Lanham, MD: Lexington Books.

Cybriwsky, R. 1991. *Tokyo. The Changing Profile of an Urban Giant.* World Cities series, edited by R. J. Johnson and P. L. Knox. London, UK: Belhaven.

Daly, M. T. and R. Stimson. 1992. "Sydney: Australia's Gateway and Financial Capital." In *New Cities of the Pacific Rim,* edited by E. Blakely and T. J. Stimpson. Berkeley: University of California, Institute for Urban & Regional Development.

Daniels, Peter W. 1985. *Service Industries: A Geographical Appraisal.* London, UK, and New York: Methuen.

———. 1991. "Producer Services and the Development of the Space Economy." Pp. 108–17 in *The Changing Geography of Advanced Producer Services,* edited by Peter W. Daniels and Frank Moulaert. London, UK, and New York: Belhaven.

Dauhajre, A., E. Riley, R. Mena, and J. Guerrero. 1989. *Impacto Economico de las Zonas Francas Industriales de Exportación en la Republica Dominicana*. Santo Domingo, Dominican Republic: Fundacion Economia y Desarrollo.

Davis, Mike. 2006. *Planet of Slums*. London: Verso.

———. 1999. *Ecology of Fear: Los Angeles and the Imagination of Disaster*. New York: Vintage Editions.

Dear, Michael. 2001. "Los Angeles and the Chicago School: Invitation to a Debate." *Cities and Communities* (1)1:5–32.

Deecke, H., T. Kruger, and D. Lapple. 1993. "Alternative Szenarien der Wirtschaftlichen Strukturentwicklung in der Hamburger Wirtschaft unter Raumlichen Gesichtspunkten." Final Report for the City of Hamburg. Hamburg, Germany: Technische Universität Hamburg Harburg.

Deere, Carmen Diana, Peggy Antrobus, Lynn Bolles, Edwin Melendez, Peter Phillips, Marcia Rivera, and Helen Safa. 1990. *In the Shadows of the Sun: Caribbean Development Alternatives and U.S. Policy*. Boulder, CO: Westview.

Derudder, B. and Taylor, P.J. 2005 "The cliquishness of world cities." *Global Networks* 5(1):71–91.

Delauney, Jean Claude and Jean Gadrey. 1987. *Les Enjeux de la Societé de Service*. Paris, France: Presses de la Fondation des Sciences Politiques.

Demographia. 2005. "Western Europe: Metropolitan Area & Core Cities 1965 to Present." Belleville, IL: Wendell Cox Consultancy. Retrieved December 7, 2005 (http://www.demographia.com/db-metro-we1965.htm).

Desfor, Gene, and Roger Keil. 2004. *Nature and the City: Making Environmental Policy in Toronto and Los Angeles*. Tempe, AZ: University of Arizona Press.

Dogan, M. and J. D. Kasarda, eds. 1988. *A World of Giant Cities*. Newbury Park, CA: Sage.

Dore, Ronald. 1986. *Flexible Rigidities: Industrial Policy and Structural Adjustment in the Japanese Economy, 1970–1980*. London, UK: Athlone.

Drache, D. and M. Gertler, eds. 1991. *The New Era of Global Competition: State Policy and Market Power*. Montreal, Canada: McGill-Queen's University Press.

Drainville, Andre. 2004. *Contesting Globalization: Space and Place in the World Economy*. London, UK: Routledge.

Drennan, Mathew P. 1989. "Information Intensive Industries in Metropolitan Areas of the United States." *Environment and Planning A* 21:1603–18.

———. 1992. "Gateway Cities: The Metropolitan Sources of U.S. Producer Service Exports." *Urban Studies* 29(2):217–35.

Duarte, R. 1989. "Heterogeneidade no Setor Informal: Um Estudo de Microunidades Produtivas em Aracaju e Teresina." *Estudios Economicos*, Fipe 19(Numero Especial):99–123.

Duneier, M. 1999. *Sidewalk*. New York: Farrar, Strauss & Giroux.

duRivage, Virginia L., ed. 1992. *New Policies for the Part-Time and Contingent Workforce*. Washington, DC: Economic Policy Institute.

Eade, John. 1997. *Living the Global City: Globalization as a Local Process*. New York: Routledge.

Economic Policy Institute (EPI). 2005a. *The State of Working America 2004–05*. Washington, DC: EPI.

———. 2005b. Income Picture: August 31, 2005. Washington DC: EPI. Retrieved December 7, 2005 (http://www.epinet.org/content.cfm/webfeatures_econindi cators_income20050831).

Edel, Matthew. 1986. "Capitalism, Accumulation and the Explanation of Urban Phenomena." Pp. 19–44 in *Urbanization and Urban Planning in Capitalist Society*, edited by Michael Dear and Allen Scott. New York: Methuen.

Ehrenreich, Barbara and Arlie Hochschild, eds. 2003. *Global Woman*. New York: Metropolitan Books.

El-Shakhs, Salah. 1972. "Development, Primacy and Systems of Cities." *Journal of Developing Areas* 7(October):11–36.

Enterprise Florida. 2005a. Global Advantages: Florida's Foreign Affiliated Companies. Retrieved December 7, 2005 (http://eflorida.com/globaladvantages/ foreign_companies1.asp?level1=25&level2=120).

———. 2005b. Global Advantages: Global Linkages. Retrieved December 7, 2005 (http://www.eflorida.com/globaladvantages/default.asp?level1=25&leve 12=124).

Ernst, Dieter. 2005. "The New Mobility of Knowledge: Digital Information Systems and Global Flagship Networks." Pp. 89–114 in *Digital Formations: IT and New Architectures in the Global Realm*, edited by Robert Latham and Saskia Sassen. Princeton, NJ: Princeton University Press.

Espinoza, V. 1999. "Social Networks Among the Poor: Inequality and Integration in a Latin American City." In *Networks in the Global Village: Life in Contemporary Communities*, edited by Barry Wellman. Boulder, CO: Westview Press.

Eurocities. 1989. *Documents and Subjects of Eurocities Conference*. Barcelona, Spain, April 21–22.

EUROSTAT. 2005. *The Urban Audit*. Retrieved October 14, 2005 (http://www .urbanaudit.org).

European Institute of Urban Affairs. 1992. *Urbanisation and the Functions of Cities in the European Community: A Report to the Commission of the European Communities, Directorate General for Regional Policy (XVI)*. Liverpool, UK: Liverpool John Moores University.

Fainstein, S. 1993. *The City Builders*. Oxford, UK: Blackwell.

———. 2001. *The City Builders*. 2d ed. Lawrence, KS: University of Kansas Press.

——— and Dennis Judd, eds. 1999. *Urban Tourism*. New Haven, CT: Yale University Press.

———, N. Fainstein, R. C. Hill, D. R. Judd, and M. P. Smith, 1986. *Restructuring the City*, 2d ed. New York: Longman.

———, I. Gordon and M. Harloe. 1992. *Divided Cities: Economic Restructuring and Social Change in London and New York*. New York: Blackwell.

Farrer, Gracia Liu. (In Process). "From Corporate Employees to Business Owners: Chinese Immigrant Transnational Entrepreneurship in Japan." Ph.D. Dissertation, Department of Sociology, University of Chicago.

Feldbauer, P., E. Pilz, D. Runzler, and I. Stacher, eds. 1993. *Megastädte: Zur Rolle von Metropolen in der Weltgesellschaft.* Vienna, Austria: Boehlau Verlag.

"Feminism and Globalization: The Impact of the Global Economy on Women and Feminist Theory." 1996. *Indiana Journal of Global Legal Studies* 4(1, Special issue).

Fernandez-Kelly, M. P. and A. M. Garcia. 1989. "Informalization at the Core: Hispanic Women, Homework, and the Advanced Capitalist State." Pp. 247–64 in *The Informal Economy: Studies in Advanced and Less Developed Countries,* edited by A. Portes, M. Castells, and L. Benton. Baltimore, MD: Johns Hopkins University Press.

────── and S. Sassen. 1992. "Immigrant Women in the Garment and Electronic Industries in the New York–New Jersey Region and in Southern California." Final Research Report presented to the Ford, Revson, and Tinker Foundations, June, New York.

────── and J. Shefner. 2005. *Out of the Shadows.* College Station, PA: Penn State University Press.

Fisher, Melissa. 2004. "Corporate Ethnography in the New Economy: Life Today in Financial Firms, Corporations, and Non-profits." *Anthropology News* 45(4):294–320.

Fitzgerald, R. 2005. "Welcome to the World's Favourite Metropolis." *The Australian,* July 27, 2005.

Florida Agency for Workforce Innovation. 2005. Labor Market Statistics, Current Employment Statistics Program. Miami-Dade County, Department of Planning and Zoning, Research Section (July). Retrieved December 7, 2005 (http://www.labormarketinfo.com/library/ces/current/miamidiv.xls).

Florida, Richard. 2004. *Cities and the Creative Class.* New York: Routledge.

──────, 2006. *The Flight of the Creative Class.* New York: Collins.

"The Forbes Global 2000." 2005. *Forbes Magazine.* March 31, 2005.

Fortin, N. M. and T. Lemieux 1997. "Institutional Changes and Rising Wage Inequality: Is There a Linkage?" *Journal of Economic Perspectives* 11 (2):75–96.

Freeman, R., ed. 1994. *Working under Different Rules.* New York: Russell Sage Foundation.

Friedmann, John. 1986. "The World City Hypothesis." *Development and Change* 17:69–84.

────── and G. Wolff. 1982. "World City Formation: An Agenda for Research and Action." *International Journal of Urban and Regional Research* 15(1):269–83.

"From Chatham House Man to Davos Man." 1997. *The Economist,* 342(February 1):18ff.

Frost, Martin and Nigel Spence. 1992. "Global City Characteristics and Central London's Employment." *Urban Studies* 30(3):547–58.

Frug, Gerald E. 2001. *City Making: Building Communities without Building Walls.* Princeton, NJ: Princeton University Press.

Fujita, Kuniko. 1991. "A World City and Flexible Specialization: Restructuring of the Tokyo Metropolis." *International Journal of Urban and Regional Research* 15(1):269–84.

Gad, Gunther. 1991. "Toronto's Financial District." *Canadian Urban Landscapes* 1:203–207.

Gans, Herbert. 1984. "American Urban Theory and Urban Areas." Pp. 308–26 in *Cities in Recession*, edited by Ivan Szelenyi. Beverly Hills, CA: Sage.

Garcia, D. Linda. 2002. "The Architecture of Global Networking Technologies." Pp. 39–69 in *Global Networks/Linked Cities*, edited by Saskia Sassen. New York and London, UK: Routledge.

Garofalo, G. and M. S. Fogarty. 1979. "Urban Income Distribution and the Urban Hierarchy-Inequality Hypothesis." *Review of Economics and Statistics* 61:381–88.

GaWC (Globalization and World Cities Study Group and Network). 2005. Retrieved December 7, 2005 (http://www.lboro.ac.uk/departments/gy/research/gawc.html).

Gereffi, Gary, John Humphrey, and Timothy Sturgeon. 2005. "The Governance of Global Value Chains." *Review of International Political Economy (Special Issue: Aspects of Globalization)* 12(1):78–104.

—— and Miguel Korzeniewicz. 1994. *Commodity Chains and Global Capitalism*. Westport, CT: Praeger.

Gerlach, Michael. 1992. *Alliance Capitalism: The Social Organization of Japanese Business*. Berkeley, CA: University of California Press.

Gershuny, Jonathan and Ian Miles. 1983. *The New Service Economy: The Transformation of Employment in Industrial Societies*. New York: Praeger.

Giarini, Orio, ed. 1987. *The Emerging Service Economy*. Oxford, UK, and New York: Pergamon.

Giddens, A. 1991. *The Consequences of Modernity*. Oxford, UK: Polity.

Giesecke, Gerald. 2005. "The Day after Tomorrow." Retrieved December 7, 2005 (http://www.zdf.de/ZDFde/inhalt/1/0,1872,2342977,00.html).

Gilbert, Allan, ed. 1996. *Cities in Latin America*. Tokyo, Japan: United Nations University Press.

Gillette, A. and A. Sayad. 1984. *L'immigration Algerienne en France*. 2d ed. Paris, France: Editions Entente.

Glickman, N. J. 1979. *The Growth and Management of the Japanese Urban System*. New York: Academic Press.

—— and A. K. Glasmeier. 1989. "The International Economy and the American South." Pp. 60–89 in *Deindustrialization and Regional Economic Transformation: The Experience of the United States*, edited by L. Rodwin and H. Sazanami. Winchester, MA: Unwin Hyman.

—— and D. P. Woodward. 1989. *The New Competitors: How Foreign Investors Are Changing the U.S. Economy*. New York: Basic Books.

"Global 500." 2005. *Fortune*, July 25, 2005.

"Global City: Zitadellen der Internationalisierung." 1995. *Wissenschafts Forum* 12(2, Special Issue).

Goddard, J. B. 1993. "Information and Communications Technologies, Corporate Hierarchies and Urban Hierarchies in the New Europe." Presented at the Fourth International Workshop on Technological Change and Urban Form: Productive and Sustainable Cities, April 14–16, Berkeley, CA.

Goldsmith, William V. and Edward J. Blakely. 1992. *Separate Societies: Poverty and Inequality in U.S. Cities.* Philadelphia, PA: Temple University Press.

Goldthorpe, John, ed. 1984. *Order and Conflict in Contemporary Capitalism.* Oxford, UK: Clarendon.

Gordon, I. R. 1996. "The Role of Internationalization in Economic Change in London over the Past 25 Years." Paper presented to the World Cities Group, CUNY Graduate School, New York.

—— and Saskia Sassen. 1992. "Restructuring the Urban Labor Markets." Pp. 105–28 in *Divided Cities: New York and London in the Contemporary World,* edited by S. Fainstein, I. Gordon, and M. Harloe. Oxford, UK: Blackwell.

——, Nick Buck, Alan Harding, and Ivan Turok, eds. 2005. *Changing Cities: Rethinking Urban Competitiveness, Cohesion, and Governance.* New York: Palgrave Macmillan.

Gottschalk, P. and T. Smeeding. 1997. "Cross-National Comparisons of Earnings and Income Inequality." *Journal of Economic Literature* 35:633–87.

Graham, Edward M. and Paul R. Krugman. 1989. *Foreign Direct Investment in the United States.* Washington, DC: Institute for International Economics.

Graham, Stephen. 2003. *The Cybercities Reader.* London: Routledge.

—— and Simon Marvin. 1996. *Telecommunications and the City: Electronic Spaces, Urban Places.* London, UK: Routledge.

Granovetter, Mark. 1985. "Economic Action and Social Structure: The Problem of Embeddedness." *American Journal of Sociology* 91:481–510.

Gravesteijn, S. G. E., S. van Griensven, and M. C. de Smidt, eds. 1998. "Timing Global Cities." *Nederlandse Geografische Studies* 241(Special issue).

Gregory, Derek and John Urry, eds. 1985. *Social Relations and Spatial Structures.* London, UK: Macmillan.

Grosfoguel, Ramon. 1993. "Global Logics in the Caribbean City System: The Case of Miami and San Juan." Pp. 156–70 in *World Cities in a World System,* edited by P. Knox and P. Taylor. New York: Cambridge University Press.

Grosz, E. 1992. "Bodies-Cities." Pp. 241–53 in *Sexuality & Space,* edited by Beatriz Colomina. Princeton Papers on Architecture. Princeton, NJ: Princeton Architectural Press.

Gu, Felicity Rose and Zilai Tang. 2002. "Shanghai: Reconnecting to the Global Economy." Pp. 273–308 in *Global Networks/Linked Cities,* edited by Saskia Sassen. New York and London, UK: Routledge.

Gugler, Joseph. 2004. *World Cities beyond the West.* Cambridge, UK: Cambridge University Press.

Hagedorn, John, ed. 2006. *Gangs in the Global City: Exploring Alternatives toTraditional Criminology.* Chicago, IL: University of Illinois at Chicago.

Hajnal, Peter I. 2002. "Civil Society Encounters the G7/G8." Pp. 215–42 in *Civil Society in the Information Age,* edited by Peter I. Hajnal. Aldershot, UK: Ashgate.

Hall, Peter. 1964. *Greater London.* London, UK: Faber & Faber.

——. 1966. *The World Cities.* New York: McGraw-Hill.

Hall, Peter. 1988. *Cities of Tomorrow*. Oxford, UK: Blackwell.

———. 2002. *Cities of Tomorrow* (3rd Ed.). Oxford, UK: Blackwell.

——— and D. Hay. 1980. *Growth Centers in the European Urban System*. London, UK: Heinemann Educational Books.

Hall, Rodney Bruce. *National Collective Identity*. 1999. New York: Columbia University Press.

Hall, S. 1991. "The Local and the Global: Globalization and Ethnicity." Pp. 19–40 in *Current Debates in Art History 3. Culture, Globalization and the World-System: Contemporary Conditions for the Representation of Identity*, edited by Anthony D. King. New York: State University of New York at Binghamton, Department of Art and Art History.

Hardoy, J. E. 1975. *Urbanization in Latin America*. Garden City, NJ: Anchor.

——— and D. Satterthwaite. 1989. *Squatter Citizen: Life in the Urban Third World*. London, UK: Earthscan.

Harris, R. 1991. "The Geography of Employment and Residence in New York Since 1950." Pp. 129–52 in *Dual City: Restructuring New York*, edited by J. Mollenkopf and M. Castells. New York: Russell Sage.

Harrison, B. and B. Bluestone. 1988. *The Great U-Turn*. New York: BasicBooks.

Hartmann, Heidi, ed. 1987. *Computer Chips and Paper Clips: Technology and Women's Employment*. Washington, DC: National Academy Press.

Harvey, David. 1985. *The Urbanization of Capital*. Oxford, UK: Blackwell.

———. 1989. *The Condition of Postmodernity*. Oxford, UK: Blackwell.

———. 2000. *Spaces of Hope*. Berkeley, CA: University of California Press.

Harvey, Rachel. (In process). "Global Cities of Gold." Ph.D. Dissertation, Department of Sociology, University of Chicago.

Hausserman, Hartmut and Walter Siebel. 1987. *Neue Urbanität*. Frankfurt: Suhrkamp Verlag.

Henderson, Jeffrey. 2005. "Governing growth and inequality: the continuing relevance of strategic economic planning." Pp. 227–36 in *Towards a Critical Globalization Studies*, edited by R. Appelbaum and W. Robinson. New York: Routledge.

Henderson, Jeff and Manuel Castells, eds. 1987. *Global Restructuring and Territorial Development*. London, UK: Sage.

Herzog, Lawrence A. 1990. *Where North Meets South: Cities, Space, and Politics on the United States-Mexico Border*. Austin, TX: University of Texas Press.

———. 2006. *Return to the Center: Culture, Public Space, and City-Building in a Global Era*. Austin, TX: University of Texas Press.

Hill, R. C. 1989. "Comparing Transnational Production Systems: The Case of the Automobile Industry in the United States and Japan." *International Journal of Urban and Regional Research* 13(3):462–480.

Hino, Masateru. 1984. "The Location of Head and Branch Offices of Large Enterprises in Japan." *Science Reports of Tohoku University* (Senday, Japan), Geography Series 34(2):1–22.

Hirst, Paul and Jonathan Zeitlin. 1989. *Reversing Industrial Decline?* Oxford, UK: Berg.

Hitz, H., R. Keil, U. Lehrer, K. Ronneberger, C. Schmid, and R. Wolff, eds. 1995. *Capitales Fatales*. Zurich, Switzerland: Rotpunkt.

Hollifield, James F. 1992. *Immigrants, Markets, and States: The Political Economy of Postwar Europe*. Cambridge, MA: Harvard University Press.

—— and Dietrich Thränhardt. 2006. *Beyond Exceptionalism: Immigration and National Traditions in the United States and Germany*. New York: Palgrave Macmillan.

Hondagneu-Sotelo, Pierrette, ed. 2003. *Gender and U.S. Immigration: Contemporary Trends*. Berkeley, CA: University of California Press.

——. 1994. *Gendered Transitions: Mexican Experiences of Immigration*. Berkeley, CA: University of California Press.

Hoover's Handbook of World Business. 1998. Austin, TX: Reference Press.

Hymer, Stephen and Robert Rowthorn. 1970. "Multinational Corporations and International Oligopoly." Pp. 57–91 in *The International Corporation*, edited by Charles P. Kindleberger. Cambridge, MA: MIT Press.

Inda, Jonathan Xavier, Louis F. Miron, and Rodolfo D. Torres. 1999. *Race, Identity, and Citizenship*. Oxford, UK: Blackwell.

—— 2005. *International Bank Lending by Country*. Washington, DC: IMF.

International Labor Organization. 2005. *LABORSTA: On-line Statistics*. Geneva, Switzerland: ILO. Retrieved December 7, 2005 (http://laborsta.ilo.org/).

Industrial Institute for Economic and Social Research (Stockholm, Sweden). 2005. Retrieved December 7, 2005 (http://www.iui.se).

IMF (International Monetary Fund). 1999. *International Capital Markets Report*. Washington, DC: IMF.

International Organization for Migration (IOM). 1998. *Trafficking in Migrants*. Geneva: IOM.

INURA, ed. 2003. *The Contested Metropolis*. New York: Birkhauser.

Ishizuka, H. and Ishida, Y. 1988. *Tokyo: Urban Growth and Planning, 1968–1988*. Tokyo, Japan: Tokyo Metropolitan University, Center for Urban Studies.

Isin, Engin F., ed. 2000. *Democracy, Citizenship and the Global City*. London, UK, and New York: Routledge.

Ito, Tatsuo and Masafumi Tanifuji. 1982. "The Role of Small and Intermediate Cities in National Development in Japan." Pp. 71–100 in *Small Cities and National Development*, edited by O. P. Mathur. Nagoya, Japan: United Nations Centre for Regional Development.

Iyotani, Toshio. 1989. "The New Immigrant Workers in Tokyo." Typescript, Tokyo University of Foreign Studies. Tokyo, Japan.

—— 1998. "Globalization and Immigrant Workers in Japan." In NIRA Review (Winter 1998). Tokyo: National Institute for Research Advancement. Retrieved December 13, 2005 (http://www.nira.go.jp/publ/review/98winter/index.html. Last accessed December 13, 2005).

——, Naoki Sakai and Brett de Bary, eds. 2005. *Deconstructing Nationality*. Ithaca, NY: Cornell University East Asia Program

Iyotani, Toshio and Toshio Naito. 1989. "Tokyo no Kokusaika de Tenkan Semarareru Chusho Kigyo" [Medium- and small-sized corporations under pressure of change by Tokyo's internationalization]. *Ekonomisuto,* September 5:44–49.

Japan Ministry of Internal Affairs and Communications, Statistics Bureau. 2005. *Monthly Statistics of Japan* No. 530. Tokyo: MIAC. Retrieved December 7, 2005 (http://www.stat.go.jp/english/data/geppou/#g).

Japan Ministry of Labor. Various years. *Monthly Labor Statistics and Research Bulletin.* Tokyo, Japan: Ministry of Labor.

Jenkins, Rhys. 1991. "The Political Economy of Industrialization: A Comparison of Latin American and East Asian Newly Industrializing Countries." *Development and Change* 11:197–231.

Jessop, Robert. 1999. "Reflections on Globalization and Its Illogics." Pp. 19–38 in *Globalization and the Asian Pacific: Contested Territories,* edited by Kris Olds, Peter Dicken, Philip F. Kelly, Lilly Kong, and Henry Wai-Chung Yeung. London, UK: Routledge.

———. 2003. *The Future of the Capitalist State.* Cambridge, UK: Polity Press.

Jonas, S. 1992. *The Battle for Guatemala: Rebels, Death Squads, and U.S. Power.* Boulder, CO: Westview.

Jones, Steve and Philip N. Howard, eds. 2004. *Society Online: The Internet in Context.* London: Sage Publications.

Kahnert, Friedrich. 1987. "Improving Urban Employment and Labor Productivity." World Bank Discussion Paper No. 10. Washington, DC: World Bank.

Kasarda, John D. and Edward M. Crenshaw. 1991. "Third World Urbanization: Dimensions, Theories and Determinants." *Annual Review of Sociology* 17:467–501.

Kasinitz, Philip. 1992. *Caribbean New York.* Ithaca, NY: Cornell University Press.

Kazepov, Yuri, ed. 2005. *Cities of Europe: Changing Contexts, Local Arrangements, and the Challenge to Urban Cohesion.* London, UK: Blackwell.

Keil, Roger. 1999. *Los Angeles: Globalization, Urbanization and Social Struggles.* Hoboken, NJ: John Wiley & Sons.

——— and Klaus Ronneberger. 1992. "Going up the Country: Internationalization and Urbanization on Frankfurt's Northern Fringe." Presented at the UCLA International Sociological Association, Research Committee 29, *A New Urban and Regional Hierarchy? Impacts of Modernization, Restructuring and the End of Bipolarity,* April 24–26, Los Angeles, CA.

——— and ———. 1995. "The City Turned Inside Out: Spatial Strategies and Local Politics." In *Capitales Fatales,* edited by H. Hitz, R. Keil, V. Lehrer, K. Ronneberger, C. Schmid, and R. Wolff. Zurich: Rotpunkt.

Kelly, Maryellen R. 1989. "Alternative Forms of Work Organization under Programmable Automation." Pp. 235–46 in *The Transformation of Work?* edited by Stephen Wood. London, UK: Unwin-Hyman.

King, A. D. 1990. *Urbanism, Colonialism, and the World Economy; Culture and Spatial Foundations of the World Urban System.* International Library of Sociology. London, UK, and New York: Routledge.

King, A. D., ed. 1996. *Re-presenting the City. Ethnicity, Capital and Culture in the 21st Century*. London, UK: Macmillan.

Klier, Thomas and William Testa. 2002. "Locational Trends of Large Company Headquarters during the 1990s." *Federal Reserve Bank of Chicago: Economic Perspectives* (26)2. Chicago, IL: Federal Reserve Bank of Chicago.

Klopp, Brett. 1998. "Integration and Political Representation in a Multicultural City: The Case of Frankfurt am Main." *German Politics and Society* 16(4): 42–68.

Knight, R. V. and G. Gappert, eds. 1989. *Cities in a Global Society*, vol. 35. Urban Affairs Annual Reviews. Newbury Park, CA: Sage.

Knox, P. and P. Taylor, eds. 1995. *World Cities in a World-System*. New York: Cambridge University Press.

—— and Linda McCarthy. 2005. *Urbanization : An Introduction to Urban Geography*. New York: Prentice Hall.

Komai, Hiroshi. 1992. "Are Foreign Trainees in Japan Disguised Cheap Laborers?" *Migration World* 10(1):13–17.

Komlosy, A., C. Parnreiter, I. Stacher, and S. Zimmerman, eds. 1997. *Ungeregelt und Unterbezahlt: Der Informelle Sektor in der Weltwirtschaft*. Frankfurt, Germany: Brandes & Apsel/Sudwind.

Komori, S. 1983. "Inner City in Japanese Context." *City Planning Review* 125:11–17.

Kothari, Uma. 2006. *A Radical History of Development Studies: Individuals, Institutions and Ideologies*. London: Zed Books.

Kotkin, J. 2005. *The City: A Global History*. New York: The Modern Library.

Kowarick, L., A. M. Campos, and M. C. de Mello, 1991. "Os Percursos de Desigualdade." In *São Paulo, Crise e Mudanca*, edited by R. Rolnik, L. Kowarick, and N. Somekh. São Paulo, Brazil: Brasiliense.

Krause, Linda and Patrice Petro, eds. 2003. *Global Cities: Cinema, Architecture, and Urbanism in a Digital Age*. New Brunswick, NJ, and London, UK: Rutgers University Press.

Kunzmann, K. R. and M. Wegener. 1991. "The Pattern of Urbanisation in Western Europe 1960–1990." Report for the Directorate General XVI of the Commission of the European Communities as part of the study *Urbanisation and the Function of Cities in the European Community*. Dortmund, Germany: Institut für Raumplanung.

KUPI (Kobe Urban Problems Institute). 1981. *Policy for Revitalization of Inner City*. Kobe, Japan: KUPI.

Kuttner, Robert. 1991. *The End of Laissez-Faire*. New York: Knopf.

Landell-Mills, Pierre, Ramgopal Agarwala, and Stanley Please. 1989. *Sub-Saharan Africa: From Crisis to Sustainable Growth*. Washington, DC: World Bank.

Lang, Robert. 2000. *Office Sprawl: The Evolving Geography of Business (Data Sets Appendix)*. Washington, DC: The Brookings Institution. Retrieved December 7, 2005 (http://www.brookings.edu/es/urban/officesprawl/13regions .pdf).

Lash, Scott M. 2002. *Critique of Information*. London: Sage Publications.

—— and John Urry. 1987. *The End of Organized Capitalism*. Cambridge, UK: Polity.

—— and ——. 1994. *Economies of Signs and Space*. London, UK: Sage.

Lavinas, Lena and Maria Regina Nabuco. 1992. "Economic Crisis and Flexibility in Brazilian Labor Markets." Presented at the UCLA International Sociological Association, Research Committee 29, *A New Urban and Regional Hierarchy? Impacts of Modernization, Restructuring and the End of Bipolarity,* April 24–26, Los Angeles, CA.

Lazzarato, Maurizio. 1997. *Lavoro Immateriale.* Verona, Italy: Ombre Corte.

Leborgne, D. and A. Lipietz. 1988. "L'après-Fordisme et son Espace." *Les Temps Modernes* 43:75–114.

Lee, Kyu Sik. 1989. *The Location of Jobs in a Developing Metropolis: Patterns of Growth in Bogota and Cali, Colombia.* New York: Oxford University Press.

LeGates, R. T. and F. Stout, eds. 2003. *The City Reader.* New York: Routledge.

Levine, Marc V. 1990. *The Reconquest of Montreal: Language Policy and Social Change in a Bilingual City.* Philadelphia, PA: Temple University Press.

Levy, Frank and Richard Murname. 1992. "U.S. Earnings Levels and Earnings Inequality: A Review of Recent Trends and Proposed Explanations." *Journal of Economic Literature* 30(3):1333–81.

Leyshon, A., P. Daniels, and N. Thrift. 1987. "Large Accountancy Firms in the U.K.: Spatial Development." Working Paper, St. David's University College, Lampeter, UK, and University of Liverpool.

———, Roger Lee, and Colin C. Williams, ed. 2003. *Alternative Economic Spaces.* London: Sage Publications.

Light, Ivan. 2006. *Deflecting Immigration: How Los Angeles Tamed Globalization.* New York: Russell Sage Foundation Publications.

———. and E. Bonacich. 1988. *Immigrant Enterprise.* Berkeley: University of California Press.

Lim, L. Y. C. 1982. "Women Workers in Multinational Corporations: The Case of the Electronics Industry in Malaysia and Singapore." Pp. 109–36 in *Transnational Enterprises: Their Impact on Third World Societies and Cultures,* edited by Kumar Krishna. Boulder, CO: Westview Press.

Linn, Johannes F. 1983. *Cities in the Developing World: Policies for Their Equitable and Efficient Growth.* New York and Oxford: Oxford University Press.

Lipietz, A. 1988. "New Tendencies in the International Division of Labor: Regimes of Accumulation and Modes of Regulation." Pp. 16–40 in *Production, Work, Territory,* edited by A. Scott and M. Storper. Boston, MA: Allen and Unwin.

Lloyd, Richard. 2005. *Neo-Bohemia: Art and Commerce in the Post-Industrial City.* New York and London: Routledge.

Lo, Fu-chen and Y. Yeung, eds. 1996. *Emerging World Cities in Pacific Asia.* Tokyo, Japan: United Nations University Press.

Logan, J. R. and H. Molotch. 1987. *Urban Fortunes.* Berkeley, CA: University of California Press.

——— and T. Swanstrom, eds. 1990. *Beyond the City Limits: Urban Policy and Economic Restructuring in Comparative Perspective.* Philadelphia, PA: Temple University Press.

Lomnitz, Larissa. 1985. "Mechanisms of Articulation between Shantytown Settlers and the Urban System." *Urban Anthropology* 7(2):185–205.

Lozano, Beverly. 1989. *The Invisible Work Force: Transforming American Business with Outside and Home-Based Workers.* New York: Free Press.

Lozano, Wilfredo and Isis Duarte. 1991. "Proceso de Urbanización, Modelos de Desarrollo y Clases Sociales en Republica Dominicana: 1960–1990." Paper presented at the seminar on Urbanization in the Caribbean in the Years of Crisis, May 29–June 1, Florida International University, Miami, FL.

Lustiger-Thaler, Henri, ed. 2004. "Social Movements in a Global World." *Current Sociology* (52)4:657–74.

Machimura, Takashi. 1992. "The Urban Restructuring Process in the 1980s: Transforming Tokyo into a World City." *International Journal of Urban and Regional Research* 16(1):114–28.

———. 2003. "Narrating a 'Global City' for 'New Tokyoites': Economic Crisis and Urban Boosterism in Tokyo." Pp. 196–212 in *Japan and Britain in the Contemporary World: Responses to Common Issues*, edited by Hugo Dobson and Glenn D. Hook. London: Routledge Curzon.

Mahler, Sarah. 1995. *American Dreaming: Immigrant Life on the Margins.* Princeton, NJ: Princeton University Press.

Mansell, Robin and Uta When. 1998. *Knowledge Societies: Information Technology for Sustainable Development.* Oxford: Oxford University Press.

Marcuse, Peter. 1986. "Abandonment, Gentrification, and Displacement: The Linkages in New York City." Pp. 153–77 in *Gentrification of the City,* edited by Neil Smith and Peter Williams. Boston, MA: Allen and Unwin.

———. 2003. *Of States and Cities: The Partitioning of Urban Space.* New York: Oxford University Press.

——— and Ronald Van Kempen. 2000. *Globalizing Cities: A New Spatial Order.* Oxford, UK: Blackwell.

Marie, Claude-Valentin. 1992. "Les Etrangers Non-Salaries en France, Symbole de la Mutation Economique des Années 80." *Revue Européenne des Migrations Internationales* 8(10):27–38.

Markusen, A. 1985. *Profit Cycles, Oligopoly, and Regional Development.* Cambridge, MA: MIT Press.

——— and Gwiasda, V. 1993. "Multipolarity and the Layering of Functions in the World Cities: New York City's Struggle to Stay on Top." Working Paper #55. New Brunswick, NJ: Rutgers University, Center for Urban Policy Research.

———, P. Hall, S. Campbell, and S. Deitrick, eds. 1991. *The Rise of the Gunbelt.* New York: Oxford University Press.

———, P. Hall, and A. Glasmeier. 1986. *High Tech America: The What, How, Where and Why of the Sunrise Industries.* London, UK, and Boston, MA: Allen and Unwin.

———, Yong-Sook Lee, and Sean Digiovanna, eds. 1999. *Second Tier Cities: Rapid Growth beyond the Metropolis.* Minneapolis, MN: University of Minnesota Press.

Marlin, John Tepper, Immanuel Ness, and Stephen T. Collins. 1986. *Book of World City Rankings*. New York: Macmillan.

Marshall, J. N., N. Thrift, P. Wood, P. Daniels, A. Mackinnon, J. Batchelor, P. Damesick, A. Gillespie, A. Leyshon and A. Green. 1986. "Uneven Development in the Service Economy: Understanding the Location and Role of Producer Services." Report of the Producer Services Working Party, Institute of British Geographers and the ESRC, August.

Martin, Philip. 1997. "Economic Integration and Migration: The Case of NAFTA." In *Proceedings of the Conference on International Migration at Century's End: Trends and Issues*, Barcelona Spain, May 7–10, 1997. Liege, Belgium: The International Union for the Scientific Study of Population.

Marcotullio, Peter and Fu-Chen Lo. 2001. *Globalization and the Sustainability of Cities in the Asia Pacific Region*. New York: United Nations University Press.

Martinelli, Flavia and Erica Schoenberger. 1991. "Oligopoly Is Alive and Well: Notes for a Broader Discussion of Flexible Accumulation." Pp. 117–33 in *Industrial Change and Regional Development: The Transformation of New Industrial Spaces*, edited by Georges Benko and Mick Dunford. London, UK, and New York: Belhaven/Pinter.

Masser, I., O. Sviden, and M. Wegener. 1990. "Europe 2020: Long-Term Scenarios of Transport and Communications in Europe." Unpublished paper for the European Science Foundation.

Massey, Doreen. 1984. *Spatial Divisions of Labour: Social Structures and the Geography of Production*. London, UK: Macmillan.

———. 2005. *For Space*. London: Sage Publications.

Massey, Douglas S. and Nancy Denton. 1998. *American Apartheid: Segregation and the Making of the Underclass*. Cambridge, MA: Harvard University Press.

Mayer, Margit. 1992. "The Shifting Local Political System in European Cities." Pp. 255–274 in *Cities and Regions in the New Europe*, edited by Mick Dunford and Grigoris Kafkalas. London: Belhaven Press.

———. 1999. "Urban Movements and Urban Theory in the Late 20th Century." Pp. 209–239 in *The Urban Moment*, edited by Sophie Body-Gendrot & Bob Beauregard. Thousand Oaks, CA: Sage Publications.

Mayne, S. 2005. "The Demise of Corporate Melbourne." *Crikey Daily*, June 15, 2005.

McDowell, Linda. 1997. *Capital Culture*. Oxford, UK: Blackwell.

———. 2005. *Hard Labour: The Forgotten Voices Of Latvian Migrant 'Volunteer' Workers*. London: University College London Press.

Mele, Christopher. 1999. "Cyberspace and Disadvantaged Communities: The Internet as a Tool for Collective Action." Pp. 264–89 in *Communities in Cyberspace*, edited by Marc A. Smith and Peter Kollock. New York and London: Routledge.

Melendez, E., C. Rodriguez, and J. B. Figueroa. 1991. *Hispanics in the Labor Force*. New York: Plenum.

Meridian Securities Markets. 1998. *World Stock Exchange Fact Book*. Morris Plains, NJ: Electronic Commerce.

Meyer, David R. 1991. "Change in the World System of Metropolises: The Role of Business Intermediaries." *Urban Geography* 12(5):393–416.

———. 2002. "Hong Kong: Global Capital Exchange." Pp. 249–72 in *Global Networks/Linked Cities*, edited Saskia Sassen. London: Routledge.

Meyer, John R. and James M. Gustafson, eds. 1988. *The U.S. Business Corporation: An Institution in Transition*. Cambridge, MA: Ballinger.

Miami-Dade County, Florida (2003). *General Statistical Data*, p. 6. Retrieved December 7, 2005 (http://www.co.miami-dade.fl.us/finance/library/genstat03.pdf).

Mignaqui, Iliana. 1998. "Dinamica Immobiliaria y Transformaciones Metropolitanas." Pp. 255–84 in *Ciudades y Regiones al Avance de la Globalización*, edited by S. Sorenstein and R. Bustos Cara. Bahia Blanca, Argentina : UNS (Universidad Nacional del Sur).

Mingione, E. 1991. *Fragmented Societies: A Sociology of Economic Life beyond the Market Paradigm*. Oxford, UK: Blackwell.

Mingione, E. and E. Pugliese. 1988. "La Questione Urbana e Rurale: Tra Superamento Teorico e Problemi di Confini Incerti." *La Critica Sociologica* 85:17–50.

Mioni, Alberto. 1991. "Legittimita ed Efficacia del Progetto Urbano." *Dis T Rassegna di Studi e Ricerche del Dipartimento di Scienze del Territorio del Politecnico di Milano* 9(September):137–50.

Mitchell, Matthew and Saskia Sassen. 1996. "Can Cities Like New York Bet on Manufacturing?" In *Manufacturing Cities: Competitive Advantage and the Urban Industrial Community*, a symposium given by the Harvard Graduate School of Design and the Loeb Fellowship, May 1996.

Mitter, S., ed. 1989. *Information Technology and Women's Employment: The Case of the European Clothing Industry*. Berlin and New York: Springer-Verlag.

Miyajima, Takashi. 1989. *The Logic of Receiving Foreign Workers: Among Dilemmas of Advanced Societies* (Gaikokujin Rodosha Mukaeire no Ronri: Senshin shakai no Jirenma no naka de). Tokyo, Japan: Akashi Shoten.

Montgomery, Cynthia A. and Michael E. Porter, eds. 1991. *Strategy: Seeking and Securing Competitive Advantage*. Boston, MA: Harvard Business School Press.

Morita, Kiriro. 1990. "Japan and the Problem of Foreign Workers." Research Institute for the Japanese Economy, Faculty of Economics. Tokyo, Japan: University of Tokyo-Hongo.

———. 1993. "Foreign Workers." Unpublished paper, Department of Economics, University of Tokyo, Tokyo-Hongo.

Morita, Kiriro and Saskia Sassen. 1994. "The New Illegal Immigration in Japan, 1980–1992." *International Migration Review* 28(1):153.

Morris, M. 1992. "Great Moments in Social Climbing: King Kong and the Human Fly." Pp. 1–51 in *Sexuality and Space,* edited by Beatriz Colomina. Princeton Papers on Architecture. Princeton, NJ: Princeton Architectural Press.

Moser C. 1989. "The Impact of Recession and Structural Adjustment Policies at the Micro-level: Low Income Women and Their Households in Guayaquil, Ecuador." *Invisible Adjustment* 2:137–66. New York: UNICEF.

Mowery, David, ed. 1988. *International Collaborative Ventures in U.S. Manufacturing*. Cambridge, MA: Ballinger.

Munger, Frank, ed. 2002. *Laboring Under the Line.* New York: Russell Sage Foundation.

Nabuco, M. R., A. F. Machado, and J. Pires. 1991. *Estrategias de Vida e Sobrevivencia na Industria de Confeccoes de Belo Horizonte.* Belo Horizonte, Brazil: Cedeplar/ UFMG.

Nakabayashi, Itsuki. 1987. "Social-Economic and Living Conditions of Tokyo's Inner City." *Geographical Reports of Tokyo Metropolitan University* 22:275–92.

Nanami, Tadashi and Yasuo Kuwabara, eds. 1989. *Tomorrow's Neighbors: Foreign Workers* (Asu no Rinjin: Gaikokujin Rodosha). Tokyo, Japan: Toyo Keizai Shimposha.

Nelson, J. I. and J. Lorence. 1985. "Employment in Service Activities and Inequality in Metropolitan Areas." *Urban Affairs Quarterly* 21(1):106–25.

Nepomnyaschy, Lenna and Irwin Garfinkel. 2002. "Wealth in New York City and the Nation: Evidence from the New York Social Indicators Survey and the Survey of Income and Program Participation." *Social Indicators Survey Center Working Paper.* New York: Columbia University School of Social Work.

Neuwirth, Robert. 2004. *Shadow Cities: A Billion Squatters, A New Urban World.* London: Routledge.

New South Wales Department of State and Regional Development. 2005. "Facts & Statistics: B17. Australian and Foreign-Owned Banks—Australian Cities, 2005." Retrieved December 7, 2005 (http://www.business.nsw.gov.au/facts Reports.asp?cid=31&subCid=69).

Nijman, Jan. 2000. "The Paradigmatic City." *Annals of the Association of American Geographers* 90(1):135–45.

———. 1996. "Breaking the rules: Miami in the urban hierarchy." *Urban Geography* 17(1):5–22.

Noyelle, T. and A. B. Dutka. 1988. *International Trade in Business Services: Accounting, Advertising, Law and Management Consulting.* Cambridge, MA: Ballinger.

O'Connor, K. 1990. *State of Australia.* Clayton, Australia: National Centre for Australian Studies, Monash University.

———. 2003. "Rethinking Globalisation and Urban Development: The Fortunes of Second-ranked Cities." *Australasian Journal of Regional Studies* 8:247–60.

OECD (Organization for Economic Cooperation and Development). 1993. *Main Economic Indicators.* Paris: OECD.

———. 1996. *Main Economic Indicators.* Paris: OECD.

———. 2005. *Main Economic Indicators.* Paris: OECD.

Office for National Statistics. 2002. *Census 2001.* London: ONS.

Olds, Kris, Peter Dicken, Philip F. Kelly, Lilly Kong, and Henry Wai-Chung Yeung, eds. 1999. *Globalization and the Asian Pacific: Contested Territories.* London, UK: Routledge.

Oliver, Nick and Barry Wilkinson. 1988. *The Japanization of British Industry.* Oxford, UK: Blackwell.

O'Neill, P. M. and P. McGuirk. 2002. "Prosperity Along Australia's Eastern Seaboard: Sydney and the Geopolitics of Urban and Economic Change." *Australian Geographer* 33(30):241–61.

Ong, Aihwa. 2003. *Buddha Is Hiding: Refugees, Citizenship, the New America*. Berkeley, CA: University of California Press.

Ong, Aihwa and Donald Nonini, eds. 1997. *Underground Empires*. New York: Routledge.

Orr, J. and Rae Rosen. 2000. "New York–New Jersey Job Expansion to Continue in 2000." Federal Reserve Bank of New York: *Current Issues in Economics and Finance* 6(5, April 2000):1–6.

Orum, Anthony and Xianming Chen. 2002. *Urban Places*. Malden, MA: Blackwell.

Paddison, Ronan, ed. 2001. Introduction. *Handbook of Urban Studies*. London, UK: Sage.

Palumbo-Liu, David. 1999. *Asian/American*. Stanford, CA: Stanford University Press.

Parkinson, M., B. Foley, and D. R. Judd, eds. 1989. *Regenerating the Cities: The U.K. Crisis and the U.S. Experience*. Glenview, IL: Scott, Foresman.

Parnreiter, Christof. 2002. "Mexico: The Making of a Global City." Pp. 145–82 in *Global Networks/Linked Cities*, edited by Saskia Sassen. New York: Routledge.

Parrenas, Rhacel Salazar, ed. 2001. *Servants of Globalization: Women, Migration and Domestic Work*. Stanford, CA: Stanford University Press.

Peraldi, M. and E. Perrin, eds. 1996. *Reseaux Productifs et Territoires Urbains*. Toulouse, France: Presses Universitaires de Mirail.

Perez-Sainz, J. P. 1992. *Informalidad Urbana en America Latina: Enfoques, Problematicas e Interrogantes*. Caracas, Venezuela: Editorial Nueva Sociedad.

Perez-Stable, Marifeli and Miren Uriarte. 1993. "Cubans and the Changing Economy of Miami." Pp. 133–59 in *Latinos in a Changing U.S. Economy: Comparative Perspectives on Growing Inequality*, edited by Rebecca Morales and Frank Bonilla. Sage Series on Race and Ethnic Relations, Vol. 7. Newbury Park, CA: Sage.

Pessar, P. R. and S. J. Mahler. 2003. "Transnational Migration: Bringing Gender In." *International Migration Review* 37(3):812–846.

Petrella, R. 1990. "Technology and the Firm." *Technology Analysis & Strategic Management* 2(2):99–110.

Pickvance, C. and Preteceille, E., eds. 1991. *State Restructuring and Local Power: A Comparative Perspective*. London, UK: Pinter.

Polanyi, Karl. 1975. *The Great Transformation: The Political and Economic Origins of Our Time*. Boston, MA: Beacon.

Portes, Alejandro, ed. 1988. *The Economic Sociology of Immigration: Essays on Networks, Ethnicity and Entrepreneurship*. New York: Russell Sage Foundation Publications.

——, M. Castells, and L. Benton, eds. 1989. *The Informal Economy: Studies in Advanced and Less Developed Countries*. Baltimore, MD: Johns Hopkins University Press.

—— and M. Lungo, eds. 1992a. *Urbanización en Centroamerica*. San José, Costa Rica: Facultad Latinoamericana de Ciencias Sociales.

——, eds. 1992b. *Urbanización en el Caribe*. San José, Costa Rica: Facultad Latinoamericana de Ciencias Sociales.

Portes, Alejandro and Ruben G. Rumbaut. 2001. *Legacies: The Story of the Immigrant Second Generation.* Berkeley, CA: University of California Press.

———, eds. 1997. *Immigrant America: A Portrait.* Berkeley, CA: University of California Press.

——— and S. Sassen-Koob. 1987. "Making It Underground: Comparative Material on the Informal Sector in Western Market Economies." *American Journal of Sociology* 93(1):30–61.

——— and Alex Stepick. 1993. *City on the Edge: The Transformation of Miami.* Berkeley, CA: University of California Press.

——— and Min Zhou. 1992. "Gaining the Upper Hand: Economic Mobility among Immigrant and Domestic Minorities." *Ethnic and Racial Studies* 15(October): 492–522.

Powell, Walter. 1990. "Neither Market nor Hierarchy: Network Forms of Organization." Pp. 295–336 in *Research in Organizational Behavior,* edited by Barry M. Straw and Larry L. Cummings. Greenwich, CT: JAI.

Pozos Ponce, Fernando. 1996. *Metropolis en Reestructuración: Guadalajara y Monterrey 1980–1989.* Guadalajara, Mexico: Universidad de Guadalajara, con Apoyo de El Fondo para la Modernización de la Educación Superior.

Prader, T., ed. 1992. *Moderne Sklaven: Asyl und Migrationspolitik in Österreich.* Vienna, Austria: Promedia.

PREALC (Regional Employment Program for Latin America and the Caribbean). 1982. *Mercado de Trabajo en Cifras: 1950–1980.* Santiago de Chile: International Labour Office.

———. 1987. *Ajuste y Deuda Social: Un Enfoque Estructural.* Santiago de Chile: International Labour Office.

Preteceille, E. 1986. "Collective Consumption, Urban Segregation, and Social Classes." *Environment and Planning D: Society and Space* 4:145–54.

Prigge, Walter. 1991. "Zweite Moderne: Modernisierung und Städtische Kultur in Frankfurt." Pp. 97–105 in *Frankfurt am Main: Stadt, Soziologie und Kultur,* edited by Frank-Olaf Brauerhoch. Frankfurt, Germany: Vervuert.

Pugliese, Enrico. 1983. "Aspetti dell' Economia Informale a Napoli." *Inchiesta* 13(59–60):89–97.

———. 2002. *L'Italia tra Migrazioni Internazionali e Migrazioni Interne.* Bologna, Italy: Il Mulino.

Pyle, Jean L. and Kathryn Ward. 2003. " Recasting our Understanding of Gender and Work During Global Restructuring." *International Sociology* 18(3): 461–89.

Queiroz Ribeiro, Luis Cesar de. 1990. "Restructuring in Large Brazilian Cities: The Center/Periphery Model in Question." Research Institute of Urban and Regional Planning, Federal University of Rio de Janeiro, Brazil.

Rae, Douglas W. 2003. *City: Urbanism and Its End.* New Haven, CT: Yale University Press.

Rakatansky, M. 1992. "Spatial Narratives." Pp. 198–221 in *Strategies in Architectural Thinking,* edited by J. Whiteman and R. Burdett. Chicago, IL, and Cambridge, MA: Chicago Institute for Architecture and Urbanism and MIT Press.

Ramirez, Nelson, Isidor Santana, Francisco de Moya, and Pablo Tactuk. 1988. *Republica Dominicana: Población y Desarrollo 1950–1985.* San José, Costa Rica: Centro Latinoamericano de Demografia (CELADE).

RECLUS. 1989. *Les villes européennes.* Rapport pour la DATAR. Paris, France: RECLUS.

Reich, Robert B. 1991. *The Work of Nations: Preparing Ourselves for 21st Century Capitalism.* New York: Knopf.

Renooy, P. H. 1984. "Twilight Economy: A Survey of the Informal Economy in the Netherlands." Research Report, Faculty of Economic Sciences, University of Amsterdam, The Netherlands.

Ribas-Mateos, Natalia. 2005. *The Mediterranean in The Age of Globalization: Migration, Welfare, and Borders.* Somerset, NJ: Transaction.

Rimmer, P. J. 1986. "Japan's World Cities: Tokyo, Osaka, Nagoya or Tokaido Megalopolis?" *Development and Change* 17(1):121–58.

———. 1988. "Japanese Construction and the Australian States: Another Round of Interstate Rivalry." *International Journal of Urban and Regional Research* 12(3):404–24.

Roberts, B. 1973. *Organizing Strangers: Poor Families in Guatemala City.* Austin, TX: University of Texas Press.

———. 1976. *Cities of Peasants.* London, UK: Edward Arnold.

———. 1995. *The Making of Citizens: Cities of Peasants Revisited.* New York: Edward Arnold.

——— and Portes, A. 2006. "Coping with the Free Market City: Collective Action in Six Latin American Cities at the End of the Twentieth Century." (On file with author).

Roberts, Susan. 1994. "Fictitious Capital, Fictitious Spaces: The Geography of Off-Shore Financial Flows." Pp. 91–115 in *Money, Power and Space,* edited by S. Corbridge, R. Martin, and N. Thrift. Oxford, UK: Blackwell.

Rodriguez, N. P. and J. R. Feagin. 1986. "Urban Specialization in the World System." *Urban Affairs Quarterly* 22(2):187–220.

Rolnik, R., L. Kowarick, and N. Somekh, eds. 1991. *São Paulo Crise e Mudanca.* São Paulo, Brazil: Brasiliense.

Roncayolo, M. 1990. *L'imaginaire de Marseille.* Marseille, France: Chambre de Commerce et d'Industrie de Marseille.

Rosen, F. and D. McFadyen, eds. 1995. *Free Trade and Economic Restructuring in Latin America* (NACLA reader). New York: Monthly Review Press.

Ross, R. and K. Trachte. 1983. "Global Cities and Global Classes: The Peripheralization of Labor in New York City." *Review* 6(3):393–431.

Rotzer, Florian. 1995. *Die Telepolis: Urbanität im Digitalen Zeitalter.* Mannheim, Germany: Bollman.

Roulleau-Berger, Laurence. 1999. *Le travail en friche.* La Tour d'Aigues, France: Editions de l'Aube.

Roulleau-Berger, ed. 2003. *Youth and Work in the Post-Industrial City of North America and Europe.* Boston, MA: Brill Academic Publishers.

Roy, Olivier. 1991. "Ethnicité, bandes et communautarisme." *Esprit* (February): 37–47.

Russell, Alan and Jan Rath. 2002. *Unravelling the Rag Trade: Immigrant Entrepreneurship in Seven World Cities.* Oxford, UK: Berg.

Rutherford, Jonathan. 2004. *A Tale of Two Global Cities: Comparing the Territorialities of Telecommunications Developments in Paris and London.* Aldershot, UK, and Burlington, VT: Ashgate.

Sachar, A. 1990. "The Global Economy and World Cities." Pp. 149–60 in *The World Economy and the Spatial Organization of Power,* edited by A. Sachar and S. Oberg. Aldershot, UK: Avebury.

———. 1996. "European world cities." Pp. 135–152 in *The Spatial Impact of Economic Changes in Europe,* edited by W. Lever & A. Bailly. Aldershot, UK: Avebury.

Saidam, Sabri. 2004. "On Route to an E-Society: Human Dependence on Technology and Adaptation Needs." A report for the Social Science Research Council's Committee on Information Technology and International Cooperation. Accessible at: [http://www.ssrc.org/programs/itic/publications/knowledge_report/memos/sabri.pdf].

Salmon, Scott. 2006. "Gentrification, Globalization and Governance: The Reterritorialization of Sydney's City-State." Chapter 7 in *Relocating Global Cities: From the Center to the Margins,* edited by Mark M. Amen, Kevin Archer, and M. Martin Bosman. New York: Rowman & Littlefield.

Salzinger, Leslie. 1995. "A Maid by Any Other Name: The Transformation of 'Dirty Work' by Central American Immigrants." Pp. 139–60 in *Ethnography Unbound: Power and Resistance in the Modern Metropolis,* edited by Michael Burawoy. Berkeley, CA: University of California Press.

———. 2003. *Genders in Production: Making Workers in Mexico's Global Factories.* Berkeley, CA: University of California Press.

Samers, Michael. 2002. "Immigration and the Global City Hypothesis: Towards an Alternative Research Agenda." *International Journal of Urban and Regional Research* 26(2, June):389–402.

Sanchez, Roberto and Tito Alegria. 1992. "Las Cuidades de la Frontera Norte." Departamento de Estudios Urbanos y Medio Ambiente, El Colegio de la Frontera Norte, Tijuana, Mexico.

Sandercock, Leonie. 2003. *Cosmopolis II: Mongrel Cities in the 21st Century.* New York and London, UK: Continuum.

Santos, Milton, Maria Adelia A. De Souze, and Maria Laura Silveira, eds. 1994. *Territorio Globalizacao e Fragmentacao.* São Paulo, Brazil: Hucitec.

Santoso, Oerip Lestari Djoko. 1992. "The Role of Surakarta Area in the Industrial Transformation and Development of Central Java." *Regional Development Dialogue* 13(2):69–82.

Saskai, Nobuo. 1991. *Tocho: Mo Hitotsu no Seifu* (The Tokyo Metropolitan Government: Another Central Government). Tokyo, Japan: Iwanami Shoten.

Sassen, Saskia. 1988. *The Mobility of Labor and Capital: A Study in International Investment and Labor Flow.* New York: Cambridge University Press.

———. 1995. "Immigration and Local Labor Markets." Pp. 87–127 in *The Economic Sociology of Immigration: Essays on Networks, Ethnicity, and Entrepreneurship,* edited by Alejandro Portes. New York: Russell Sage.

———. 1996. *Losing Control? Sovereignty in an Age of Globalization.* The 1995 Columbia University Leonard Hastings Schoff Memorial Lectures. New York: Columbia University Press.

———. 1998. *Globalization and Its Discontents: Selected Essays.* New York: New Press.

———. 1999. "Global Financial Centers." *Foreign Affairs* 78(1):75–87.

———. [1991] 2001. *The Global City: New York, London, and Tokyo,* 2d ed. Princeton, NJ: Princeton University Press.

———, ed. 2002. *Global Networks, Linked Cities.* London and New York: Routledge.

———. 2003. "The Repositioning of Citizenship: Emergent Subjects and Spaces for Politics." *Berkeley Journal of* Sociology 46:4–26.

———. 2004a. "The migration fallacy." *The Financial Times* December 27, 2004.

———. 2004b. "Local Actors in Global Politics." *Current Sociology* 52(4):657–674.

———, ed. 2006. "Human Settlement Development." in *Encyclopedia of Life Support Systems* (EOLSS), Developed under the auspices of the UNESCO. Oxford, UK: EOLSS Publishers [http://www.eolss.net].

———. 2006. *Territory, Authority, Rights: From Medieval to Global Assemblages.* Princeton, NJ: Princeton University Press.

——— and Robert Latham. 2005. *Digital Formations: IT and New Architectures in the Global Realm.* Princeton, NJ: Princeton University Press.

Sassen-Koob, Saskia. 1980. "Immigrants and Minority Workers in the Organization of the Labor Process." *Journal of Ethnic Studies* 8(Spring):1–34.

———. 1982. "Recomposition and Peripheralization at the Core." Pp. 88–100 in *The New Nomads: Immigration and Change in the International Division of Labor,* edited by Marlene Dixon and Susanne Jonas. San Francisco: Synthesis. (Reprinted in *Contemporary Marxism,* vol. 4.).

———. 1984. "The New Labor Demand in Global Cities." Pp. 139–71 in *Cities in Transformation,* edited by M. P. Smith. Beverly Hills, CA: Sage.

Saxenian, Anna-lee. 1996. *Regional Advantage: Culture and Competition in Silicon Valley and Route 128.* Cambridge, MA: Harvard University Press.

Savitch, H. 1988. *Post-Industrial Cities.* Princeton, NJ: Princeton University Press.

———. 1996. "Cities in a Global Era: A New Paradigm for the Next Millennium." Pp. 39–65 in *Preparing for the Urban Future: Global Pressures and Local Forces,* edited by M. Cohen, B. Ruble, J. Tulchin, and A. Garland. Washington, DC: Woodrow Wilson Center Press (Distributed by Johns Hopkins University Press).

Sayer, Andrew and Richard Walker. 1992. *The New Social Economy: Reworking the Division of Labor.* Cambridge, MA: Blackwell.

Schiffer, Sueli Ramos. 2002. "Sao Paulo: Articulating a cross-border regional economy." Pp. 209–36 in *Global Networks/Linked Cities*, edited by Saskia Sassen. New York and London, UK: Routledge.

Sclar, Elliott D. and Walter Hook. 1993. "The Importance of Cities to the National Economy." Pp. 48–80 in *Interwoven Destinies: Cities and the Nation*, edited by Henry G. Cisneros. New York: Norton.

Scott, Allen J. 2001. *Global City-Regions*. Oxford, UK: Oxford University Press.

———. 1988. *Metropolis: From the Division of Labor to Urban Form*. Berkeley, CA: University of California Press.

——— and Michael Storper, eds. 1986. *Production, Work, Territory*. Boston, MA: Allen and Unwin.

Sennett, R. 1990. *The Conscience of the Eye: The Design and Social Life of Cities*. New York: Knopf.

———. 1996. *Flesh and Stone: The Body and the City in Western Civilization*. New York: Norton.

———, 2006. *The Culture of the New Capitalism*. New Haven, CT: Yale University Press. "The Service 500." *Fortune*, May 31, 1993, Pp. 199–230.

Shank, G., ed. 1994. "Japan Enters the 21st Century." *Social Justice* 21(2, Special issue).

Sheets, R. G., S. Nord, and J. J. Phelps. 1987. *The Impact of Service Industries on Underemployment in Metropolitan Economies*. Lexington, MA: D. C. Heath.

Short, J. R. and Y. H. Kim. 1999. *Globalization and the City*. New York: Longman.

Siebel, W. 1984. "Krisenphänomene der Stadtentwicklung." *arch + d* 75/76: 67–70.

Silver, H. 1984. "Regional Shifts, Deindustrialization and Metropolitan Income Inequality." Presented at the Annual Meeting of the American Sociological Association, August, San Antonio, TX.

———. 1993. National conceptions of the new urban poverty: social structural change in Britain, France and the United States. *International Journal of Urban and Regional Research* 17(3):336–54.

——— and R. Bures. 1997. "Dual cities? Sectoral shifts and metropolitan income inequality, 1980–90." Service Industries Journal 17(1):69–90.

Simon, David. 1995. "The World City Hypothesis: Reflections from the Periphery." Pp. 132–55 in *World Cities in a World-System*, edited by P. Knox and P. Taylor. New York: Cambridge University Press.

Singelmann, J. 1974. "The Sectoral Transformation of the Labor Force in Seven Industrialized Countries, 1920–1960." Ph.D. dissertation, University of Texas, Austin, TX.

——— and H. L. Browning. 1980. "Industrial Transformation and Occupational Change in the U.S., 1960–70." *Social Forces* 59:246–64.

Singh, Surjit. 1994. *Urban Informal Sector*. Jaipur, India: Rawat.

Skeldon, R. 1997. "'Hong Kong: Colonial City to Global City to Provincial City?" *Cities* (14)5:265–71.

Skeldon, R., ed. 1994. *Reluctant Exiles?: Migration from Hong Kong and the New Overseas Chinese.* Armonk, NY: M. E. Sharpe.

———. 2000. "Trends in international migration in the Asian and Pacific region." *International Social Science Journal* 52(165):369–82.

Sklair, Leslie. 1985. "Shenzhen: A Chinese 'Development Zone' in Global Perspective." *Development and Change* 16:571–602.

———. 1991. *Sociology of the Global System: Social Changes in Global Perspective.* Baltimore, MD: Johns Hopkins University Press.

———. 2001. *The Transnational Capitalist Class.* Malden, MA: Blackwell Publishers.

Smeeding, T. 2002. "Globalization, Inequality, and the Rich Countries of the G-20: Evidence from the Luxembourg Income Study (LIS)." *Luxembourg Income Study Working Paper No. 320.* Prepared for the G-20 Meeting, Globalization, Living Standards and Inequality: Recent Progress and Continuing Challenges, Sydney, Australia, May 26–28, 2002.

Smith, Anthony, ed. 1992. *The Apartheid City and Beyond: Urbanization and Social Change in South Africa.* London, UK: Routledge/Witwatersrand University Press.

Smith, Carol A. 1985. "Theories and Measures of Urban Primacy: A Critique." Pp. 87–116 in *Urbanization in the World-Economy,* edited by M. Timberlake. Orlando, FL: Academic Press.

Smith, David. 2004. "Global Cities in East Asia: Empirical and Conceptual Analysis." *International Social Science Journal* 56(3):399–412.

———. 1995. "The New Urban Sociology Meets the Old: Rereading Some Classical Human Ecology." *Urban Affairs Review* 30(3):432–57.

——— and Michael Timberlake. 2001. "World City Networks and Hierarchies, 1977–1997: An Empirical Analysis of Global Air Travel Links." *American Behavioral Scientist* 44(10):1656–79.

———, S. Solinger, and S. Topik, eds. 1999. *States and Sovereignty in the Global Economy.* London, UK: Routledge.

Smith, M. P. and J. R. Feagin. 1987. *The Capitalist City: Global Restructuring and Territorial Development.* London, UK: Sage.

———. 1996. *The New Urban Frontier; Gentrification and the Revanchist City.* London: Routledge.

——— and P. Williams. 1986. *Gentrification of the City.* Boston, MA: Allen and Unwin.

Smith, Robert C. 1997. "Transnational Migration, Assimilation, and Political Community." Pp. 110–32 in *The City and the World,* edited by Margaret Crahan and Alberto Vourvoulias-Bush. New York: Council on Foreign Relations.

———. 2005. *Mexican New York: Transnational Lives of New Immigrants.* Berkeley. CA: University of California Press.

Solinger, Dorothy. 1999. *Contesting Citizenship in Urban China: Peasant Migrants, the State, and the Logic of the Market.* Berkeley, CA: University of California Press.

Sonobe, M. 1993. "Spatial Dimension of Social Segregation in Tokyo: Some Remarks in Comparison with London." Paper presented at the meeting of the Global City Project, Social Science Research Council, March 9–11, New York.

SOPEMI (Systeme d'Observation Permanente pour les Migrations). 1999–2005. *Trends in International Migration*. Paris, France: OECD, Directorate for Social Affairs, Manpower and Education.

Stanback, T. M., Jr., P. J. Bearse, T. J. Noyelle, and R. Karasek. 1981. *Services: The New Economy*. Montclair, NJ: Allenheld, Osmun.

—— and T. J. Noyelle. 1982. *Cities in Transition: Changing Job Structures in Atlanta, Denver, Buffalo, Phoenix, Columbus (Ohio), Nashville, Charlotte*. Montclair, NJ: Allenheld, Osmun.

Statistics Canada. 2005. "Employment by Industry." Table 282–0008. Ontario: Statistics Canada. Retrieved December 7, 2005 (http://www40.statcan.ca/l01/cst01/econ40.htm?sdi=employment%20sector).

Stimson, Robert J. 1993. "The Process of Globalisation and Economic Restructuring and the Emergence of a New Space Economy of Cities and Regions in Australia." Presented at the Fourth International Workshop on Technological Change and Urban Form: Productive and Sustainable Cities, April 14–16, Berkeley, CA.

Stopford, John M., ed. 1992. *Directory of Multinationals*. London, UK: Macmillan.

Stren, R. E. and R. R. White. 1989. *African Cities in Crisis: Managing Rapid Urban Growth*. Boulder, CO: Westview.

Stren, Richard, Barney Cohen, Holly E. Reed, and Mark R. Montgomery (eds). 2003. *Cities Transformed: Demographic Change and Its Implications in the Developing World*. Washington, D.C.: National Academies Press.

Susser, Ida. 1982. *Norman Street, Poverty and Politics in an Urban Neighborhood*. New York: Oxford University Press.

——. 2002. "Losing Ground: Advancing Capitalism and the Relocation of Working Class Communities." Pp. 247–90 in *Locating Capitalism in Time and Space: Global Restructurings, Politics, and Identity*, edited by David Nugent. Stanford, CA: Stanford University Press.

Tabak, Faruk and Michaeline A. Crichlow, eds. 2000. *Informalization: Process and structure*. Baltimore, MD: The Johns Hopkins Press.

Tardanico, Richard and Mario Lungo. 1995. "Local Dimensions of Global Restructuring in Urban Costa Rica." *International Journal of Urban and Regional Research* (19)2:223–249.

Taylor, Peter J. 2000. "World Cities and Territorial States Under Conditions of contemporary Globalization." *Political Geography* (19)5:5–32.

——. 2004. *World City Network: A Global Urban Analysis*. New York: Routledge.

——, D. R. F. Walker, and J. V. Beaverstock. 2002. "Firms and Their Global Service Networks." Pp. 93–116 in *Global Networks, Linked Cities*, edited by Saskia Sassen. New York: Routledge.

Taylor, Peter J., Gilda Catalano, and Michael Hoyler. 2002. "Diversity and power in the world city network." *Cities* (19)4:231–42.

Teresaka, Akinobu, Itsuki Wakabayashi, and Abe Kazutoshi. 1988. "The Transformation of Regional Systems in an Information-Oriented Society." *Geographical Review of Japan* 61(1):159–73.

Thomas, Margaret. 1983. "The Leading Euromarket Law Firms in Hong Kong and Singapore." *International Financial Law Review* (June):4–8.

Thomson Financials. 1999. *International Target Cities Report*. New York: Thomson Financial Investor Relations.

Thrift, N. 1987. "The Fixers: The Urban Geography of International Commercial Capital." Pp. 219–47 in *Global Restructuring and Territorial Development*, edited by J. Henderson and M. Castells. London, UK: Sage.

———. 2005. *Knowing Capitalism*. London: Sage Publications.

——— and Ash Amin. 2002. *Cities: Reimagining the Urban*. Cambridge, UK: Polity Press.

Timberlake, M., ed. 1985. *Urbanization in the World Economy*. Orlando, FL: Academic Press.

Tinker, I., ed. 1990. *Persistent Inequalities: Women and World Development*. New York: Oxford University Press.

Todd, Graham. 1993. "The Political Economy of Urban and Regional Restructuring in Canada: Toronto, Montreal and Vancouver in the Global Economy, 1970–1990." Ph.D. dissertation, Department of Political Science, York University, Toronto, Canada.

———. 1995. " 'Going Global' in the Semi-periphery: World Cities as Political Projects. The Case of Toronto." Pp. 192–214 in *World Cities in a World-System*, edited by P. Knox and P. Taylor. New York: Cambridge University Press.

Topel, Robert. 1997. "Factor Proportions and Relative Wages: The Supply Side Determinants of Wage Inequality." *Journal of Economic Perspectives*. Spring: 55–74.

Torres, R., L. Miron, and J. X. Inda, eds. 1999. *Race, Identity, and Citizenship*. Oxford: Blackwell.

Toulouse, Christopher. 1992. "Thatcherism, Class Politics and Urban Development in London." *Critical Sociology* 18(1):57–76.

Trejos, J. D. 1991. "Informalidad y Acumulación en el Area Metropolitana de San José, Costa Rica." In *Informalidad Urbana en Centroamerica: Entre la Acumulación y la Subsistencia*, edited by J. P. Perez-Sainz and R. Menjivar Larin. Caracas, Venezuela: Editorial Nueva Sociedad.

Tribalat, M., J.-P. Garson, Y. Moulier-Boutang, and R. Silberman. 1991. *Cent Ans d'Immigration: Etrangers d'Hier, Français d'Aaujourd'hui*. Paris, France: Presses Universitaires de France, Institut National d'Etudes Demographiques.

Tyner, James. 1999. "The Global Context of Gendered Labor Emigration from the Philippines to the United States." *American Behavioral Scientist*. 42(40): 671–694.

Union Bank of Switzerland. 2003. *Price and Earnings around the Globe*. Zurich, Switzerland: UBS.

UNCTC (United Nations Center on Transnational Corporations). 1991. *World Investment Report: The Triad in Foreign Direct Investment*. New York: United Nations.

———. 1992. *The Determinants of Foreign Direct Investment: A Survey of the Evidence*. New York: United Nations.

UNCTAD (United Nations Conference on Trade and Development), Programme on Transnational Corporations. 1992. *World Investment Report 1992: Transnational Corporations as Engines of Growth*. New York: United Nations.

———. 1993. *World Investment Report 1993: Transnational Corporations and Integrated International Production*. New York: United Nations.

———. 1997. *World Investment Report 1997: Transnational Corporations, Market Structure and Competition Policy*. New York: United Nations.

———. 1998. *World Investment Report 1998: Trends and Determinants*. New York: United Nations.

———. 2004. *World Investment Report 2004: The Shift Towards Services*. New York: United Nations.

United Nations. Department for Economic and Social Affairs, Policy Analysis. 2003. *Urban and Rural Areas, 2003*. New York: United Nations.

———. 1994. *Urban Agglomerations and Rural Agglomerations, 1994*. New York: United Nations.

United Nations. Department of Economic and Social Affairs, Population Division. 2004. *Urban Agglomerations, 2003*. New York: United Nations.

———. 1996. *Urban Agglomerations, 1996*. New York: United Nations.

United Nations. Department for International Economic and Social Affairs. 1988. *Prospects of World Urbanization*. New York: United Nations.

———. 2003. *Prospects of World Urbanization*. New York: United Nations.

Urban Age. 2005. The Future of Cities Conference Series. London: The Cities Program, London School of Economics (http://www.urban-age.net).

U.S. Bureau of the Census. 2004a. *Income, Poverty, and Health Insurance Coverage in the United States: 2003*. Washington DC: U.S. Government Printing Office.

———. 2004b. *Money Income in The U.S.: 2001*. Washington, DC: U.S. Government Printing Office.

———. 1997. *U.S. Census Update*. Washington, DC: U.S. Government Printing Office.

U.S. Bureau of Labor Statistics. 1998. *U.S. Bureau of Labor Statistics Data*. Washington, DC: U.S. Government Printing Office.

———. 2005. *U.S. Bureau of Labor Statistics: Labor Force Statistics from the Current Population Survey*. Washington, DC: U.S. Bureau of Labor Statistics. Retrieved December 7, 2005 (http://www.bls.gov/home.htm).

U.S. Department of Commerce, Office of the U.S. Trade Representative. 1983. *U.S. National Study on Trade in Services*. Washington, DC: U.S. Government Printing Office.

U.S. Department of Commerce. 1992. *U.S. Direct Investment Abroad: 1989 Benchmark Survey, Final Results*. Washington, DC: U.S. Government Printing Office.

U.S. Department of Commerce. 1985. *U.S. Direct Investment Abroad: 1982 Benchmark Survey Data*. Washington, DC: U.S. Government Printing Office.

U.S. Department of Housing and Urban Development. 2005. *State of the Cities Data Systems*. Washington DC: HUD. Retrieved December 6, 2005 (http://socds .huduser.org/index.html).

U.S. Department of State. 2004. *Trafficking in Persons Report*, released by the Office to Monitor and Combat Trafficking in Persons. Washington, D. C.: U.S. Department of State.

Valle, Victor M. and Rodolfo D. Torres. 2000. *Latino Metropolis*. Minneapolis, MN: University of Minnesota Press.

van den Berg, L., R. Drewett, L. H. Klaassen, A. Rossi, and C. H. T. Vijverberg. 1982. *Urban Europe: A Study of Growth and Decline*. Oxford, UK: Pergamon.

Veltz, Pierre. 1996. *Mondialisation Villes et Territories*. Paris, France: Presses Universitaires De France.

Vidal, Sarah, Jean Viard, et al. 1990. *Le Deuxième Sud, Marseille ou le Present Incertain*. Arles, France: Editions Actes Sud, Cahiers Pierre-Baptiste.

Vieillard-Baron, Herve. 1991. "Le Risque du Ghetto." *Esprit*(February):14–22.

Von Petz, U. and K. Schmals, eds. 1992. *Metropole, Weltstadt, Global City: Neue Formen der Urbanisierung*. Dortmund: Dortmunder Beiträge zur Raumplanung Vol. 60. Dortmund, Germany: Universität Dortmund.

Wacquant, L. 1997. "Inside the Zone." *Theory, Culture, and Society* (15)2:1–36.

———. 2006. *Deadly Symbiosis: Race and the Rise of Neoliberal Penalty*. London: Polity Press.

———. 2007; forthcoming. *Urban Outcasts*. London: Polity Press.

Waldinger, Roger. 1996. *Still the Promised City? African-Americans and the New Immigrants in Postindustrial New York*. Cambridge, MA: Harvard University Press.

Walter, I. 1989. *Secret Money*. London, UK: Unwin Hyman.

Walters, Pamela Barnhouse. 1985. "Systems of Cities and Urban Primacy: Problems of Definition and Measurement." Pp. 63–86 in *Urbanization in the World-Economy*, edited by M. Timberlake. Orlando, FL: Academic Press.

Walton, John and David Seddon. 1994. *Free Markets & Food Riots: The Politics of Global Adjustment*. Cambridge, MA: Blackwell.

Ward, K. 1991. *Women Workers and Global Restructuring*. Ithaca, NY: Cornell University Press.

——— and Jean Pyle. 1995. "Gender, Industrialization and Development." Pp. 37–64 in *Women in the Latin American Development Process: From Structural Subordination to Empowerment*, edited by Christine E. Bose and Edna Acosta-Belen. Philadelphia, PA: Temple University Press.

Warkentin, Craig. 2001. *Reshaping World Politics: NGOs, the Internet, and Global Civil Society*. Lanham, MD: Rowman & Littlefield.

Weinstein, Liza. (In process). "Making Mumbai: Resident Participation and the Making of a Global City." Ph.D. dissertation, Department of Sociology, University of Chicago, IL.

Wentz, Martin, ed. 1991. *Stadtplanung in Frankfurt: Wohnen, Arbeiten, Verkehr*. Frankfurt, Germany, and New York: Campus.

Werth, M. and H. Korner, eds. 1991. *Immigration of Citizens from Third Countries into the Southern Member States of the European Community. Social Europe*. Supplement 1/91. Luxembourg: Office for Official Publications of the European Communities.

Whiteman, J., J. Kipnis, and R. Burdett. 1992. *Strategies in Architectural Thinking.* Chicago, IL, and Cambridge, MA: Chicago Institute for Architecture and Urbanism/MIT Press.

WIACT (Workers' Information and Action Centre of Toronto). 1993. "Trends in Employee Home Employment." Toronto, Canada: WIACT (Mimeo).

Wigley, M. 1992. "Untitled: The Housing of Gender." Pp. 327–90 in *Sexuality and Space,* edited by Beatriz Colomina. Princeton Papers on Architecture. Princeton, NJ: Princeton Architectural Press.

Wihtol de Wenden, Catherine, ed. 1988. *La Citoyenneté.* Paris, France: Edilic, Fondation Diderot.

Willoughby, K. W. 1990. *Technology Choice.* Boulder, CO, and San Francisco, CA: Westview.

Wilpert, Czarina. 1998. "Migration and Informal Work in the New Berlin: New Forms of Work or New Sources of Labor?" *Journal of Ethnic and Migration Studies* 24(2):269–94.

Wilson, W. J. 1997. *The Truly Disadvantaged: The Inner City, the Underclass and Public Policy.* Chicago, IL: University of Chicago Press.

———. 1987. *When Work Disappears.* New York: Alfred A. Knopf.

Wonders, Nancy A. and Raymond Michalowski. 2001. "Bodies, Borders, and Sex Tourism in a Globalized World: A Tale of Two Cities—Amsterdam and Havana." *Social Problems* 48(4):545–71.

World Bank. 1991. *Urban Policy and Economic Development: An Agenda for the 1990s.* Washington, DC: World Bank.

———. 1998. *World Development Indicators.* Washington, DC: World Bank.

———. 2005. *World Development Indicators.* Washington, DC: World Bank.

———. 2006. *Global Economic Prospects: Economic Implications of Remittances and Migration.* Washington, DC: The World Bank. "World Business." 1989. *Wall Street Journal.* September 22, R23.

———. 1992. *Wall Street Journal.* September 24, R27.

———. 1998. *Wall Street Journal.* September 28, R25–27.

———. 2004. *Wall Street Journal.* September 27, R20.

World Federation of Exchanges. 2003. *Annual Statistics for 2003.* Paris: World Federation of Exchanges.

———. 2004. *Annual Statistics for 2004.* Paris: World Federation of Exchanges.

——— 2005. *Annual Statistics for 2004.* Paris: World Federation of Exchanges

Wright, Talmadge. 1997. *Out of Place.* Albany, NY: State University of New York Press.

Yamanaka, Keiko. 2004. "New Worlds, New Lives: Globalization and People of Japanese Descent in the Americas and From Latin America in Japan." *Journal of Asian Studies* 63(4):1080–2.

Yeung, Yue-man. 2000. *Globalization and Networked Societies.* Honolulu, HI: University of Hawaii Press.

Yuval-Davis, N. 1999. "Ethnicity, Gender Relations and Multiculturalism." Pp. 112–25 in *Race, Identity, and Citizenship,* edited by R. Torres, L. Miron and J. X. Inda. Oxford, UK: Blackwell.

Yuval-Davis, N. 2006; forthcoming. *Gender and Nation* (updated 2nd ed). London: Sage Publications.

Zelinsky, Wilbur. 1991. "The Twinning of the World: Sister Cities in Geographic and Historical Perspective." *Annals of the Association of American Geographers* 81(1):1–31.

Zukin, Sharon. 2005. *Point of Purchase: How Shopping Changed American Culture.* New York: Routledge.

———. 1991. *Landscapes of Power.* Berkeley, CA: University of California Press.

Index

Note: Entries marked with *E* indicate Exhibits.